*Dawn was born in Launceston,
Tasmania, and spent most of her
childhood on King Island in Bass
Strait. Although she began training as
a nurse, circumstances prevented her
finishing the course, and she now
describes herself as a writer with an
interest in psychic research.*

*Dawn lives on a small farm in
Tasmania with her husband, Craig,
and a large collection of animals.*

WITH A LITTLE HELP FROM MY FRIENDS

**Dawn Shelley Thomas
writing as Dawn Hill**

**PAN
AUSTRALIA**

First published 1991 by Pan Macmillan Publishers
This Pan edition published 1994 by Pan Macmillan Australia Pty Limited
St Martins Tower, 31 Market Street, Sydney

Reprinted 1993, 1994

National Library of Australia
cataloguing-in-publication data:

Hill, Dawn, 1946-
With a little help from my friends.
ISBN 0 330 27245 4.
1. Parapsychology. 2. New Age movement.
3. Spiritualism. I. Title.
133

Typeset in 11/12 pt Baskerville by Post Typesetters
Printed in Australia by McPherson's Printing Group

To Craig, my best friend and life partner,
who taught my heart to laugh
With love

And now I see with eye serene
The very pulse of the machine;
A being breathing thoughtful breath,
A traveller between life and death.

From 'She Was a Phantom of Delight'
by William Wordsworth

CONTENTS

CHAPTER ONE

How to rearrange the universe, scandalise the neighbourhood and terrify the cat

Are you looking for a clear sense of meaning in your life? Me too. Want to find where you belong? Same here. Do you feel as though your life so far has been one long search? I know how that feels, too.

What are you searching for? People started asking me that question when I was still only a child. They've been asking me the same question ever since. At first, the only answer I could give was, 'I don't know yet, but I'll know when I find it, because I'll *feel* it... in here', indicating a point in the area of my midriff. I couldn't say exactly what it was that I needed to find, because it wasn't anything that could be defined intellectually. There was a gut feeling, a sense of something missing, an incompleteness about life in general, and the world of reality as it was explained to me did not fill in the gaps. I felt restless and unsatisfied, but I could not explain why, not in words. Whenever I tried to express my feelings verbally, it came out all wrong, but the feelings didn't go away, even when people told me that I was living in a world of fantasy and ought to get my head together. I tried hard to be normal and to act like everyone else, but somehow it never felt quite right. Have you had those feelings, too?

Today, it is easy enough for anyone to recognise that the need I could not express in words was originating in the non-verbal right hemisphere of my brain, which was telling me that the logical, left-brain oriented definitions of reality as impressed on me by the outside world were only giving me half of the picture, but I am now in my mid-forties. When I was a child, and even when I reached young adulthood, split-brain research was unheard of and psychic awareness was the fabric of fantasy. Little girls who guilelessly revealed their knowledge of adult matters which were not discussed in front of children were not recognised as being psychic; they were accused of listening at keyholes and being precocious. The inner hunger that I felt, my restlessness and dissatisfaction with life in general were simply regarded as antisocial attitudes. I didn't understand those inner feelings myself; I only knew that I wasn't happy with life in this world.

It isn't difficult to put labels on the things we are searching for, like 'love' and 'happiness', but how do you define the words? What answer do you give when you have said that you're looking for love and someone answers, 'But you're surrounded by people who love you. Why isn't that enough for you?' If, in the eyes of those around you, you have everything a person needs in order to be happy, but you still feel restless and unfulfilled, do you have problems trying to justify your feelings, even to yourself? You might be surprised to know just how many people there are who know exactly how you feel. They know because they feel the same way, too.

You might be one of the more fortunate souls who have found what they're looking for and don't feel that restless hunger any more. In that case, there are a lot of other people who would love to know the secret of your success. You would be a very unusual person, however, if you had never felt that inner longing or could not remember how it feels.

What draws you and me together at this point is a sense of recognition. The feelings I have just described are familiar, you can recognise them within yourself. I am not being fantastically psychic, merely stating a fact: most of us have those feelings, or have had them in the past. We aren't all that different, really, underneath the surface. Perhaps we learn to put a veneer over our feelings and present an acceptable facade to the outside world, but that doesn't stop us from searching for the elusive butterfly ... something that will make the pieces fit and give our lives a sense of order, meaning and purpose. Some people seek it in places where it cannot be found, in a quest for fame, money, prestige and power, but no matter how many of those acquisitions they may accumulate, the inner hunger is not assuaged because those things alone are never enough.

One of the characteristics that distinguishes New Age people is a readiness to carry the quest beyond the confines of everyday reality and to explore the horizons of their own minds. We realise that the world of form and substance cannot give us all the answers. Not all New Age people think of themselves as being psychic, but most are quite open-minded and accepting of the subject. A lot of other people may think we're slightly crazy, and maybe we are by their standards, but when you take a good look at what the world 'out there' accepts as normality, the question of craziness

3

becomes highly debatable. People firing missiles at each other, children being allowed to starve to death in famine-stricken countries while other nations dump surplus food to rot, ecological destruction, toxic waste, global chaos... this is sanity? I'd rather talk to my friendly spooks and play with the pixies, if it's all the same to you!

So what if other people think there's something odd or abnormal about you, what do you care about the opinions of others? No matter how you may act on the surface, if you're like most of us, you probably care quite a lot. Everyone needs to feel a sense of belonging and self-worth. People with a natural inclination towards the esoteric and New Age ideals are characterised by high levels of sensitivity, and sensitive people can be strongly affected by the thoughts and attitudes of others for reasons that are not entirely due to vulnerable emotions. Sensitivity is a faculty of sensation and perception: you are able to see and hear because your eyes are sensitive to light and your ears have a sensitivity to soundwaves. The senses react to stimuli in the surrounding atmosphere, and we all have a number of senses beyond the 'normal' five that are attuned to wavelengths limited to the physical spectrum. We call these 'extra' senses psychic, because they pertain to phenomena and conditions that appear to operate outside the domain of physical reality. Perhaps you may not consider yourself to be psychic to the extent of foretelling the future or conversing with the spirit world, but nevertheless, your psychic senses react to subtle influences which are undetectable to the physical senses. You will feel those reactions within yourself and you will be affected by them, even if you don't quite understand how or why you feel the way you do at times.

This quality of sensitivity extends to the atmospheric vibrations generated by the thoughts and feelings of other people. Thought is energy, so is emotion, and all forms of energy have an effect on other energies in the surrounding atmosphere, seen and unseen. Think of a television set: if you have an item of equipment that contains the required sensory and conversion mechanisms, and you bring it to life by circulating an energy through its circuits (in this case electricity) it will detect complex audio and visual vibrations in the atmosphere, which are nonexistent as far as your physical senses are concerned, and it will convert those vibrations into sounds and images within your range of physical perception. The difference between the energy principles that make your television set do what it does and the principles governing the function of your psychic senses is really only a matter of degree.

If you are in the company of people who share an affinity with you, understand the way you think, and give you support, encouragement and a feeling of being valued, you feel good. Your energy levels are high, your frame of mind is positive and your emotions are uplifted. In the company of people who regard you as an oddity, criticise your attitudes, ridicule your belief system and undermine everything that holds value for you, your energies droop, life becomes lonely and miserable. An inhospitable atmosphere can even make you physically ill.

After I wrote my first book, *Reaching for the Other Side*, in which I told of the experiences that led me to investigate the nature and purpose of psychic phenomena, and my encounters with spirit beings who helped me to understand such things, I received a lot of letters from people who thanked me for coming out into the open. These people told me that in writing of my experiences, my reactions to them and my outlook on life in general, 'You have put into words the things I have been thinking and feeling'. They said that it was a relief for them to discover another ordinary person who had similar ideas and experiences to their own. 'I thought I was the only person who encountered such things,' wrote one reader. 'Now I know that I'm not insane, and there are other people like me, I don't feel so alone any more.'

If they had only known it, the readers who wrote to thank me for the reassurances they found in my book were giving me exactly the kind of reassurance that *I* needed. When I wrote the book, I didn't know anyone else who shared my particular outlook on life. I had met other psychics and people who claimed an affinity with the realms of spirit, but their philosophy on life in general didn't seem to be much different from what I had encountered elsewhere, except that they incorporated psychic activity into their system of belief. To me, it had always seemed that the mere fact of being psychic could not be an end in itself. While it was gratifying to know that there really is a life hereafter and we can communicate with spirits from beyond the veil, there had to be more to it. I was searching for deeper levels of meaning, and more practical purposes to which they could be applied. It was more than just being psychic, and certainly much more than being religious, although it incorporated elements of both. It was an attitude of mind, a way of looking at life. The people I knew all seemed to think of me as being too intense about it all, too complex in my ways of thinking and too deep in my feelings of involvement.

My husband at that time, Roland, was a gifted trance medium, and it was through his mediumship that the spirit guides were able to communicate with me in those early days. They explained the natural laws that govern the function of psychic energy, taught me how to work safely with those energies and helped me to develop my own psychic faculties so that I could work independently without the need for assistance from trance mediums. Roland provided a channel for all of that spiritual intercourse and he was intrigued by the psychic elements involved in the process, but even he couldn't come to terms with the degree of spiritual commitment that I felt so deeply. The spiritual implications of our activities didn't interest him at all: he was content to explore the potential benefits of psychic phenomena, but if I tried to discuss spiritual principles with him he rapidly grew bored and irritated.

It was the people who read my book who gave me the feedback I needed, along with the assurance that I was not an alien in this world, as I had come to believe. In their letters, they reflected my own thoughts and feelings back to me in their own words. They gave me the reinforcement and the encouragement that I needed to continue, and they taught me to have faith in myself. In the years to follow, when my faith and my strength were being tested almost beyond the limits of my endurance, when I reached the pits of despair and even the husband I adored had become a hostile stranger, friends from near and far, most of whom I had never met in person, were my lifeline. They reminded me of the purpose, they gave me love and light when all around me was darkness and betrayal. Most of them will never know just how much they did to help me when I needed it the most, but I will never forget.

We all have to deal with challenges, setbacks and heartbreaks, and every difficult situation that we face is a test for our strength and faith in everything we believe. Writing books about the New Age experience didn't win me any exemptions: I'm still human and I face my share of trials and heartaches like anyone else. The only difference, if there is one, is that because I have written those books, a lot of people tend to assume that I have all the answers and my life should be a picture of bliss, a rose garden without any thorns, which is not the case at all. There are joys aplenty, to be sure, but there are troubles too, and spiritual principles that are simple to understand in theory aren't always easy to apply in practice. That is the kind of thing we learn through trial and error. Some of those trials are hard and very painful, and no matter how high our spiritual ideals may be, we still have to deal with life in this world. Being spiritual by nature and inclination isn't difficult: applying that spirituality in a world that seems designed to defeat us at every turn is a much more challenging prospect. We all have to do it; that is how we grow in strength and wisdom, but no one gets it easy. If we don't have the reassurance of knowing there are friends who care enough to believe in us, we can all too easily lose faith in ourselves, lose heart . . . and lose the way.

I have had to face my share of fearsome trials, but I haven't lost my way, and people like you are a large part of the reason why. When I get a letter from someone who tells me that a book of mine has picked them up when they were at a point of low ebb, I feel recognition as well as happiness, because that is what people like you have done for me, many times over. Perhaps I've been of help to some of you, but you have helped me, too. You have always been there when I have needed you the most.

I didn't know it would be like this when I wrote the first book. I wasn't really sure of anything back then, except my trust in the spiritual truths I was learning from my spirit guide, David, and the other entities who worked with him. At that time, I believed that my spirit companions were the only real friends I had. There were people in my life who called themselves my friends, but I couldn't talk with them about things that were important to me and receive any real understanding in return. They would pat me on the head and tell me that they loved me in spite of my strange ways, but I didn't feel loved, and I was always trying to justify myself, or making excuses for being different.

Writing the books provided me with an avenue in which I could be myself without feeling obliged to make excuses or justify my ways of thinking. Writers have the advantage of a certain degree of anonymity; in most cases people see our words, not our faces. Even the most popular authors have a reasonable chance of walking down city streets without being recognised. For a person who tends to be shy and tongue-tied in the presence of other people, writing is an excellent means of expression.

I don't get so tongue-tied these days, however, and this is largely due to the friends my books have made for me. A few months ago, I presented a seminar in Hobart, and just before we were to commence, one of the organisers asked me if I would like him to introduce me before I began to speak. I know that is the usual way of doing things, but it also tends to set a rather formal atmosphere and I didn't feel like being formal. I felt like enjoying myself with a group of like-minded people, which is what I usually do at a seminar. So I asked for the formalities to be dispensed with, perched myself cheerfully on a table at the front of the room and said to the assembled audience, 'If you don't know who I am, you've come to the wrong address'. People chuckled and the seminar was under way with a minimum of formality.

What a difference from the time, in a motel room in Melbourne, about an hour before I was due to make my very first public appearance, when the enormity of what I was about to undertake hit me like the gentle caress of a runaway truck. Crying and shaking in terror, I fell to my knees and clutched Roland by the legs, howling, 'I can't *do* it! All those people staring at me ... I'll freeze up! I'll do something stupid! I'll *die*! I can't ... I can't face it!' I had to face it of course, and I managed to muddle through somehow, although I sincerely doubt that the members of the audience were particularly impressed. People, quite frankly, scared me to death. Most people seem to feel quite at ease with other human beings, but scared of ghosts. With me, it was the other way around. Spooks are okay; even the troublesome ones can be confronted with a minimum of trepidation, but people in *this* world had me completely bamboozled!

I am aware that being at ease with the spiritual but uncomfortable with the physical world was not a balanced condition in which to be. I realised this at the time, but I really didn't know how to be any different. If my spirit friends neglected to warn me in advance that, as a direct result of writing books, I would be placed in a situation that forced me to come to terms with my fear of other people, I don't hold it against them. They knew me better than I knew myself, and they knew when they suggested that I write these books that it was the most expedient way of helping me to become more balanced and at ease in all worlds. So, while I was industriously beavering away to help other people come to terms with the supernatural, the readers were helping me learn to enjoy my life in this

10

world. I have been fortunate enough to meet some of those readers in person and a few have become close friends, of the kind who truly understand how I think and feel, and who love me just the way I am. Others, I have known only through the mail, but every person who ever cared enough to write, or come to see me at a public meeting, has helped me to find a balance, a sense of belonging and a feeling of self-worth, all of which are as essential to anyone's well-being as an understanding of the worlds of spirit.

Spirituality is our nature, and learning to understand ourselves as spiritual beings is necessary for an understanding of life itself. At the same time, we live in a physical world and we need to have equilibrium at all levels of our existence. Just as we cannot fully understand life in the physical world without possessing some knowledge of the spiritual universe, we cannot be in a healthy state of balance as spirits if we do not come to terms with physical life, and for a very great number of us, that isn't easy.

We need to know just how much we really have in common with other people in order to have a feeling of kinship and belonging, but our society is set about with so many artificial standards and expectations, and people feel obliged to maintain their masks of conformity, so it becomes very difficult to see beyond the surface and discover how very much alike we really are. These masks really don't help at all, they only prevent us from getting to know each other as we need to do, and they lead to a very unhappy problem, which is epitomised in a letter I received recently:

Dear Dawn

Just read your books Reaching for the Other Side *and* Edge of Reality. *I identified with many things you spoke of, especially with your experience as a five-year-old, being told that you couldn't talk with Jesus . . .*

'. . . from that time onward I learned to live with hopelessness, despair and rejection.'

'I felt unworthy to be loved by my Creator.'

'. . . suddenly my life became something fearful.'

Your words have prompted this letter. Although I don't demonstrate any outward signs of being psychic and haven't encountered any 'strange beings' or had unusual experiences, I do feel like a lost child in a busy shopping complex. Anchored to the spot in sheer terror, I look to find familiar faces — I see none. No one smiles — no one looks remotely interested. People seem to be rushing around, obviously knowing where they are going, getting on with business. I'm desperate, and I feel total panic.

My sadness and grief rise in my throat, where they tighten and strangle my screams of despair. My heart is breaking. I am alone. I must find home. But who will I ask? Which way will I go?

This pathetic scenario describes the feelings of a thirty-five-year-old UNKNOWN HOUSE-WIFE, outwardly meeting the demands of the Horror Stretch of life, raising three kids and looking after a husband in downtown suburbia.

Until I read your books — my mind and emotions found no rest. The constant chatter kept up with a fierce pace. Maybe now I can

look for landmarks that will lead me home.
Perhaps someone might even take my hand for
a while. I think I'd like that.

Wish me well on my journey as I know you
will. God bless you and your family.

Your sister in Christ
Barbara

What I find most saddening about Barbara's letter
is that there are so many Barbaras, all striving to
meet the demands of their lives, rushing around,
getting on with business, outwardly seeming to
know what it's all about, and inwardly crying for
the touch of a friendly hand. If Barbara only knew
it, the people she sees around her only *appear* to
have their lives together. Most of them are wearing
the masks they believe that they *must* wear in order
to fit in and be accepted, but underneath it all they
are as lonely and despairing as all the other
Barbaras.

When people's lives are restricted to the boundaries of home, family and workplace, it is difficult for them to know how much of their thoughts,
feelings and the events in their lives are specific to
them and how much is common to the rest of
humanity; how much is due to their own attitudes
and actions and how much is subject to cosmic
tides and seasons that affect millions of other
people everywhere. If you were to be granted a
perspective that allows you to see the events that
befall you occurring simultaneously in the lives of
many others, a completely different prospect
would be revealed.

To give an illustration, think of an event that
has a significant effect in the life of anyone who
has to undergo the experience. When a marriage

ends, for instance, the two people most directly concerned will believe that the cause lies solely in the way they have treated each other, and nowhere else. What other causes could there possibly be, you might ask? I would have felt the same once, but because I have been given that extra dimension of perspective, I have noticed something that provides a great deal of food for thought. When I called an end to my marriage with Roland, I felt that it was due to nothing more than the personal differences between us and there was no other factor remotely involved, but as the situation progressed I noticed that the same thing was happening to a lot of other people, under very similar circumstances. Women who had hitherto been patiently giving their best in long-term marriages that seemed outwardly stable and reasonably happy, were suddenly deciding that they needed to be free, and the conditions they had accepted for years just weren't good enough any more. I saw it in letters from my readers, heard it from women at seminars, and a clinical psychologist remarked to me that 'There must be something cosmic about all this'.

'All of a sudden,' she said, 'the majority of my clients are men whose wives have walked away from them. I know marriages are breaking up all the time, but there is something different about this. There's usually a balance between the number of marriages that end because the wife leaves, and the ones where the husband leaves, and usually the proportion of husbands who leave is higher. Now, the balance has been completely overturned. It's the wives who are leaving, the number of marital break-ups has increased by some considerable amount, and the men are falling apart because they can't cope. I haven't seen anything like this before... it's almost an

14

epidemic, yet there seems to be a purpose to it, a pattern of some kind.' During the same period, a television current affairs programme featured an item about this trend, calling it 'The Runaway Wife Syndrome'.

When one person gets fed up with an unhappy marriage and calls an end to it, there is no reason to see it as anything but an isolated occurrence, but to discover that the same thing is happening on such a wide scale and under such similar circumstances places a different complexion on the matter. We begin to see that there are larger forces at work and we are not alone in our responses to them. When millions of other people are sharing the same kind of experiences and feelings, we cannot be as unusual or as isolated as we may have believed. We can see ourselves as part of a bigger pattern. There is a wider perspective, and while there must undoubtedly have been factors within each relationship which played a large part, there was some kind of cosmic tide taking effect as well. Not only does this raise some thought-provoking questions; it indicates that there is quite a large number of people who would like to know the answers. The times are changing, and all of us are feeling the effects of those changes, but we can only understand the tide of events if we are able to see the same influences at work in the lives of our fellow human beings.

I chose divorce as my example because it is a significant event in any person's life, but I could give any number of different examples from my experience alone (not all as cataclysmic in nature) of events, experiences, ideas and feelings that are shared by an immense number of other people. We seem to have more things in common than most of us even begin to suspect. I know before I write a word about any of my thoughts, feelings and experiences that, when those words are read, there will

15

be a chorus of readers' voices crying 'Yes, me too!' This doesn't happen because there is anything special or unique about me: it can only happen because there isn't.

Whatever happens to me, it will be happening to countless others as well. Whatever I think, others are thinking, and my feelings are theirs also. This is not because I am causing anything to happen, it is only that I am a part of what is happening, like millions of other people. It is eminently comforting to know that there are people everywhere who understand exactly how it feels to be me, but a lot of other people aren't so fortunate. They still feel the way I *used* to feel, before I started writing books and found out how many kindred spirits there are in this world of ours. People like the lady who wrote the following letter:

Dear Dawn

Thank you so much for making your books available to me, I can't begin to tell you the profound changes they've brought to me. I know you are modest in your attitudes, but I do think you are truly wise, you would have to be to follow the teachings of your spirit guide and, although you are only human and make mistakes, you've chosen an enlightened path. I believe (for what it's worth) that once you're on that path you must *continue on it. I think that is a natural universal law. You can progress from ignorance to enlightenment but you can't progress from enlightenment back to ignorance.*

I think I've stepped on to the path (you may see me struggling up the rear if you look

16

behind you!) and as much as I feel like deviating at times, I know it's impossible and I have to confront all manner of obstacles, self-imposed and otherwise. Of course, as you warned in your books, I've felt incredibly lonely. I remember going shopping once with my Mum, who lives with my husband, myself and our little boy. Mum and I went into a bookshop and I happened upon your book. Mum purchased what she was looking for and I told her I'd meet her outside. After she had left, I guiltily purchased your first book and hid it in my bag. At a later date, I purchased your other two books as well and kept them hidden in my bedroom dresser. It's been pretty tough, keeping all your invaluable knowledge hidden. I've since 'spilled the beans' on my beliefs and, of course, as I instinctively knew, I'm a bit of a laughing stock now. There is no religious background in my family, they're all confirmed atheists, and have fought for various political causes over the years, feminism and socialism etc. I do respect their beliefs and adhere to some of them, but I feel they're only necessary band-aid structures until human consciousness evolves as a whole.

I have had a few psychic incidents since I've practised your meditation techniques and I think I've been in touch with my spirit guide (a Red Indian man), but I'm not sure. After all, it could be all in my mind. Everyone around me thinks I'm nutty and I've got no one to bounce my ideas off. It's sometimes easy for me to become discouraged and to believe I'm deluding myself. When I feel like that, it's as if a rug has been pulled out from under me and I've

17

spent many a night crying myself to sleep. At times like that, I find it impossible to meditate and my 'prayers' to my guardian spirit to bring me tangible proof of his existence don't seem to be heard. I realise I'm creating my own blockages by not trusting my instincts, but how can I possibly believe I'm right and everyone around me is wrong? If my guardian spirit could only tell me his name, show me his face, that would give me a little hope. How do I weather this storm, Dawn? The funny thing is, I can't stop trying. I feel if I do stop, I'll be slipping back into 'sleep-walking' my way through life and I don't want that!

I realise you can't answer all letters, but just by writing to you, I feel I've reached out to the one sympathetic spirit in my world and I'm eternally grateful to you.

Love
Diana

If you can read that letter without wanting to weep, that is something you and I do *not* have in common. That Diana has to feel that I am the only sympathetic spirit in her world is a tragic indictment of the conditions that exist in our society. It is small comfort for someone in Diana's position to be told that these conditions are changing. For her, they haven't changed yet, and she has to cope with the daily reality. When I read letters like this, and Diana's is not the only one by any means, I can't help wanting to do something that might make things better, however small my contribution may be.

If reading one person's account of her experiences and ideals as a New Age person can be of help and comfort to someone like Diana, I wonder how much more helpful and encouraging it might be to share in the stories of more than one? Readers are always telling me that they get pleasure from my 'conversational' style of writing, because it's friendly and personal. I know lots of other people who are just as friendly and as willing to share, and I met the majority of them in the letters they wrote to me after reading my books, so we all have a lot of things in common.

When a group of people combines to share ideas and experiences, there is so much more to be shared. For instance, many people have written to ask me for more information about the Earth Religion, but because I am not a follower of that religion I don't have a comprehensive knowledge of the subject, therefore any information I can give is second-hand and explained from an observer's point of view. More informative and enlightening by far, is to have it explained by someone with an intimate working knowledge of that philosophy. Have you ever wondered what it might be like to be regressed to a past life, and what effects it might have on a person's life this time around? I have never been regressed, so I can only theorise, but I know someone who can tell about it from the viewpoint of a participant. What about a committed Christian who experiences communication with spirits from other dimensions, recognises the value and validity of that experience but wishes to remain committed to the Christian philosophy: how does a person in that situation find a workable balance? I'm sure a lot of people would be interested in hearing how that can be achieved, and I know someone who can tell about it, first-hand. I know lots of people with interesting stories to share. In fact, when I let it be known that I was collecting material to be used in this book, so

19

many people provided so much information that I now have much more than I can use in just one volume.

Even the idea of inviting others to participate with me in the writing of this book was given to me by a friend. His name is Bruce Clarke and he's a sound technician who works for a television station. We have never met in person, but that is no hindrance to our friendship. We exchange letters periodically and share an amiable 'kindred spirit' kind of communication. Bruce has a way of reading the feelings behind my words, and he wrote to me soon after the publication of my third book, *Lifting the Veil*, referring to a problem that had been vexing me for some time, which has been classified as 'guruism'.

People need to understand the forces which influence their lives, know that having psychic experiences and New Age beliefs does not make them odd or abnormal in any way, and feel encouraged to develop their spiritual abilities, to use them in ways that can be of benefit to everyone concerned. For this to be made possible, information needs to be shared. If, for instance, a person hears voices out of thin air and sees images that are invisible to the people around her, and every person she knows tells her that what she is perceiving is impossible and she's losing her grip on reality, that is what she will eventually be forced to believe, which will cause a lot of unnecessary mental, emotional and psychological torment for her. Furthermore, because nobody around this person understands the phenomena of clairaudience and clairvoyance, there will be no one who can explain to her the need to clear her channels and shield them so that unwanted and harmful influences are screened out, much less tell her how this can be done. This leaves her in a vulnerable and dangerous situation, where she can be exposed to very real harm. This is not merely a hypothetical situation: psychiatric hospitals contain a lot of people who have been damaged in this way. If you knew that things like this are happening, and you had been given the kind of information that could help people to prevent it from happening to them, or to their children, would you keep that information to yourself, or would you share it?

I was asked to share by the spirit teacher who had given me the understanding I needed. I can remember what I went through when there was nobody who could understand or explain what was happening to me, and how I felt when the lifeline of information was extended to me. How could I refuse to offer the same lifeline to anyone else who needs it and still smile at my reflection in a mirror?

I didn't set out to impose my opinions on anyone else. My message, in essence, has always been 'I am an ordinary, everyday human being and these things have happened to me. Maybe they happen to you also, and maybe, like me, you'd like to understand more about them and hear from someone else who knows how it feels. Perhaps we can be of help to each other.'

From my point of view, it is not only preferable for people to understand that I am not a guru and there is nothing about me that makes me different from anyone else; it is *essential*. The very core of my message is that the things I have learned and experienced are not unusual but characteristic of a natural phase in human development that happens to millions and millions of ordinary people all the time. We are currently emerging from a period of spiritual darkness and ignorance that has lasted for centuries, during which human beings have had their natural spirituality stifled and repressed, often quite ferociously. This has left us a legacy of ignorance and prejudice that needs to be lifted for all our sakes, and that process will not be assisted by people who want to believe that they are special and different just because they happen to be psychic. In order to reinforce this belief with regard to themselves, those people have to convince people like us that it is not normal for ordinary human beings to possess such abilities, and that is not true. If I let people believe there is anything special or unusual about me, I would undermine the very message that I most want to get across to people, so I spend a lot of time reminding people that I am an ordinary person, very much like everybody else, with no special gifts or abilities. Nevertheless, there are always some people who seem to think that I am able to do things they cannot do, which causes me a certain amount of concern.

By the same token, like anyone else I feel good when someone tells me they have enjoyed my work and found it helpful, and I like to share my good feelings with those close to me. In the past, if I received letters that made me feel particularly uplifted, I used to read passages aloud to my friends so that they could enjoy the feeling too, but a number of those former acquaintances saw this as a display of egotism. They told me that I was flaunting myself, displaying conceit and making myself out to be better than everyone else. That wasn't what I had meant to do, but I felt that if sharing in that way was giving a false impression, I had better stop doing it.

There is another way in which I am the same as most other people. I have feelings, and when people I have regarded as friends make harsh accusations, those feelings can be hurt. This is what Bruce addressed in his letter and, in suggesting a solution for me, he came up with an idea that has potential benefits in other ways, for a lot of other people. Here is his letter.

Dear Dawn

Well, it's near midnight, can't sleep, the urge to write this won't go away and I know better than to ignore the 'urge'.

Thank you, thank you for your new book. The phrase 'pulling the strings together' hit me in the first chapter and by surprise (!), out comes that phrase further on in the book.

Why is it, Dawn, that your book never holds any surprises? I don't get the luxury of thinking 'That's interesting', 'That's new' or 'Good theory'. No, not with your books. I'm too busy crying 'Yes! Yes! Yes!' every time I turn a page. Out of a mishmash of scrambled thoughts, ideas and images in my mind, a parallel mind has the ability to put it down on paper in logical, practical order.

No wonder people cry when they read your books. It must be out of sheer relief, that you have the ability to say what others can only feel. Thank you.

All this adulation (I wrote the original letter half-way through the book so I won't change it, yet another Dawn surprise) which leads me on to the next topic. Guruism. (This may make you feel better.) Here is an analogy for you.

A group of people find themselves in a darkened room. They stumble about, knocking things over, looking for switches, desk lamps etc., then somebody strikes a match and lights a candle. Now, the first thing everybody is going to do is turn towards *the light. The person with the candle has become the centre of attention. Why? Firstly, this person provided a solution to the problem. Secondly, this person had the foresight to carry the candle and matches. Now you get guruism, or is it? It appears to be a problem for both sides, but the people stumbling around in the dark have had their problem solved. They turn to the person holding the candle out of admiration more than anything else. Not being able to take the admiration, the candle holder says, 'Oh, I always carry a candle in my pocket. Most of my friends do, too'. Some will say 'How clever!' or 'Why didn't I think of that?' and others would say 'Smart-arse bitch!' It's all relevant.*

Where is this heading, you might ask? I don't know, I'm only transcribing these thoughts. Being in your position, it is extremely difficult not to have people drawn to you. Call it guruism or just plain admiration or need, you have a problem. As this letter unfolds, there may be an answer, but first . . .

Being in television, I have had the opportunity to observe 'celebrities'. I have experienced this myself in a small way. There is the up side and the flip side. The up side is fame, fortune, doors being opened. The down side is lack of privacy, people seeing you as special, larger than life, and there is an inability for friends to cope. Another story . . .

A dear friend of mine desired to read the main weekday news bulletin, and so it came to pass. As you may know, to be a newsreader is to be a media guru, simply because hundreds of thousands of people hang on every word you say. The down side of this attention or 'centring' was the decline of friends around him. Not through malice or jealousy, they just thought, now being a 'celebrity', he would be too busy to see them. The upshot was that he became very lonely. Kick me in the pants if I am getting out of line, but I think you're in that position and it upsets you. You know and I know that we are only doing God's work. I would be pretty angry with God if He/She didn't let you take a bow and be admired, nay revered, for having the courage to light the candle for so many people.

Here comes the crunch. You need 'back-up', as they say in the police shows. Take the 'goo' out of guru... dilute it... spread the load. Normal people are passing through this spiritual awakening; some starting, some half-way through, some even further. Hence Book Four **With a Little Help from My Friends**. *I know Roland says you will do well at fantasy, but hear me out. To give the 'spiritual revolution' more punch, and show it as a perfectly natural evolutionary condition, I am prepared, as I'm sure many of your readers would be, to put my name, occupation and my experiences on paper. From all walks of life, from all points of the globe, the same story can be told, thus giving credibility, and that is also relative to those who need it. It would be an opportunity to compare notes, gather support, reduce the isolation and, more importantly, give courage to those who are just awakening.*

Let there be many candles to light the way.

Many candles indeed! Why not? The more ordinary people who stand up and say, 'I'm another ordinary person and these things happen to me', the more other people will be encouraged, and the more knowledge we will all have to share. It has to start somewhere, and the people who have made a contribution to the writing of this book, by allowing their experiences to be shared, have made a start. All of these people share my hope that those who read the book will be encouraged to continue, in their own way, lighting their candles in their own corner of the world. Who knows what a difference it can make until we do it? Nobody can do it all alone, but nobody is expected to do anything more than try. You have a candle in your pocket, too, and maybe someone near you needs to see it shine. In any case, the friends who have joined me in the writing of this book have not done so out of any desire for acclamation, but simply because they care, and they want to do whatever they can to share their light with others. They have shared with me, and my life has been enriched beyond measure because of them. I hope it will be that way for you, too, and that whether you need reassurance, encouragement or just food for thought, you will find whatever you need in the pages to follow.

CHAPTER TWO

Cosmic consciousness — 'May the Force be with you!'

Dawn

I would like to talk to you about a situation which has arisen over the past few months. I am not sure how to deal with it, and it covers energies which I feel familiar with, am afraid of, and am beginning to feel I am attracting. I'm not exactly sure how this letter is going to go, as I'm just writing it as it comes. I figured that if I tried to plan it, it wouldn't work. Reading back over that last bit, you'd swear I was a kitten of about sixteen or seventeen. I am thirty-five years old, and I've always had a tendency to attract people who are in circumstances they are either unsure about dealing with or are frightened of, and I have usually found that they wander away after a bit of a chat and their lives have changed, their attitudes have been transformed, and they are looking at things much more positively. I haven't worked at it, and sometimes I get a bit nervous because I often find myself saying things I didn't know I knew, but when I've said them I find I did know them, but I don't know where they came from.

I have always felt — I was about to say 'a bit' different, but that's actually a lie. I've always felt a lot different. I've never quite been able to do things the way other people do things, and I've always felt this feeling inside myself that simply won't go away and, in spite of everything, I don't want it to go away, either. I have also, on a few occasions, and they are only a few, felt that I should just drop all the crap about the value of life and humanity, and accept that basically people are bastards and there's not a bloody thing I can do, so why don't I just join the public service or get a job like a 'normal' person. It never works. Almost invariably I'll find myself going to a movie to 'escape from the real world', and I end up seeing things like Star Wars *or* Star Trek: The Movie, *which really reinforces my sense of the energy, relaxes me, and puts me back on the 'different' track I seem to be on. I am also aware, in some way, that I'm not really on a different track; more I suppose, that I see the track differently.*

Now, after that little rave, down to nitty gritty. I keep getting the feeling that I can't hold down the energy any more (as I say that, I can almost feel you jumping up and down, saying, 'Of course you shouldn't, you silly bitch!') without causing major damage to myself, to what I'm working on, and the people I'm working with and, damn it, to everything else as well. I feel sometimes like maybe all I've got is a massively over-inflated ego and all this internal energy is just a really weak thing, jumping up and down, trying to draw attention to itself/myself. I guess what it comes down to is, I'm scared. I can feel this energy and sometimes it is so strong it hurts. I can't pull telepathic stunts, I'm not precognitive, I'm not anything definable, though I get feelings about people which are almost invariably correct, and I have learned to trust them a lot more than the little brain saying 'Now hold on, dear, you don't really know these people, do you? Give them a chance'. Of course, when I do sense something wrong and give 'them' a chance, invariably, sometimes even years later, it becomes clear I had not been mistaken at all.

off track. Often, when I think about intellectualising. It's a really ute, but it's starting to run a d, of course, it never really

king at the development tech-given in Edge of Reality, and lf feeling really uneasy about not have a belief in a personal cription at all. I am aware of a rgy which surrounds, binds and everything, but I feel that put-onality on it is very destructive. I constant hassles with my family over tter, with my sister saying on occasions, if you don't believe in God, you must eve in the Devil', when in truth, I don't believe in either. I am aware of an energy field which goes so far beyond a 'personality of godhead' but it is not definable according to anything more than what we create it to be. I find the concept of receiving white light from a personality is equally difficult. In your book, you mentioned that you had used the name of

Christ simply because it suited you. I do not have a nametag I can place on the energy, and saying the word 'God' or any other such title I find completely throws my intents, because it is a reality I have no link with.

To try and take it a little further, I once had a vision (I don't know what else to call it). I wasn't exactly asleep and I wasn't exactly awake, and I saw the entire universe as a human shape, with the Earth being located on the little finger of the right hand. Every part of that shape was integral and creative in its own right. The shape did not make its individual parts, nor did the individual parts make the shape, they simply were. I realised that using a human shape was simply to put it into a framework I could accept. But this shape did not have a name, it did not have a religion or belief structure, it was simply the sum total of its parts, and its shape was defined by those parts. That shape was also surrounded by other shapes. I am assuming our universe is not alone, but that there are other universes existent in, for want of a better term, dimensions other than our own.

I can't put a name to that shape. If I were to term it God, it would be a lie because it is not the God most people accept, because it is not a personality. It does not have any more or less love for us than what we create. It is too impartial to be personalised. The White Light Meditation talks of a creator; the Invocation to the Spirits of Light calls on a personality in Christ. I don't know what nametag I can put on what I believe in. The closest I can come to says it's me, which will probably put me well in line for the next trip to the loony-bin, but I don't feel I can separate myself from it by putting a name on it. I can't even think what word could be used. Perhaps you may be able to give me some support with that. I am also really nervous about tapping in to my own energy without guidance. I was wondering whether you know of any groups or individuals you could recommend in my area. I am terrified that if the energies that I have been keeping well and truly held inside myself for a lot of years were suddenly to explode out with no guidance apart from my own fairly limited awareness, I could really hurt someone.

This may have no relevance, but I feel it is pertinent in some ways. I have occasionally done some rebirthing, and I have a certain skill in finding my own voice while I'm doing it. Two things keep coming up. One is a 'memory', if you like, of being chained to a wall in a place under the ground, while the 'scribes' and the 'ruler' demanded that I use my skills to punish and destroy their enemies. I refused, they tortured me, and finally I broke; I destroyed not only the building, but them as well. As I destroyed them, I felt it like a ripping out of part of my own insides. The other memory is of a fire and a stake, and you know the usual procedure they used. I can remember feeling the burning, and feeling strengthened by it, and screaming inside myself, 'You can never destroy me. What I am will continue for ever.' I have a feeling that the energies which raise themselves within those sessions are alive and well, and living inside me, but I find I'm scared. I don't want to let them out with no one else around.

I was about to say that I realise this sounds a

31

bit wacky, but I suppose it doesn't really. I seem to continually attract to myself people with quite extraordinary energies, but I can't find anyone who isn't either afraid of them, unwilling to accept them, or simply unaware that they're even there. And then of course there are the ones who say they know exactly what's happening, and act like they've got some hidden whammo tucked up their sleeves. I am a bloody sight more sus about them than about the other ones. I am also aware that my own fear makes the connection terribly difficult and probably more dangerous. I am also aware of all the stuff that says if you're interested in the higher good, you will be safe, and I have a feeling that's more like candy-floss than tin tacks.

I think I've put down enough. I often wish I could be like 'Miss Average', but I don't think the energies within and surrounding me will ever allow me to forget who I am. I just don't know what the hell to do about it.

Dawn, I hope you can sort this letter out. If you are still here on the last page, congratulations, you've just completed an epic. I hope I may hear from you.

Yours sincerely
Margaret

Fortunately for me, Margaret provided a telephone number in her letter. I'm not in the habit of ringing people to answer their letters as a rule, but when I read what Margaret had written, I wanted to include it in this book. She is not the only person who has told me of this difficulty with relating to the universe as a personality, and I suspect there are many more who can identify with her situation. However, I was running short on time to meet my publisher's deadline, and there were matters I wanted to discuss with Margaret prior to writing this chapter. Hence the telephone call.

'This is going to sound very simplistic, until I explain myself,' I told her, 'but it seems to me that your dilemma can be defined by one word... semantics.'

'Really?' Her voice sounded hopeful.

'It's a matter of words. You can't relate to a god, but "god" is a word. Energy is energy; it doesn't change, no matter how often people change the words they use to describe it. An alternative term for God could be the cosmos. Do you know what cosmos means?'

'Oh darn! Someone told me that only a few days ago, and I've forgotten,' came her chagrined reply.

'Never mind, I've got a dictionary in front of me. Cosmos means the world, or the universe, as an ordered system: order, harmony, a harmonious system...'

'Yes, I can relate to that,' came her keen response.

'And how about "the force"?' I suggested.

Margaret laughed. 'That's what I always keep *wanting* to call it, but I've been a bit reluctant to do that, because of the connotations of "power *over*".'

'Nup,' I demurred. 'Think of Luke Skywalker. Think Yoda.'

'I've got you!' came her response, ringing with relief and merriment.

'You know,' I continued, in a reflective tone. 'I knew a lady some years ago who you'd have liked. We were both fans of *Star Wars* and we were in the habit of saying, "May the Force be with you" to

33

each other. When she was leaving my place one day, she said it as usual, then she grinned and said, "Who am I kidding? We *are* the Force!"'

'*Exactly*!' exulted Margaret. 'I can relate to that, with no problems.'

'Thought you would,' I answered cheerfully.

For years untold, human beings have looked to the Source of All Life, and attempted to define it in terms they can understand and relate to. This quest for knowledge of the infinite has given rise to religions, sciences and philosophies without number. The process continues today, and no doubt for as long as human beings exist this quest will continue.

Some people look at what they know, or think they know, about the Source of All Life, and they call it God. 'God' has many names, in many different languages, but the energy that is the Source remains unchanged. Scientists have reached the stage of saying that, ultimately, all is chaos... which seems to mean, in essence, that just when they think they've caught the secret and they can predict what will happen next, the universe pulls a switch on them. Still the Source goes on being what it has always been. Scientific theories haven't altered it, nor have religious doctrines.

The 'spiritual quest' is essentially the search for greater understanding about the nature of life, and a striving to achieve a state of union with our Source. Sciences, religions and philosophies are systems of thought through which we attempt to define the indefinable. Difficulties arise when people start confusing labels with the reality. The way to the Ultimate isn't a matter of finding one religion, science or way of thought that is right for everyone, but rather finding the keys that unlock your own deeper understanding. Margaret's letter demonstrates how easily words can get in the way.

Cosmic principles remain cosmic principles: words and intellectual concepts are only ways of expressing the principles. We can alter the words to suit our individual perceptions, but the words don't alter the principles. Energy remains energy, and controlling it intelligently is really just a matter of becoming familiar with its principles of function and applying them appropriately to the way we live our lives. It may be easier said than done, but the doing is of necessity a matter of time, practice and perseverance. These energy principles can be expressed in the languages of science and religion, or equally as well in the language of fantasy.

One person may say 'God is within All that Is' while another says 'There is a pervading energy which surrounds, binds and interconnects All that Is', and each person is saying the same thing. They are merely using different words to describe their perceptions. Just think of all the religious wars that human beings have fought over the words we use to describe that which none of us fully understands!

I know quite a number of people who cannot relate to the idea of being religious disciples, but when they are asked if they can relate to being 'Jedi knights' there is an immediate lighting up in their eyes. Why not? The idea is not as far-fetched as some people might imagine.

In the language of *Star Wars*: there is the Force, an all-pervading energy that surrounds, binds, interconnects and energises All that Is. Many people are unaware that the Force exists, some regard it as nothing more than an ancient myth. Those who are aware learn that the Force is quite real, utterly impartial but infinitely powerful, and it can be tapped and directed to achieve tangible physical results through the power of the human mind. The Force can be directed to harm and enslave others, as it is by the dastardly Darth Vader, or it can be directed to uplift and to heal. When it is used to cause harm, this power takes its toll on the user. With every act of harm that he perpetrates, Darth Vader must suffer the progressive destruction of his own personality. Is there any difference between the *Star Wars* Force and the cosmic energies in New Age philosophy?

In *Star Wars*, there is psychic communication, as when Luke Skywalker hears the voice of his mentor, Ben Kenobi, speaking in his mind after Ben Kenobi's physical body has been killed. This speaks of life after death, telepathy and communication beyond the grave. How much different is it for a psychically sensitive person to mentally 'hear' spirit voices through clairaudience?

There are cosmic energy streams that we can tap and focus with the power of our minds, which can be directed to achieve tangible physical results. Whether we refer to these energies as the Force or the Holy Spirit makes no difference to the energies. They flow in accordance with the cosmic laws of nature, as they have always done and will always continue to do. It is possible to place too much importance on the words we use to define the energies, when really it is how we use those energies, and how much we understand about the way they work, that should be of the greatest importance. If words get in the way of your understanding and inhibit your ability to work harmoniously with cosmic energies, there is a simple solution: change the words.

Margaret has reached a level of psychic awareness at which she is conscious of her union with the Source, which is why she finds it difficult to separate herself from it by giving it a name. In truth, she would be ill-advised even to try achieving that kind of separation, for it would constitute a retrograde step in her development. That sense of oneness is what millions of other people are striving to achieve through the process of psychic and spiritual development.

Margaret's awareness of the tremendous currents of power flowing into and around her arouses a fear that if the energies were to erupt forth from her without control she could hurt someone. She is aware that if this were to happen she would harm herself, but she also senses that any attempt to repress the energy would lead to major damage. It is vital for her to have an understanding of the ways in which she can safely channel those energies for the highest good of all concerned. If it helps to think of it as attuning to 'the Force' then that is what she would be best advised to do.

Her rebirthing 'memories' suggest that, in other life experiences, Margaret has already acquired the level of inward control that will enable her to safely harness and direct the energies that flow within her. The 'torture chamber' experience shows an imprint in her subconscious awareness that to cut loose and destroy is to self-destruct. She describes the feeling as like having a part of her own insides ripped out. Perhaps we can learn a lesson in this respect from the bee, who also loses a part of her insides when she uses her sting, and must then crawl away to die.

The second 'memory', of being burned at the stake, indicates that Margaret also has the degree of self-control that she needs. Burning at the stake constitutes torture in itself, and it was almost invariably preceded by other forms of gruesome torture. In this episode, however, Margaret's experience is not of breaking under the torment, but holding in the rising power and, even in extremity, being aware that she can never be destroyed, regardless of what is done to her physical body.

With these 'memories' so strongly ingrained in her, along with her natural tendency to give in a helpful, uplifting way and her desire to use her abilities positively, it is highly doubtful that Margaret would knowingly use her psychic energies destructively. What she fears is that lack of knowledge may be her undoing. She needs to know how to use the energies so that the pressure doesn't build up inside her, and she needs to be confident that when she allows them to flow, it will happen in a beneficial manner. In this case, the difference between knowing and not knowing is simply a matter of finding the right terminology to define that which she is already perceiving inwardly.

While there is certainly an element of 'candy-floss' in the saying that 'if you're interested in the higher good, you'll be safe', there is also truth. Thought creates reality: if your thoughts are focused on the higher good, that is the direction in which your energies will tend to flow. Like attracts like; therefore a benevolent outlook attracts benign influences. Having an awareness of these factors and focusing one's energies accordingly can be a lot of help in maintaining a level of safety. Of course, we need to bear in mind that, as humans, our self-control can slip and there are times when we may not feel particularly well disposed towards our fellow humans, so we need to explore all possible methods of ensuring that we neither release nor attract bursts of negative energy.

What keeps coming back to my mind is the principle that thought creates reality, and it is possible, with the use of mental techniques, to create mechanisms for safety. Years ago, when I was doing a lot of work with psychic rescue, I had one experience in which a hostile entity gained control of the medium's body, sufficient to rise from the chair and start lurching towards me with an obvious intent to do harm. The situation was effectively defused without injury, but I didn't want to experience anything like that again. The next time I saw a hostile entity trying to raise the medium's body from the chair, I 'imagined' a glowing golden bar blocking the way, and mentally focused on the message, 'You cannot rise from the chair. You cannot pass the barrier'. It was intriguing to see the entity causing the medium's body to grunt and strain, exactly as though he were pushing against a solid obstruction, yet I spoke no words aloud, nor did I make any gestures. The effect was created by thought energy alone, and I used that technique quite a number of times, with different entities; none ever succeeded in passing the barrier. All I did was *think* it. Anyone else can do the same, with appropriate alterations to suit the circumstances at any given time.

From a spiritual perspective, thought not only creates reality, thought IS reality.

To control and direct the universal energies, we use the power of thought. *We* govern the effects of any 'psychic' energies that flow through us, and/or around us. The imagery can be altered to suit the individual, but in general we can use 'imagination' to create channels through which the energies are directed. We can choose directions for that energy that bring positive benefits to everyone they touch, or we can direct them in ways that cause harm. *We* do the choosing.

White light can be summoned with or without the use of any formal structures of thought. An example of the latter is given in a letter I received a few years ago from a lady named Lisa.

Dear Dawn

I just had to write and let you know of the wonderful experience I just had. I wanted to ring my Mum and tell her, but it's too late and I can't contain it any longer, so that's why I'm writing this letter.

I read your last book a few months ago and found it very helpful in pointing me in the right direction. At the moment I'm in the middle of your second book, which brings me to my wonderful news.

First of all, I decided to try cleansing my aura with white light. I didn't expect much to happen as I've tried meditating before but I don't seem to have the patience or time, with a two-year-old daughter around me all the time. Anyway, I waited for my husband and daughter to go to sleep and gave it a try. First, I lay down and relaxed my body and imagined myself in a sort of plastic bubble.

Next, I tried to imagine myself under a white waterfall, but I kept seeing myself floating around in space, so I went with it. Next, I saw white light coming towards me from space, and it didn't just flow, it zoomed, all around and through my body, almost like electricity.

Then I saw myself from outside, looking into my 'bubble' and I sealed it off with a mirror surface. Then I went back inside the bubble and, next minute, my whole body went hot, from my toes up, like a flush, and I went all tingly over my body, and sort of exploded. I know this sounds extremely crude, but it was almost like an orgasm, except in my mind.

All these tiny sparks of white light shot out and started to rain down, and when I looked

*down, they were raining on to the Earth, just
like you see it from space. And I remember
thinking that one particular spark was for the
Ayatollah (Khomeini, of Iran). I thought, 'The
poor man needs a lot of white light'. And all
the time, my mind was saying, 'Peace and love.
Peace and love.'*

*When I opened my eyes, I had tears rolling
down my cheeks. It was one of the most wonderful experiences I've ever had. I hope you
don't mind me writing like this, I couldn't
wait, I had to tell someone.*

*I'm going to practise that every day, and
hopefully try some of your other exercises later.*

Thanks again.

*Yours sincerely
Lisa*

The basic White Light Meditation is given further
on in this book, and it should be noted that Lisa
did not perform the exercise *exactly* as given. She
incorporated the *basic principles*, adapted them to
suit herself, and went with her natural flow. She
did not have to think in advance about what she
would do with the light energy, it happened spontaneously, and she went with it because it felt good
and right for her to do so. Had it felt wrong,
harmful or threatening in any way, she would just
as spontaneously have resisted it and brought herself out of the meditation. Had it happened in that
other way, it might have frightened her, but her
own natural inclinations would not have allowed
her to go with it. In this sense, having a strong
focus on the highest good for all concerned offers
quite a lot of effective protection.

Note also that during the induction period of

41

her meditation Lisa did not invoke God, Christ or any other deity. First, she focused on the relaxation of her body, then she 'imagined' herself in a plastic bubble. Next, she focused on the white light, and the light responded with the speed of thought.

As Margaret has pointed out: when I wrote my second book, back in 1986, I said that as a part of my own protective procedures I used the name of Christ, because it felt right for me to do so. For myself. I also pointed out that the names we use are essentially a matter of choice. At the level of energy upon which we desire to call, names are irrelevant because communication is non-verbal. Here, all communication is through the power of thought, for thought is reality.

Why, then, is the use of certain 'names of power' recommended at all? Because it helps us to focus *our own* thought energies in such a way that we will succeed in contacting the level of energy signified in our own minds by the names we use. At our level, names are not irrelevant; we communicate through the spoken word. When a person has learned how to focus thought energy directly on to the desired level of frequency the use of names becomes an option, but I find that it helps.

Are the words we use really of such vital importance? If Margaret and I are mentally attuning ourselves to exactly the same source of energy, does it make any difference that I call it Christ and she calls it the Force? Energy is energy.

To my mind, it is of greater importance that we recognise the light in each other, and this applies to anyone with whom I come into contact. Names are words: they are helpful when they make us focus our thought energy in the ways that it needs to be focused, but when words block the way to true understanding and mutual recognition, they are merely a nuisance.

For instance, the concept of a universal consciousness that is completely impartial, and therefore impersonal, might seem foreign to some people, but what happens if we change the words yet retain the essential meaning? If that cosmic mind is truly as balanced, ordered and fair as we conceive it to be, how could it be anything *but* impartial? Wouldn't anything else signify a condition of *imbalance*?

To be completely rational and impartial does not necessarily have to be equated with being unloving. Too often, when we use the word love, we think in terms of feelings that are based on emotion. These might be beautiful, caring feelings of the highest possible order, but they are still seated in the emotions. The cosmos does not operate on emotion, but on order and balance, and the qualities of *universal* love cannot be perceived at the level of emotion. Perhaps we should be thankful that this is so; emotions can sometimes let us down, but the cosmos is always there, steady and constant. If it were not, I would feel cause for insecurity. Thinking about what the words *mean* helps us to reach beyond the barriers of misunderstanding.

If the New Age is to achieve its highest possible potential, then the people of the New Age need to have a communication and an understanding of each other that is not impeded by words. We *need* words for our day-to-day communication, but for deeper levels of understanding, we need to look beyond the words, and see each other as we really are on the inside where it counts.

In previous books, I have written of the need for us to come together, to share our thoughts and feelings, and to pool our energies to achieve the kind of world in which we all wish to live. In this book, these ideas are now coming together. Other people's experiences, even their ideas, may not be exactly the same as yours or mine, but very often those differences will only be a matter of words and mental concepts. Ultimately, the reality is the same for all of us, and often when you hear something explained in someone else's words, things that may not have been entirely clear to you will gently click into place. Always, in the words we share here, the aim is for a greater understanding of ourselves and each other, along with increased levels of awareness and perception.

Maybe the words in this book will not alter the situation that Margaret has to deal with, but in the sharing of ideas, she may find that there is a greater amount of light shining on her path, so that she can find her way forward in confidence. If this can be achieved for Margaret, it will be achieved for many, many others also. It is my hope that this will bring more of us even more closely together at the levels where it counts.

MAY THE LIGHT BE WITH YOU!

CHAPTER THREE

My very best friend

'I've got something to ask you,' said Craig.

I spooned sugar into two mugs of steaming coffee. 'Ask away,' I answered cheerfully. Craig looked uncertain.

'It's kind of serious,' he ventured.

'So, we're friends aren't we? What's the problem?'

'Well, it's not exactly a problem.'

Whenever friends tell me there's a serious question that isn't exactly a problem, it usually means they *have* a problem, but they need to talk it through in their own words, without prompting from me. At times like that, a cup of coffee is very useful. I can sip it slowly while I wait for the other person to collect words together, and if they need a breathing space to do so, they can take their time about sipping their drink. Craig took a few moments. I waited, saying nothing.

'Since you and Roland separated, have you been having any second thoughts? I mean, you were together for fifteen years . . . are you sure you weren't just giving him some shock treatment when you asked him to leave?'

I shook my head. 'I had all my second thoughts before we separated, Craig, and the time for shock treatment would have been quite some time ago. It's too late now. Look, I know you're a friend and you probably mean well and want to help, but you can't mend this broken marriage. It's over. Dead. Let it be. I appreciate your concern, but . . . '

'No, it isn't that,' he assured me hurriedly. 'It's just . . . well, I wondered if you're really sure of your feelings.'

'I'm sure. Why?'

'Well, now that you're single again, word's going to get around, and before long you're going to have a line of fellas at your door wanting to come courting.'

I couldn't help laughing with some irony. 'Such optimism!' I chortled. 'At my age, I hardly think that's likely.'

'You're not that old,' he protested.

'I'm forty-three, Craig, but thanks for the compliment. Are you concerned about my reputation, is that it?'

'No-o, not exactly.'

'Then what is it?'

'I'd like to be first in line.'

I set my coffee mug down on to the table.

Very carefully.

When things like this happen in the movies, the actors always seem to find wonderfully appropriate and clever things to say. This wasn't a movie. It was my cheerful, slightly muddled and boringly normal kitchen. At least, it had *seemed* normal until a few moments ago. Now it was me who grabbed for the coffee mug and Craig who waited, while I struggled frantically for words. Any words.

'Just exactly what are you telling me, Craig?' I managed to ask, finally.

'That I think you're a beautiful lady,' his voice was steady. 'And a lady like you shouldn't be allowed to be as unhappy as you've been. You deserve to be happy and I think I could give you happiness, if you'll let me. I'm asking for the chance to try.'

'You're thinking in terms of a *relationship*?'

'Of course! Did you think I'd just want to seduce you or something?'

'No, I... Craig, I'm sorry. I didn't mean to offend you, I just don't know what to think! I'm used to us being friends... the idea of anything else hadn't... I mean, there's the age difference... have you considered that when you're forty-seven, I'll be sixty?'

'I've had longer to think about it than you have, Dawn,' he told me quietly, his gaze steady. 'Age is on the outside; it's the inside that matters, the qualities a person has, and they don't age. I've known what qualities I wanted in a life partner right from the start. That's why I've never been married... I never found all those qualities in one lady before.'

'And I have them?'

He smiled. 'Every single one.'

I took another sip of my coffee, trying to muster a sense of reality. 'Craig, how long have you felt...' I hesitated, lost for words.

'How long have I wanted you to be my lady?'

I nodded.

He looked thoughtful. 'Do you really think you're ready to know?'

'I'm... not sure.'

'I didn't think so,' he remarked. 'Look, I know you're surprised, and you need time to think. I don't expect an answer straight away, I just had to tell you how I feel, because I can't keep coming here as your friend and not tell you the truth. I'm only asking you to think about giving me a chance. I want to make you happy, Dawn, and be happy with you. I wouldn't hurt you, I promise. Will you think about it?'

'Yes, Craig,' I agreed. 'Yes, I'll think about it.'

Have you ever tried to think rationally when your mind is behaving like a windmill in a hurricane?

47

What does a person think in a situation like the one I found myself in?

When my marriage to Roland had finally shattered into irretrievable fragments, I had prepared myself mentally and psychologically to live alone for the rest of my life. I had once loved Roland more than life itself, and it had taken a very long time for me to admit to myself that our paths had diverged, our interests and ideals were no longer compatible, we were going through the motions, but the differences had become too great, the arguments were not going to stop, and things weren't going to get better. That was my second attempt at marriage and, by the time it ended, I felt emotionally battered, bruised, hurt, disillusioned and very, very tired. I had vowed that I would never allow myself to be so vulnerable to any man ever again. The scars were too recent. The idea of another relationship had simply not been on my agenda and, even if it had, I would not have expected to be considering it with Craig. Not that there was anything wrong with Craig, he was a pleasant, easygoing, good-humoured young man, whose company I enjoyed, and we were very good friends.

Friends!

Young man!

Impossible!

Why me?

How long had he been harbouring deeper feelings for me, and why had I noticed no sign of them before? Over and over in my mind, I retraced the course of our friendship. I had met him almost a year before at an art exhibition organised by his mother's art group. It was Roland who made contact with her; he had a talent for drawing and had done an art course in Queensland not long before we moved to Tasmania. When he learned about the local art group and its annual exhibition, he contacted Craig's mother to ask if some of his pictures could be placed on display. She agreed, and a friendly acquaintanceship was formed.

When opening night arrived, I was feeling wretched. I had a fierce headache and, as a chronic migraine sufferer, I recognised all the danger signs. I felt like crawling into bed and I knew I should, but although Roland said he understood, it was clear that he felt I would be letting him down if I did not attend the opening night with him. Feeling guilty for even thinking of staying home, I swallowed some painkillers, put on a bright smile, and went along with him.

During the evening, Roland and I drifted in different directions and for the most part I stayed in the background, nursing my headache and giving Roland the space to enjoy his big night. At some stage in the proceedings, I made my way across to him, hoping to suggest that we leave. He was engaged in conversation with an earnest-looking young man and, when he saw me nearby, he made the introduction: 'Craig, I'd like you to meet my wife. Dawn, this is Craig...'

I managed to smile a polite hello, then withdrew. It was clear that Roland was not yet ready to leave and, despite the introduction, I knew he did not like me to interrupt his conversations by joining in unless he specifically invited me to do so, and an introduction constituted a courtesy, not an invitation.

By the time we arrived home, I felt as though a volcano was erupting in my head. Roland called the doctor, who ordered me admitted to hospital, so I spent the rest of the night and a large part of the following day in a hospital bed, drowsy from the painkilling injections. When I got home, Roland was alight with exuberance, bursting to

49

tell me about the encouraging comments he had received for his artwork.

'Oh, and Craig called in this morning,' he remarked.

'Craig?' I echoed vaguely, still feeling dazed.

'The chap I introduced you to last night,' he reminded me. 'Do you know, he's epileptic, too, like me. We even share the same specialist.'

'That's nice,' I answered feebly. 'It's good to see you making some friends.'

When Craig visited again, I made coffee and polite conversation, but kept myself very much on the sidelines, not wanting Roland to feel that I was intruding on his friendship. Craig would often address a remark to me in what I saw as a chivalrous attempt to help me feel included, but with a careful eye to Roland's moods, I kept my responses to a minimum.

As time went by and the chasm between Roland and me grew rapidly wider and more impassable, Roland spent more and more time secreted away in his studio, presumably absorbed in his drawings. For a while, he would emerge if I tapped on his door to let him know that a visitor had called, but eventually he issued strict instructions that I was not to disturb him for any reason. No matter who might be visiting, he wanted to be left alone.

It fell to me to entertain any visitors who arrived, including Craig. At first I felt diffident about being a poor substitute for Roland but, when I apologised, Craig only grinned. 'Never mind, I like talking to you, too, and you're prettier than Roland anyway.'

Gradually, I learned to relax with Craig, and to enjoy his company. With his easy-going attitude and wry good humour, he often had me laughing in spite of my inner tensions. If I began to feel a lift of the spirits when I heard his familiar knock at the door, I put it down to my pleasure at the prospect of forgetting my worries for an hour or so. I didn't speak to him about my marital problems and he didn't ask. As far as I could tell, he might have been sublimely unaware that anything was amiss. His manner remained the same whether or not Roland was present when he called. Because I still tended to regard him as being primarily Roland's friend, I half expected a negative reaction when he learned of our impending separation, but when he heard the news he showed equal concern for both of us.

Thinking back over the time I had known Craig, I could not recall anything that might have hinted at anything more than friendship in his feelings for me, and I was frankly puzzled. I am not usually so deficient in sensitivity that I would fail to notice something of such magnitude; people just don't hide their feelings that well, and I am accustomed to noticing subtle flickers of expression. Why had I seen nothing with Craig? More perplexing still, why had I *felt* nothing? Any person's energy field is continually broadcasting emanations that carry the pattern of their emotions, thoughts, moods, and their state of health. Even when a person maintains a mask on the surface, someone who is sensitive to those emanations will feel them. Having that kind of sensitivity is an aspect of my nature that has sometimes created difficulties for me; for instance, if I am in a conversation with somebody who is telling me things that he or she knows to be untrue. People don't like being made to feel that someone else knows they are hiding something, and I learned many years ago that it is not appreciated if I blurt out a remark like 'That isn't what you're really feeling' or 'You aren't telling me the truth'. That sort of thing makes people feel uncomfortable. I don't always know exactly what it is that the person is trying to conceal and, because I have an innate aversion to prying, I don't try to read those tell-tale emanations, but I can't help knowing when they are present. At least, I had usually detected them with other people in the past. Not with Craig, though. Was there something wrong with me? Had I been so immersed in the troubles and heartaches of a dying marriage that I had failed to notice what should have been obvious?

'Not at all,' Craig assured me when I spoke to him about it the next day. 'You wouldn't have noticed anything because I didn't want you to know.'

'Why not?'

He spoke in a patient, careful tone, as though explaining the facts of life to a child. 'Dawn, you were a married lady. It wouldn't have been right for me to let you see.'

'But how did you shield your aura so completely?'

'Is that what I did?' His question was guileless. I knew he had never studied any psychic techniques, nor felt it necessary to explore the subject with anything more than passing curiosity, which of course is why I was so puzzled.

'You must have done *something*, Craig. I'd have felt it if you hadn't.'

'I s'pose I must have then. I don't know about what you call shielding, but I knew you're psychic and I didn't want you reading my mind, so I just sort of pretended.'

'I don't read minds. I just feel energies, and I can *feel* it when people are pretending.'

'Not this time, you didn't,' he grinned.

What could I say?

Craig didn't press me for a decision about moving our friendship into something deeper. Having acknowledged my need for time to think, he

52

seemed content to let the matter rest. On the surface, our friendship continued as it had done before. He called in for coffee each afternoon and carried on the usual light-hearted bantering conversations as though nothing had changed. Occasionally he persuaded me to go out driving with him, to a beach or through the countryside, 'To get you out of the house, blow the cobwebs away. You spend too much time cooped up, just thinking. Scrambles your head.'

If he felt any restlessness or uncertainty, he didn't let it show, nor did he reveal in word or gesture any feelings beyond his habitual warmth and friendliness. This was not easy for me to reconcile with the feelings he had confided to me and with what I had learned of male behaviour. I can't claim an expert comprehension of the male psyche, but from my previous observations, men who feel any kind of desire usually show it in some way, even if they do not overstep the boundaries of propriety. A man who behaves like nothing more than a friend in every way usually wants to be a friend, and nothing more. I had thought that I knew Craig quite well, but his ability to put deep feelings to one side and carry on as normal was a surprise to me. When I remarked on it, he shrugged and commented that 'You get used to doing it'.

'There are things you just learn to do because you have to,' he explained. 'After I had the accident, it took a while for me to get my head together, and I could see people thinking I wasn't normal any more. You know, brain damage and all that. Wasn't much I could do about it. It hurt a bit, but you get used to it. Not much point in letting it get you down all the time, so you learn to put your feelings aside and get on with living.'

By profession, Craig is a motor mechanic and, in

his late teens, his great pleasure was riding motor-cycles. The love of his life was the Honda 750 Four and, being a motor mechanic, he knew how to modify the equipment, which meant that he rode very hot Hondas. He also liked to ride very fast. When he was eighteen years old, he was riding his favourite Honda along the highway, at a speed in the vicinity of 140km/h, when a panel-van sud-denly appeared on the road in front of him, pul-ling out from behind a billboard sign which had obscured it from Craig's view, just as he had been obscured from the van driver's field of vision. It was so close and happened so quickly that Craig had no time to take evasive action. Braking fur-iously but still travelling at high speed, he collided head-first with the rear of the van.

I can barely begin to imagine the horrific nature of Craig's head injuries. A friend who had known him since childhood and was working in the intensive care unit of the hospital to which he was taken told me that his injuries were so severe she did not recognise him when he was brought in. Nobody believed he could possibly survive, and when he had been in a coma for twelve days the doctor asked his parents for their consent to dis-connect the life support machinery. They refused. One day later, Craig woke up.

A few weeks after his discharge from hospital, Craig suffered the first of his epileptic seizures. Repeated attacks of epilepsy eventually made it impossible for him to continue in the workforce and he was placed on an invalid pension.

In high school, Craig had excelled at English, but after the accident he had speech difficulties. He had problems summoning the words he needed, and often the word that came out was not the one he meant to use but something inappropriate. His speech pattern also became hesitant, and he often had to think for some time to get a sentence together. From this, combined with a general lack of understanding about brain damage in general, people gained the impression that he had become feeble-minded. 'Not what he used to be. He's a bit slow in the head now, you know.' It is Craig's brain that was damaged, not his mind. He knew what people were thinking, but without the ability to verbalise his thoughts as clearly as he had once done, he was trapped. The brain is basically an item of physical machinery. Brilliant and sophisticated in structure and function it may be, but it is still a biological machine. Its purpose is to transmit thought impulses but it is not, as many people believe, the seat of intelligence. Intelligence comes from the mind, a manifestation of our existence as spiritual beings whose substance is the essence of thought. If the brain is damaged, the mind may not be able to communicate thought messages efficiently, but it is the *machinery* that is faulty, not the intelligence behind it. An intelligent mind operating through a damaged brain could be compared with a world-class racing driver at the wheel of a beat-up Volkswagen. No matter how well he can drive, he hasn't a chance of equalling the performance of the latest Ferrari, but it would be ludicrous to suggest that because the car doesn't perform at peak efficiency the man behind the wheel cannot drive.

The driver can get out of the Volkswagen and into a Ferrari, but Craig could not escape the consequences of his injuries. Friends who flocked to visit him in the hospital began to realise that he would never again be able to join in all their fun and games as he once used to do, and they now became conspicuous only by their absence. Other people in the small township, some of whom had known him all his life, began to regard him as a simpleton, and to treat him like one.

'I used to get angry at first,' he told me. 'But

throwing tantrums only makes things worse. People are what they are. You learn not to let your feelings get on top of you . . . put them aside, like I said, and not let them show. I suppose that's how I learned to do what you call shielding.'

'Oh, Craig,' I faltered. 'To be treated like that . . . it must hurt terribly!'

'It did,' he admitted. 'But it's not so bad now. I don't have as much trouble with talking as I used to, and there are people who take the time to listen and get to know me properly. They're good friends. Who needs the other sort?'

I wanted to weep.

'Hey!' Craig lifted my chin with his finger. 'Don't get so downhearted.'

'But it hurts to think of you suffering all that for so long.'

'It could be worse, sweetheart. I'm not in a wheelchair, I can still get around and enjoy myself, and I've got friends. Anyway, you get to be pretty good at judging a person's character; when people think you're a bit silly, they're not so careful with their . . . what do you call it when they're putting up a front?'

'Their facades?'

'Yes, facades, that's the word. You can tell who's honest and who's just out to use you. Doesn't do any harm to let them think you're silly sometimes. Had you fooled, didn't I?'

'Beast!' I protested cheerfully. 'I *never* thought you were silly.'

'No, but you didn't know I was in love with you, either.'

Instantly, I was covered with confusion. Those words came so naturally from Craig, but they caused so many conflicting feelings in me.

'I'm sorry.' He was full of contrition. 'I didn't mean to upset you.'

56

'I'm not upset, I just . . . '

'Don't know what to think?' his voice was gentle. I nodded.

'Would you like me to stay away for a while, not come around to see you?' he asked.

'Why?'

'Maybe you need space. Time to think, without me bothering you. Anyway, the neighbours are probably gossiping about you, with me coming here every day.'

'Damn the neighbours!' I declared. 'The day I let a bunch of people I don't even know dictate who I can and cannot see will be the day Hell freezes over. And you don't bother me!'

'You're sure?'

'Of course I'm sure, Craig. You confuse me sometimes, but you don't bother me. You're my friend.'

'Always.' He smiled, but his eyes were wistful, and I felt an ache in his aura that he could not conceal.

After he left, I spent a lot of time deeply immersed in my thoughts. I could see Craig's virtues clearly enough. Simple honesty and the strength of character to do what he sees as right, caring, consideration and tenderness, along with a generous heart. I knew that, if I accepted him, he would move Heaven and Earth if he could to give me happiness. I could not doubt his qualities, but if I could not return his feelings with equally wholehearted honesty, I had no right to accept what he offered. He treated me like a princess . . .

'And you're dangling him on a string!' scolded a voice in my head. I recognised the voice of truth. I hadn't done it intentionally or even knowingly, but I had been doing it nonetheless, and he deserved better. In spite of his self-control and his understanding about my state of confusion, he was being hurt. I had seen it, behind his smile. I was keeping him in suspense, and it wasn't fair.

'You bet it's not fair!' said the voice. 'Pull yourself together, girl. Give the man the chance he has asked for, or cut him loose and let him go.'

Let him go? I thought about what that would mean, and a leaden weight descended in the pit of my stomach. Craig had offered me the most precious gift he could give; his heart. If I rejected that offer, I could hardly expect him to keep coming around and acting as nothing more than a friend, as though nothing had happened. I had been trying to imagine what my life would be like if I accepted the friend as a lover and it had left me perplexed and in conflict with myself. Now I imagined what life would be like without Craig in it, and I did not like the prospect at all. Not one tiny bit!

Next afternoon, I waited for him to arrive so that I could tell him of my thoughts, but he didn't come. I was on tenterhooks as the hours crawled by and the afternoon paled into sunset. Why hadn't he called? Had he changed his mind? What if he had decided that I'd kept him waiting for too long and he didn't want to see me any more? What if? The things an imagination can do with just two words and a question mark!

Evening came, and so did Craig. I ran to answer his knock, and when he walked through the door I was as tongue-tied as a nervous schoolgirl.

'I thought you wouldn't come!' I babbled. He gave me a bewildered look.

'Why wouldn't I?' he asked.

'Yesterday, you said maybe you'd stay away. When you didn't come this afternoon, I thought...'

'That I'd stay away without talking to you about it first? Why would I do that?'

'I don't know, I just . . . Would you like a coffee?'

'Please. Hey, are you all right?'

'I'm fine.'

Flustered and perilously close to blushing (at your age, Dawn? Get a hold of yourself!) I turned away and fumbled with the electric kettle. A gentle touch on my shoulder turned me around to meet the concern in Craig's eyes.

'You're *not* all right,' he asserted. 'You're as nervous as a kitten. What's wrong?'

'Nothing's wrong. I just . . . I've been thinking about what you asked, and . . . well, there's only one way to find out if a relationship will work, and that's to have one.'

Craig went perfectly still, and his eyes searched my face for endless moments before he spoke. 'Is that what you want?'

I dropped my head, not brave enough to meet his gaze. 'I don't want to be without you,' I replied, in a timid little voice. 'I think maybe I love you. What do I do now, Craig?'

'I don't know about you, sweetheart,' he answered softly. 'But right now, I want to kiss you. Do you mind?'

If I thought that there were no more surprises in Craig, I was soon to be undeceived. A few days after our relationship had commenced on its new footing, I was working at my typewriter while Craig sat quietly beside me leafing through some of my photograph albums. I heard him utter an exclamation, and turned to see him gazing in fascination at an old newspaper clipping.

'This picture!' he declared. 'This is the one that made me start having the visions.'

'Visions? What visions?'

'They started after I saw this picture,' he explained, holding out the clipping for me to see.

59

It was about six years old, and featured an article about psychic activity, along with a photograph of me.

'When I saw that picture, I knew I had to meet you,' Craig continued. 'Then I started having dreams, and the visions.'

'Tell me about it from the beginning, Craig. Are you saying that you fell in love with a picture?'

'No, it wasn't like that. I didn't start loving you until I met you. It was like I said, I just knew I had to meet you. It wasn't that I *wanted* to meet you . . . it's hard to explain, I can't find the right words. I looked at the picture and sort of knew that I had to meet you and get to know you. Don't ask me why. I thought it was stupid myself at the time. It wasn't a wish, it was . . . like I just knew it had to happen . . . what's the word for that?'

'Premonition.'

'Yeah, a premonition. Then the visions started. Boy, did I think I was going nuts!'

'Well, I do declare,' I grinned. 'This boy is full of surprises! You've never told me about having any premonitions, Craig. I'm all ears, tell me about it!'

'It was just . . . dreams, only they didn't always happen when I was asleep. Sometimes I'd be wide awake, and it was like a dream, but not a dream. I kept seeing you with me as though we were together, like man and wife. Not romantic stuff all the time, just things that couples would do together, in the house, or the garden, or out shopping. All sorts of things. It felt so real. I thought I was being stupid . . . I mean, you weren't even living here then. You were thousands of kilometres away, somewhere. Anyway, you're a writer with your picture in the papers, and I'm just plain old Craig from up the street. Even if you lived here, you wouldn't bother with someone like me. But I kept on seeing you with me . . . it was really stupid, you know?'

60

'Not so stupid,' I remarked. 'You're here, aren't you?'

'Yes, it makes sense now,' agreed Craig. 'But it didn't at the time. Then they told me you were dead, and I really hit the pits.'

'Who said I was dead?'

'I can't remember. I was with a group of people somewhere, and one of them mentioned reading a book of yours. Then someone else said they'd heard about you being killed in a car accident somewhere on the mainland; in Victoria, I think.'

I made a grimace of distaste. 'People keep killing me off all the time! I wonder how these stories get started?'

'I don't know, but that one really got to me.' Craig flinched at the memory. 'I felt this terrible ... loss, and grief. I thought I was really going crazy then, wanting to cry my heart out over someone I'd never met. That wasn't long before you moved here. When I heard you were living here, right in my home town ... I really got the jitters!'

'What on earth for?'

'Well, I wanted to meet you, just get to know you and be able to talk to you. I could dream about it when you weren't anywhere near, but you were here ... and I thought that if I met you, you wouldn't want to know me, and I didn't know what I'd do if that happened.'

'Well, you were worrying about nothing on that score, weren't you?' I smiled. 'Why didn't you tell me about these premonitions before?'

'I couldn't, Dawn. You were with Roland,' he answered. 'How could I tell you then that I'd been dreaming about having you as my lady? After you separated, when I'd told you how I felt and you needed time to think, if I had told you then, it would have been like trying to influence you. It wouldn't have been right, you see? So I couldn't tell you, until now.'

There was speculation in my thoughts as I digested Craig's revelations. Although he had never demonstrated any scepticism with respect to psychic phenomena, Craig had not shown any noticeable interest either, and he had certainly given no hint that he had ever had any psychic experiences hitherto. I may be a romantic female, but my professional curiosity is never far from the surface, and something in the way Craig had related his experiences was causing my antennae to buzz. He said that he had not understood why he was having those premonitions in particular, but he did not say that it was unusual for him to *have* premonitions.

'How long have you known that you're psychic?' I asked, in a casual tone.

He shrugged. 'Hard to tell. I didn't think about it that way, you see. I mean, when I was a kid, I thought everybody saw things like that, so I didn't pay it much attention. It just wasn't that unusual. After a while, I find out that other people didn't see things, like the colours... and I sort of knew it wouldn't be smart to talk about it, so I didn't.'

'What do you mean, about colours?'

'People have colours around them. You know about all that stuff; you know what the colours are, around people.'

'You're talking about auras.'

'That's what I've heard you call them,' he agreed. 'But I didn't know what it meant until I heard you talking about it. To me, it was just colours.'

'None of this ever surprised you?' I queried. 'Seeing the colours, or having premonitions?'

He shrugged. 'Why should it? If something's always been there, you don't get surprised about it.'

'Do you mean you've *always* seen these things?'

'Isn't that what I said?' he enquired mildly.

The subject was literally begging to be explored! A person who has retained such vivid clairvoyance since early childhood would have intrigued me at any time, but discovering this ability in Craig was fascinating. I couldn't have been more delighted if I'd found a cache of jewels buried in my garden.

'You see my aura, I suppose?' I spoke casually, but I was as curious as anyone else would be in the same circumstances.

'Yeah,' he smiled. 'Yours is real pretty.'

'Thank you for the compliment, kind sir, but what colour is it?'

'It isn't one colour all the time, it keeps changing,' he replied. 'It's like that with everyone's colours... is that how it's supposed to be?'

'Yes. The colours change, depending on a person's moods, thoughts, health and so on, but there is a dominant colour that keeps returning.'

'That's what I see,' he agreed. 'But I didn't know if that's how it's supposed to be. Yours is usually a sort of sparkly blue... like looking at stars in the sky at summertime, only there are more stars in your aura. The blue is like a colour in the background, and your stars are really thick, there are so many of them, all silver and sparkly... so it's really more silver than blue. Sometimes there's gold, but usually it's silver, with the blue.'

'What other colours do you see?'

'All sorts of colours, but most often there's a light green. When you're in a bad mood, it goes red, and when you're feeling sexy...'

'That will do!' I was beginning to wonder about the possible disadvantages involved in living with a man who has the ability to read me at a glance. A lady likes to preserve a few mysteries after all.

Craig's eyes held a distinctly wicked twinkle. 'Want to know what colour it is now?' he grinned.

Craig tends to be reticent about his psychic perceptions, partly because of his early awareness that it would not be wise to discuss the subject freely, but also because he has never regarded his talents as being anything remarkable. As he puts it, he has always 'seen things', and he accepts this as a matter of course. As I guessed, he is also quite accustomed to having premonitions, which he also kept to himself before, partly because of his instinctive awareness that other people would not accept them as readily as he did, but also because he took them for granted. His reasoning was quite straightforward: if these things happened to someone like him, there couldn't be anything special about them, because he saw nothing special in himself. That kind of acceptance is natural, but it is not common.

Most people have a tendency to regard the manifestation of psychic abilities with something akin to awe. It is common for people to be frightened when they have psychic experiences; it is common for some to become euphoric about them, and it is common for a lot of people to regard such things as magical, but it is *not* common for someone to shrug his shoulders and regard his psychic faculties as being no more remarkable than blue eyes and brown hair. This is not false modesty on Craig's part: in order for a person to assume the cloak of modesty, there must be an element of pride involved, since false modesty is really only pride wearing a mask. Craig does not have that kind of pride. If he were asked to state his opinion of himself, his reply would be 'I'm as good as anyone else, I suppose'.

While he doesn't make a fuss about his abilities, he has no reluctance about using them if he believes it may be of some benefit to another person, even if it means doing something he has never attempted before. Several weeks ago, I had a headache. Not a migraine or anything dramatic, just an ordinary, nuisance headache. Like anyone else with a headache, I was not particularly happy about it. I had work to do, and in any case, I am not fond of pain at the best of times. So I grouched and complained a bit, as people with headaches are inclined to do.

'I hate to see you hurting,' sympathised Craig. 'Is there anything I can do to help?'

'Not unless you feel like trying your hand at psychic healing,' I groaned.

'Yeah? How do I do that?'

'You place the palm of your passive hand over the pain centre.' I indicated the part of my forehead that felt as though a little man inside my head was trying to break his way out with a sledgehammer. 'And you put your dominant hand in a similar position on the opposite side of my head.'

As I spoke, Craig was already placing his hands into position.

'Now,' I continued, 'to generate a flow of healing energy, you ... '

'I'm doing it,' he remarked. 'Let me concentrate.'

I sat still. For a minute, I could feel only the warmth of Craig's hands and I wondered how I could tactfully interrupt and point out the technique required for focusing healing energy. While I was considering this, I began to notice a slightly increased feeling of pressure in my head, then a sensation like a soft 'pop'. At once, I could feel the pain draining out of my head, like water from a sink when the plug has been removed. Within moments, the pain was gone and my head was clear.

'Yecch!' Craig surveyed his hands with an expression of disgust. 'I've got that muck in my hand! How do I get rid of it?'

'Wash your hands under running water, right

away,' I told him. 'Otherwise the condition will remain in your aura and upset your energy balance. By the way, how did you do that?'

'Just thought about it,' he replied, as he rinsed his hands at the sink. 'It was like pushing with my right hand, as though I was trying to shove the pain out of your head, only the pushing sort of came *through* my hand, if you know what I mean. Then it felt as though my left hand filled up with some sort of mucky stuff.'

No one had told Craig that the dominant hand exerts a 'pushing' energy while the passive hand attracts or draws energy to itself. He did not know, either, that in psychic healing an energy imbalance can be drawn away from the patient and 'held' in the passive hand. He had intuitively focused the healing flow correctly.

Either Craig is so far advanced that a person like me can't even see his dust, or he constitutes a fine illustration that we can sometimes get so enmeshed in complex technicalities that we forget how simply spiritual energies are meant to work. Personally, I wouldn't be surprised if I were told that Craig *is* very highly advanced, but he disputes that idea out of hand.

'I'm an ordinary sort of bloke, like anyone else,' he insists. 'Don't start making me out to be something I can't live up to.'

What I have seen in Craig so far is enough to demonstrate that people who think they can't develop any worthwhile spiritual abilities because they 'haven't got enough education' or are 'not smart enough' have no need to be concerned. Craig doesn't think he is anything special, either. He worked as a motor mechanic, not a doctor or a scientist, and he is further afflicted with a brain injury that impedes his mental processes. There is no limit to the wonders we ordinary people can

66

achieve when we allow our natural abilities to manifest, so if you are one of those who have been thinking, 'I'm just an ordinary person, I can't do anything special', I have a simple message for you. Think about Craig. Then think again!

CHAPTER FOUR
'Maybe we're twins'

'I've been talking to a lady who wants to get in touch with you,' said Adam. 'I've suggested that she write, but I think you might find it interesting to ring and have a talk with her.'

'You *do*?' My attention was guaranteed! Adam, like all of my closest friends, is scrupulous about protecting my personal space and usually makes it a rule not to act as go-between when he meets people who wish to contact me. He certainly doesn't need any help from me at a psychic level, since he is a powerful and highly skilled practitioner, and it is much more common for me to refer people to him than the other way around, so when he tells me that he thinks I'll be 'interested' in talking to someone, it's more likely that I'll be fascinated. He gave me Sandy's name and telephone number and I wasted no time before making the call.

On one or two occasions, I have had the undeniable feeling that I'm talking to an old, familiar friend when I've been speaking to someone I haven't met before in this life. It doesn't happen very often, but it happened when I spoke to Sandy, and in almost no time after the first 'Hello' we were both engulfed in gales of laughter as we discussed the many parallels between us, discovered more similarities, and even spoke in tandem more than once, both uttering the same words at the same moment.

She told me that she had written to me some months earlier, and at first I was at a loss to understand why I had failed to notice her letter. When I receive a letter from someone to whom the Powers that Be wish me to pay particular attention there is usually an almost magnetic attraction, as though the letter 'lights up' in my hands. It was difficult for me to comprehend why this had not happened with Sandy's letter, because it was obvious to both of us that the contact between us had not happened by any random chance. Fortunately Sandy has a word processor and had not erased the programme in which her original letter had been stored, so she was able to send me a copy; when I saw the date on the letter, I understood. She had written to me during the last few weeks of my marriage to Roland, when I was going through a period of intense stress and turmoil emotionally, mentally and psychically. In my state of mind at that time, I probably wouldn't have noticed if her letter had been hand delivered by the Archangel Gabriel himself. Thanks to Sandy's trusty word processor, however, her letter has not been lost, nor the accompanying account of the events which marked her spiritual awakening, which is fortunate for all of us. I think a lot of people are going to enjoy reading what she has to say, and that her words will be a source of encouragement.

Dear Dawn

Let me begin by saying that I have absolutely no idea why I am writing this letter!

I'm sure you've heard it all before — I read your books and felt an empathy that I really can't explain — *but that's mainly because I don't understand it myself. I'm sure that I will. One day. Perhaps my purpose is simply to thank you for the enjoyment and knowledge your books provided!*

In fact, during a recent reading, my Egyptian guardian interrupted the psychic to mention that I had recently experienced considerable growth through reading, and that the 'relevance to my life's path' was being cognitised (his word). He said he was very pleased about this — so, since I had been reading your books at the time, it seems they have met with the approval of at least two guardians — your David and my Ra-fera-ma. Therefore, my guardian thanks you, too!

The truth is, Dawn, that I felt compelled to write to you, and I hasten to assure you that I'm not in the habit of writing to authors or people I have never met. (I won't say 'strangers' because I don't feel that you are!) But I am so often 'compelled' to do things, with the reasons invariably being revealed later, that I have given up asking why and simply accept that these are things I must do. I must admit, however, that having been so compelled, I was really hoping that I would lapse into automatic writing and that the Powers that Be would say whatever it was I was supposed to say. No such luck!

You have, no doubt, gasped in awe at the length of this letter, but let me put your mind partly at rest — it is NOT all letter! I have drafted an account of various recent experiences for my own benefit (nothing quite as drastic as yours, I might add!) and thought I would include a copy of this with my letter. And again, I don't really know why! But don't you just LOVE people who send you REAMS of reading material when you can't even find the time to plough through your own? Course you do!

I recently viewed the Hanging Rock and Beyond video* and I DO know both you and Roland! I knew precisely what you would look like, and I am quite certain I would have said hello if I'd passed either of you in the street, and no doubt would have wondered afterwards who you were and how I knew you! But I suppose that could be put down to your excellent writing ability. If that's so, then my heartiest congratulations — and how about some tips on how to achieve this! You see, I'm also a writer!

I'm sure there's more to it, though. Do I remember you from the future, or have we known each other in another lifetime? (I'm glad you're YOU, there are some who would think I had gone totally around the bend if they read those words!) But what intrigues me is that there do seem to be an incredible amount of similarities between us.

As I said, I too am a 'writer with an interest in spiritual matters' but unlike you, so far my 'writing' and 'spiritual matters' have been kept separate. (I have only had one book published — a travel directory about your original neck of the woods, actually — Tasmania — along with various articles on nutrition and natural healing.) I am also a Libran and, although born in

*The video Sandy refers to was produced as a documentary by the Andronicus Foundation. Roland and I participated in some of the events that were filmed, at the invitation of Ian Gordon, then president of the Foundation.

71

Melbourne, I descended from a long line of Tasmanians — my mother was born in Beauty Point and spent part of her childhood on Flinders Island.

You mention penpals in one of your books, and I also had many during my teens and twenties — in fact, I'm still in touch with some of them! It would appear that your bookshelves are about as well stocked as mine — with books that, even with the best intentions, we will never get around to reading. Intentions might also be good when it comes to giving up smoking, but as yet I haven't been able to achieve such a feat — how about you? We are both animal lovers who lost a never-to-be-replaced pooch — yours, of course, was Taffy; mine Muffin. And Cliff Richard was one of the loves of my life once, too.

I could go on, but I don't want to bore the pants off you, if you'll excuse the expression! They're probably all coincidences (a word that is supposed to explain the mystery by putting a name to it!), but what was NOT a coincidence was that your books almost jumped off the bookstore shelf and landed in my arms! Well, not literally, but I did get the feeling that if I hadn't reached out to take them, they might very well have followed me out of the shop, so I had to buy them to save such embarrassment! And when I began to read them, I had the eerie feeling that I was reading my own words — not the experiences as such, but the words themselves!

We do differ in that I am not psychic. Well, that is to say, I have not developed my natural psychic abilities. I have always respected the ability of some people to see more than that of

72

which I am presently capable. However, a clairvoyant did tell me recently (among many other things that were 'spot on') that she could see a gigantic third eye opening — much to both my delight AND consternation.

Also unlike you, I never wanted to be a nurse. I have to admit that the mere sight of blood was enough to horrify me, so the profession never appealed, and I also became very disillusioned by the constant bombardment of drugs in which doctors seemed to be putting all their faith. At that time (more than twenty years ago) naturopaths and health food shops were for strange off-beat people and were really not to be taken too seriously, but in spite of this fact my interest in nutrition and natural healing methods began to steadily grow, so I was not at all surprised to learn recently that I am surrounded by a conglomeration of Red Indian guides knowledgeable in this area.

I have also been told by various clairvoyants that I am very well protected, and I know this to be true. There have been many occasions when I feel I have been guided to do certain things or prevented from doing others. I never understand why at the time but invariably discover the reasons afterwards. Although I must say that on some occasions I have found that if I don't allow myself to be guided (and I do tend to be very strong-minded and therefore don't always do what my 'instincts' tell me I should) I invariably HAVE to do them, for rather than being guided I am pushed, sometimes in a most dramatic way.

Believe me, over the years I have learned to listen! Hence, this letter!

Incidentally, I was at the Theosophical

Society recently and was told that I had missed you by weeks. What a pity. I am there so often I am beginning to think I will return to haunt the place once I have left this dimension! You were spoken of very highly by a member of the staff there, a chap who said you were 'quite down to earth and very pleasant'! (Just thought you'd like to know that, I always like to repeat compliments to people when I hear them!)

While there, I was also forced (induced? nudged?) to buy Initiation — about a young girl's initiation into the priesthood in ancient Egypt. It didn't threaten to follow me out of the shop this time, but it did fall over as I approached it, and continued to do so every time I stood it up again. Ra-fera-ma's influence again, no doubt, as with another book I picked up second-hand recently — The Ra Material!

Have you read anything of Ra? It makes very interesting reading, particularly the references to Akhenaten — an eighteenth dynasty Pharaoh who has always fascinated me! But what really intrigued me was that Ra is one of the 'Nine',* and for this reason I contacted Ian Gordon recently and had quite a lengthy phone discussion with him about it. Ian encouraged me to read Uri by Andrija Puharich, and I later discovered that Dr Puharich had worked with the authors of The Ra Material and had also endorsed the book!

I visited the Theosophical Society bookshop the following day, and the staff there went to

*The 'Nine' are said to be a group of highly evolved spiritual entities whose task is to assist in the evolution of beings who currently inhabit the third dimension.

any mount of trouble to locate a copy of *Uri*, but eventually had to give up. Already late for my creative writing class on the other side of town, I hurried off, but kept being pushed in another direction until I finally surrendered and 'went with the flow' — straight to an obscure second-hand bookshop. Of course, no time was wasted, for Puharich's *Uri* almost met me at the entrance! And considerate really is the word for my guardian, for I had complained bitterly when compelled to buy *Initiation* for $19.99. *Uri* cost me $1 — probably the cheapest book on the shelves of the second-hand book shop!

Dawn, this has been a very long letter and, as I said, I'm not even sure why I am writing it. I know that it can be gratifying to receive letters from satisfied readers, but I also believe (as I know you do) that often we are meant to do things or meet people or even just make contact, the reasons for which will not always seem obvious at the time.

I do hope that I will hear from you, but I honestly can't imagine why I would. Perhaps you will see the importance of something in either this letter or the attached draft, something I've missed! I've made half a dozen attempts at this letter, and in fact I began it almost two months ago! I'm trying to say everything without making it too lengthy and have gone to great pains to word it in such a way as not to sound like some kind of nut, but eventually had to edit the original eight pages down to these mere four! Think yourself lucky! *Précis* was never my best subject in English — two pages to be précised into one page *invariably ended up four or five. Odds on you had the same problem — I'm told it's the sign of a born novelist!*

If it's not possible to find the time to reply, then please don't give it another thought. I know how busy you must be. Maybe in years to come, one or both of us will recall this letter and realise its significance! What that could possibly be, I truly have no idea! (You're not, by any chance, the twin sister I didn't know I had, but born two years earlier than me, are you? I think I'd even be inclined to believe that!)

In the meantime, please keep up the good work, and I look forward to reading more books by you in the future.

Yours sincerely and with much gratitude
Sandy C.

Well, Sandy's puzzlement about the purpose of her letter to me should now be effectively dispelled, because I told her of my plans for this book and let her know that I felt her letter and the record of her own awakening would be ideally suited for inclusion here. Although she is rather modest about her degree of psychic awareness, she tells of experiences that are common to a significant number of people, all of whom will no doubt be encouraged to see those experiences related in such an easy and relaxed manner by another person.

I was always aware that I had a spirit guide. How, I don't really know. It was simply an acceptance of a fact — a fact that I don't recall ever thinking about to any great extent. If I did think about it, then I don't believe I imagined such a beneficial being as having form or substance, a face or a name. I imagined it to be like an airy-fairy type of spirit hovering nearby, in much the same way that a ghost haunts an old mansion.

However, I could not claim complete surprise when, during my teenage years, a clairvoyant informed me that my guide was a Red Indian. For the first time, my guide had form and a personality of its own, and that knowledge created a certain amount of personal interest.

While in London a few years later, I visited the Spiritualists Association for a reading, and another clairvoyant described my Red Indian — tall, strong, and very proud of the fact that he had saved my mother from drowning when I was only a baby. 'I did it!' the clairvoyant repeated his words, and told me he was waggling his thumb towards his chest. 'It was me, I did it!'

Strange, I thought at the time. It would seem that my spirit guide not only has form and personality, but he actually takes pride in his accomplishments — an attribute I would not have considered possible for a member of the spirit world. On my return to Australia, however, I was not at all surprised to learn that my mother had, in fact, almost found herself condemned to a watery grave when I was a mere babe. The onset of a strong cramp resulted in her thrashing about in the ocean for quite a while until suddenly, without rhyme or reason, the cramp had disappeared and she had been able to swim ashore.

During the following ten years, nothing occurred to change my mind — in either direction — regarding the existence of my guide. He was there. He was with me. What he did, when and where and how he did it, even why he did whatever it was he presumably did — I had no idea. I only knew that he was there. He was my guide. He was here to guide me. And so that, I supposed, was what he did!

It was during my thirtieth year that someone suggested I read a book entitled Many Mansions. At that time, I had not even heard of Edgar Cayce — the famed 'Sleeping Prophet'. This book was to change my way of thinking from then on. I began to develop a small understanding of reincarnation and karma, and the universal or cosmic laws which govern us and our lives in every way. I began to look at people, situations, incidents, in a completely different way. I began to understand why some people were attracted to each other, while others were mutually repelled, why some became instant friends while others never seemed to get along.

Slowly, the need for tolerance and acceptance began to seep into my conscious mind. Everything — every situation in life — was meant to be a learning experience, and was no doubt brought about through a deed, word or thought in a previous lifetime. Good, bad or indifferent, we created the building blocks for our own lifetimes, and there could be no escape other than that afforded by learning acceptance and tolerance of the situation or person involved.

A further ten years were to pass before my education continued. During this time, the influence of Edgar Cayce never left me. I cannot take credit for being an avid student, quick to learn and eager to use this knowledge in everyday life. I tried, though. Oh, how I tried. Patience. Tolerance. Acceptance. 'Walk a mile in another man's moccasins' was a phrase I was often heard to repeat to others, when in fact I was really saying, 'Do as I say, not as I do'.

A seed correctly planted, however, and provided with the right conditions, must eventually grow. It would seem that this airy-fairy being who hovered around day and night and took credit for spiritual life-saving techniques really knew my potential far better than I, for if my next lesson had occurred at any time during those ten years, I doubt that I would have given as much credence to it as I did in my fortieth year.

Although quite interested in the spiritual world of which I knew little, and in the laws of karma, my main interests up to this point had been nutrition and natural health, Stuart England and ancient Egypt. As a child, I often pored over the huge medical encyclopedia we kept in our bookcase. And I recall, during a school visit to a museum, having to be physically dragged away from a glass case containing an Egyptian mummy, and being told that I must stay with the rest of the class. I don't recall my age, I doubt it was more than eight or nine, but the incident stands out most clearly in my mind. By the time I was thirteen or fourteen, I constantly had my nose in books about the Stuart kings, particularly King Charles II, and always wondered why the rest

79

of my classmates did not share my boundless enthusiasm for this era.

My interest in nutrition and health developed much later, when I was in my early twenties, and developed steadily until, in 1987, my mother became ill and, frustrated at the failures of the medical profession to find a cause, let alone a cure, I threw myself into the study of nutrition, physiology, herbal treatments, homeopathy and a variety of other aspects of natural healing.

How many of our interests, talents and personality traits are the result of upbringing and conditioning, and how much due to past life experiences and karmic effects? Although I did not know it when I visited a clairvoyant in 1989 — the first time in over ten years — I was soon to find out.

The clairvoyant immediately began to describe my Red Indian guide. He had been very strong (I had heard that before!) and very spiritual. He had also been a great believer in natural healing, and had carried a small leather pouch around his neck in which he kept herbs and other medicinal plants. When she went on to describe another guide — a nun — I was quite confused. Another guide? What had I done to deserve a second guide? This one had possessed healing hands. 'You would have made an excellent healer!' the clairvoyant told me.

There were others, but she seemed most impressed with the Red Indian and suggested I have a sketch done of him, providing me with the name and address of the psychic artist. (I might add here that although much of her reading seemed totally trivial to me at the time, many of the things she told me were to come true within the week!) At the end of the session, I asked if she knew of anyone with whom I could undergo regression, as I was far more interested to know details of my lifetimes in Egypt and Stuart England than have a sketch made of some Red Indian. She provided me with a name and address, and warned me that I would have to wait many months for the appointment.

As luck would have it — or is there such a thing? — a cancellation meant that I could undergo regression the following week. I was pleased to learn that the procedure would not be done under hypnosis, as I doubted I would be a particularly good subject, but that it involved total relaxation followed by immediate answers (without thought, consideration or censorship) to any questions asked. I still had my doubts, but looked forward to the attempt.

On the evening of my appointment, I made every effort to put ancient Egypt out of my mind, although in so doing found that I was thereby concentrating on the very thing I wanted to forget. I did not want to have any preconceived ideas and realised how easy it would be to concoct a story prior to the session. How surprised I was when, during the session, the question 'Where are you?' resulted in the answer 'Athens'. I was even more surprised to discover that I was a male — a boy of fourteen in the year 1016.

With the guidance of the questioner, I progressed through my lifetime — the deaths

81

of my parents, my marriage, children, grandchildren, up to my own death. I was a shepherd on the outskirts of Athens. I owned twenty sheep, three goats and a donkey. I also had a pet dog, and I allowed my youngest daughter (I had three daughters, but my youngest was very ugly and would therefore never find a husband) to keep a pet hen, which she called Bubba. My only son, Costa (named after my father), learned the trade so that he could take over at my death. He married and later, when he and his children moved into the one and only bedroom I, like my father before me, moved into the storeroom off the kitchen.

I had two brothers. One had fought with my father as a youngster, and we later found his body at the base of a tall cliff. My other brother was a rather arrogant type, and had not wanted the responsibility of the farm. He had gone to Athens to seek work. I did not like him. I did not like his wife. I did not, in fact, like anyone very much (although I did admit to a fondness for my daughter-in-law, but only secretly, for I tried hard not to show it!). My wife died at a fairly young age, and my only comment was that I now had no one to do things for me.

When my brother's wife died, he came to visit me. He was lonely and asked to stay, but I turned him away. My two older daughters married and moved away, visiting me rarely. I never visited them at all. As I grew older, I spent most of my time sitting outside in the sunshine, allowing Costa and his wife, along with my ugly daughter, to do the work and take care of me. I rarely ventured in to Athens, for it was so busy there. My only true friend was my

82

old donkey. (It is interesting to note here that donkeys are now my favourite animals. I have often said that when I look at a donkey I feel that I could tell it my secrets, discuss my problems with it, and feel that it was listening and understanding. This, then, must be a result of my memories of my old donkey friend of almost a thousand years ago.)

I was taken through the dying experience, and the questioner was pleased to hear that, along with my immediate family, my brother was now at my bedside and was holding my hand. I had forgiven him. I described the scene vividly, pointing out that everyone had their heads bowed, but that no one was crying, for we had all known for quite a while that I was dying, and had accepted the fact. I was quite looking forward to it, for I had been in considerable pain. I viewed my family and my own body from a point above the bed, and described myself as having no hair at all, but very proudly pointed out that I still had a moustache, and that it was still black. I then drifted away and met up with my parents, and soon I met up with the brother who had died many years before. He apologised, for he had fallen from the cliff by accident, and he regretted that he had given us the mistaken impression that his death had been on purpose.

During the weeks following the regression I searched for information on life in or around Athens during this time period, but all to no avail. Apparently, Athens was a thriving community up to the third century AD and after that, it became nothing more than a backwater for a thousand years or so. This seemed to correspond with my continual 'Nothing much' answers whenever questioned during this regression as to 'What is going on — are there any wars, is there anything you want to tell me about?'

I did not return to watch my funeral, for there was none. 'We were not religious people,' I explained. 'They just put my body — somewhere — I'm not sure where, and went on with their lives. It was not important.'

Following my life in Athens, I was asked if I had decided on my next incarnation and I advised the questioner that I had wasted my life that time. I had cut myself off from people, and my next lesson was meant to show me how to get along with others. For this reason, I explained, I would incarnate as a female, 'for females get along better with people' I pointed out. When asked what I was now wearing on my feet, I immediately answered 'Moccasins'. (Is this why I so often, in this incarnation, used the phrase 'Walk a mile in another man's moccasins'?)

As my description of this next incarnation began, I was a twelve-year-old Apache squaw about to be married to a brave. The year was 1560. We lived on the border of what is now Canada, in the midwest, and my work was that of 'keeper of the fires'. Every night I ensured that the fires encircling the campsite were kept burning. To allow them to go out meant inviting evil spirits. But I also studied during the day, for I was learning to be a healer!

Although I knew absolutely nothing about Red Indians at the time of this regression, many of my statements were able to be checked

out later. At first, however, I was a little confused, for all the books I obtained showed the
Apache tribes living in the south-west. I rang
the gentleman who conducted the regression
and asked if I could, perhaps, have been wrong
about my tribe, but he would not hear of it. 'If
you said Apache, then Apache it was,' he told
me. Eventually I found a book which detailed
the whereabouts of various tribes BEFORE the
coming of white man, and although the majority of Apache tribes still tended towards the
south-west, one tribe of Apache was situated in
the midwest — near the border of Canada!

A reference to the campfires was located in
This Land Was Theirs — and it described how
a circle of fires was always kept alight in order
to frighten away evil spirits. A reference to the
study a healer needed to undertake can also be
found in this book — a study of physiology,
herbs, and a variety of other aspects of healing
was necessary.

When I arose in the morning, I would immediately go to the river to wash, but this I did
alone. This confused me at the time, for I
imagined such a large tribe would bathe
together. This Land Was Theirs discusses the
prayers and homage to the rising sun, pointing
out that this was always the Red Indian's first
duty, and was always done in solitude!

I gave birth to two daughters, and hastily
packed them off to live with their grandparents. I was far too busy. Then, my husband was
killed during a skirmish with another tribe — a
tribe that came too close to our territory.

I continued to study and, under the guidance
of a great healer by the name of White Cloud, I

began to undertake various healing tasks. I was no longer responsible for the fires. I moved into White Cloud's teepee, and gave birth to two more daughters. Again, they were packed off to live with my parents. My name in this incarnation was White River.

In Sun Men of the Americas, another book I obtained well after the regression, the naming process of Red Indians is described. It was their belief that the holy Father was spirit and the holy Mother was earth. Therefore, at the birth of a baby boy they would look to the heavens for a name, but to the earth when naming a girl. This certainly backs up my answers.

I seem to have progressed rapidly under the guidance of White Cloud. Soon, I was healing with vibrations, and I described this process during my regression. I massaged feet, necks and knuckles, and I felt the vibrations from my arms entering the patient's body. I spoke to the patient, chanted and soothed, and cured many people. I was very proud of this fact.

Pride, however, was one of my two major faults, and was eventually to lead to my downfall. Vanity was the other. These White Cloud often tried to correct. He continually explained that, as a healer, I was only a tool, an instrument. But my healing was so successful — I was able not only to cure, but in many cases prevent illness — that I took great pride in this accomplishment. Added to that was the fact that I was a mere woman and yet was held in very high esteem by the tribe. I was respected. 'This is most unusual,' I explained during the regression. (Could this, therefore, be the reason for my belief in this incarnation that I deserve respect?)

White Cloud also explained that, since I was a spirit in a physical vehicle, vanity, like pride, had no place in my thinking. This did not stop me from continually gazing at my reflection in the river, for I was very beautiful.

Only the chief did not extend this respect to me. Was this the reason I didn't like him? I made the excuse that 'he is very serious, grumpy. He never laughs' but I suspect that pride played a large part in my attitude. Pride comes before a fall. How many times have we heard that? I was soon to discover the meaning of such a cliché.

We lived a relatively peaceful life. Apart from the one battle in which my husband was killed there was only one skirmish, in later years, with another tribe. 'They are not our people,' I explained, 'and they came to attack us. They came on horses. We did not have horses. But there were not many of them and many of us, and we were able to defend ourselves.' (In each of the books I later read, I found many references to the Spanish using horses in North America in the 1500s but, for the most part, it would seem that the Red Indian did not have access to this means of transportation for at least another hundred years.)

'You are now fifty-five years old. Where are you?' the questioner asked.

'I am in my teepee. And I am totally alone,' I replied sadly. Why was I alone? Suddenly I blurted out that I had 'killed the chief'. There was silence for a moment. And then, angrily, I continued: 'I did NOT kill the chief. They say that I did, but I didn't. He was sick. My vibrations were negative. They knew I didn't like

*him so they said I had killed him. But I didn't
kill him. Only I couldn't save him. Now, now
they say that I have lost the power to heal, and
that I only have the power to kill. They have
turned their backs on me. I am alone.'*

*I explained that White Cloud had died a few
years before this incident, and that someone
else was now doing the healing. I didn't know
who, for I had not trained anyone. I was still, at
fifty-five quite beautiful, and still proud of that
fact. I had moved my teepee to the outskirts of
the campsite and ate whatever I could find —
vegetables, herbs, left-over scraps. I soon grew
tired of this existence, however, and determined that I would die. I sat in my teepee for
many weeks, and did not eat. I was particularly
sad at this stage that I had lost my beauty.
Eventually, I was too weak to sit, so I lay down
and simply — and eagerly — waited to die.
'Nobody comes,' I said angrily. 'They know I
am dying. They sense it. But nobody comes.
Not even my children.'*

*Shortly before my departure from my body, I
was aware that White Cloud was with me. I
stepped from my body and took his hand, and
we began to walk. 'He is angry with the tribe,' I
tell the questioner. 'Don't look back,' White
Cloud tells me as we walk away from the
teepee.*

*I subsequently read a book about the Red
Indians and their way of life, in which one
statement almost seemed to jump off the page
as I was reading. It said that when a death
occurred, members of the tribe would always
tell the departing spirit* not to look back. Presumably, since the tribe played no part in my

dying process, White Cloud took the responsibility of reminding me of this warning.

We stayed together and it was White Cloud, I explained, who was to become my guide in the next incarnation, one that I did not wish to go through. For my lesson this time would be to love even if that love was not returned. 'I loved my people,' I told the questioner. 'And they loved me, for I was beautiful and I was an excellent healer, but then they didn't love me any more, so I refused to love them. But I should have loved them even though they no longer loved me. I must remember that. I must love even if I am not loved.'

All the same, it seems I was not looking forward to my next incarnation — whether that is the present one, or another (Stuart England, perhaps?) I don't know, for after one and a half hours, the questioner felt that it was time to call a halt to the session. We discussed various aspects of the session, and he played some tapes of other regressions to me. Some were quite fascinating — two in particular in which the participants had lapsed into a foreign language unknown to them in the present. I questioned the 'vibrationary healing process' and was told that this has often been described by participants experiencing a lifetime as a Red Indian.

I was, however, a little confused that White Cloud would have been angry with the tribe, for as a spirit would he not have been above such emotions reserved for we mere mortals? 'Not so!' I was told. 'They are just like us, only they don't happen to be incarnate at the moment. They are not all-knowing or all-wise.

Not yet.' This, I must admit, did confuse me, and I was reminded of the Red Indian thumping his chest twenty years before and proudly saying, 'I did it!' (This Red Indian, I was later to learn, was not White Cloud. I was almost relieved to discover this fact. What a hypocrite he would have been, preaching to me during my lifetime that I should not be so proud, for I was no more than a tool, then taking pride in his own accomplishments!) Red Indians, I was later to learn, figure quite prominently as guides, due in the main to their spiritual life-styles before white man came to their land. Chinese guides are also quite prominent, for the same reasons.

At this stage, though, I only knew that White Cloud had been my teacher and lover, and was now my guide, so naturally I was quite interested in having the sketch done, and hastily made an appointment. In the weeks to follow, however, I read extensively — both on Red Indians and the spirit world. As could be expected, whenever I found something to which I could relate, I would gasp an audible 'Oh!' How closely our thoughts and words are monitored, I was unaware at that time, but this was soon to be made known to me.

By the time of my appointment with the psychic artist, I had gathered a considerable amount of information about the world of spirits, guides and guardians. I had discovered that we all have a guardian, along with any number of spirit guides. Book after book explained that guides are not all-knowing or all-wise. They have a certain amount of wisdom, it is true, and use their wisdom to assist us, but it is up to us to ask for the assistance we require, and if any of the guides with us at that time are not able to grant this assistance, another will be asked to do so. Usually, these guides were people we knew in other lifetimes, and they offer their assistance in return for favours or kindnesses shown to them by us in that lifetime, or to work off karma created by them if they harmed us during other lifetimes. They do not usually remain with us throughout our entire lives, but only for as long as their particular lesson lasts, or for as long as it takes to work off their karma. It is really a matter of 'You scratch my back and I'll scratch yours'. For in acting as a guide and providing assistance, our guides are, in fact, improving their own status in the spiritual world. All the same, it should be noted that they do not do this selfishly, for it is their choice to act as guides.

Our guardian, on the other hand, is someone we made an agreement with prior to birth, and this spirit remains with us throughout our entire lifetime (or incarnation). The one who acts as guardian has reached a higher status than the guides, therefore has accumulated considerably more wisdom and knowledge. Consider that, prior to birth, we know which life-lessons we intend to experience. At the moment of birth, however, the knowledge is lost to us. And this is as it should be, for knowing our life lessons would be of no benefit during the experience. Due to our loss of memory, therefore, we arrange with a spirit friend to watch over our progress and perhaps even give us a nudge from time to time if we seem to stray too far from the path we set for

91

ourselves. *And stray we often will, for we are always allowed free will, and although we plan our lives to a certain extent before incarnation, when we reach a fork in the road that we have chosen to travel we are each free to make our own decisions, choose our own experiences or routes. Due to the law of free will, of course, neither our guides nor our guardian can prevent those choices, but they can give us a subtle nudge if they feel we are wasting our opportunities to learn and experience that for which we came.*

Because our guardian is on a much higher vibrationary level than our guides, many clairvoyants who have not developed their abilities further than guide level are not able to perceive these beings. It would appear that the psychic artist, however, was not one of these.

Having previously been advised by the artist that only one guide would come forward when she began to sketch (and she later explained that her sketch was, to a great extent, the work of the spirit guides themselves and not simply her interpretation — a similar process to automatic writing) I spent two days prior to the appointment mentally asking White Cloud to come through at the sitting. Imagine my surprise when, as the artist opened the door, almost her first words were 'You have an Egyptian with you!' I was partly disappointed that White Cloud had not taken up my invitation, and partly pleased to know that there was a reason for my fascination with ancient Egypt.

When she began to sketch, however, the artist told me that my Egyptian had stepped aside, but she did not know who was coming through. The result — a magnificent portrait of a Red Indian! And her comment during the sketch was that she had the distinct impression of physical strength. His aura was greeny-blue and gold — the former denoting healing, and the latter spiritual wisdom.

The reading which followed (although she prefers not to call it a reading, as it is more of a life message from that particular guide — a nudge?) began by suggesting that the very strong presence of the Egyptian would probably indicate that he was my guardian, but that this guide was here to encourage me in the area of teaching. As this meant nothing to me, she continued to explain that the things I knew about healing I would soon be giving out in a more formalised teaching format. Only the day before, I had been asked how the correspondence course in nutrition was progressing, something I had been working on for my office for many months, and I was suddenly aware of the significance of this statement.

This Red Indian, she explained, was from Canada. Then she corrected that statement and said he was North American. Then she looked at the portrait for quite a while, seeming to be listening and again changed it back to Canada. (I understood her confusion, realising that I had placed us on the border of Canada — and that in the 1500s there had not even been a border.)

She went on to tell me that within a few years I would be joining with a group of people to form some kind of consultancy service, and I would also join with another existing group in which I would be asked to do readings, talks on *healing, spiritual experiences, etc. I found this difficult to believe, although I kept my doubts to myself, but was immediately told not to be over-awed by the prospect of such things, for they would be natural to me when they came forward.*

At one point during the reading, my Egyptian 'popped in'. The artist was telling me that I had been having some intensified growth experiences lately, and in recent months the penny had dropped as to what these were all about. Most of it had come through reading, and that I had kept thinking 'Oh!' when it all began to fit into place. The Egyptian then arrived to say that he was very happy that I had gained these understandings. 'Understandings', it would seem was the psychic's word, for she then interrupted. 'Ah, he calls it cognitise, you know, to become concrete in your mind, and the relevance of the events to your life's pattern and your life's pathway. He's very happy about that.'

She went on to describe the Red Indian as a healer, a guide who was going to help me teach healing technique, and then told me that his name was either Yellow Sun or Yellow Eagle. She was not sure which. This surprised me, for I had been certain it was White Cloud, and I questioned her further, explaining that I had recently undergone regression in which White Cloud had been my healing teacher.

'Most of the guides,' she explained 'have had past life connections with us, and it's one of the uniting bonds we have with them, it's a love link, a spiritual love link that we have from the past, and often there are things — debts that

have been owed and so their services are offered. Just as you have a guardian, you also have a number of guides around you. Where there are people who have a lot to do with healing work, you will find a gathering of guides who specialise in healing. White Cloud is easily of as much importance to you as Yellow Sun. Don't be deterred or confused at all there. Ah, he says — rejoice in the fact that you've got many.'

All the same, I was still sure this must have been the one I had invited — the references to healing and Canada convinced me, and I questioned her further.

'The best thing to do,' she replied, 'is when you get the picture home, just sit with him and ask him if it is indeed White Cloud. It's really easy.'

That easy? Really? I sat and I looked. I asked and I listened. And eventually, I gave up and reached for the book I had been reading [Edge of Reality]. I opened the page to the place I had reached before putting it aside, and the first paragraph I read was: 'Words can be wonderful tools for communication, so long as we don't allow them to get in the way... Why should you and I argue if my name for the Lord of Light is Christ and yours is Mithras? Isn't it more important that we recognise the Light in each other?'

So, there was my answer, albeit a cryptic one. Did that mean his name was White Cloud, or that it was not but it didn't matter?

While reading Sun Men of the Americas a few months later, I discovered the reason for the original confusion over Yellow Sun or

Yellow Eagle. The Red Indian believed that the eagle was the only creature able to look directly into the sun, therefore anyone of the tribe who developed psychic powers was given this name — Sun or Eagle. Since the colour yellow denoted wisdom, a wise psychic would therefore be known as Yellow Sun or Yellow Eagle. However, this still did not provide any clues about White Cloud. These were to come much later.

A few weeks after the sketch was made, I visited the Healthy Living Show, and one of my main aims was to purchase a crystal to use for healing. I had considered doing this the previous year, but realised I knew little or nothing about them, and purchased a book on crystals instead. This book, however, sat in my bookshelf for the entire year and was taken down and flicked through only the night prior to the show.

At the show, I bought a few crystals, then happened to notice a booth where clairvoyants were giving readings. Well, I thought, why not?

The first thing the clairvoyant said to me as I handed her the cross I wear around my neck was 'You have some beautiful crystals and you're going to use these for healing'.

'That's correct,' I replied, always being careful not to provide too much information.

'You know how to use these.' This was a statement, not a question.

'No,' I replied.

'Oh, yes you do,' she insisted. 'You've used them before, only you don't remember. Soon it will all come back to you. And you'll also

remember the relationship between crystals, colour and sound in healing'.

I was amazed. She had known, somehow, that I had practised healing in a previous lifetime. But crystals? I had not mentioned using crystals, had I? Or colours. Sounds, perhaps, for I had chanted. Her next revelation, however, put an abrupt end to my line of thinking.

'I can see an enormous third eye opening up.'

'Pardon?' I asked, meekly.

Jokingly, she handed the cross back to me. 'Here, you do a reading for ME!' she said.

'Ah, well, I don't think I'm quite ready for THAT!' I replied with a weak laugh.

She went on to tell me about various other guides who were with me at that time, although she did not mention my Red Indian. She told me about a Chinese man who was holding his index finger to his lips and advising, 'Pearls before the swine'. It was true, I had been telling many about my recent experiences, and had been subjected to ridicule quite often. This had not bothered me particularly, but I understood his warning all the same. Then she began to laugh. 'I have a lovely lady here at the moment,' she told me. 'She's from the Victorian age. She's wearing an off-the-shoulder dress, has her hair up, and she's saying that it's time for a change.'

'Time for a change? What does she mean by that?' I asked.

'She's telling you that it's time to start wearing nice clothes again!'

That certainly hit the mark. For the past six months, working from home, I had been living mostly in track suits and jeans, and could not remember the last time I had worn a dress.

When the book on crystals was eventually opened and read, some amazing facts became evident. First of all, crystal healing is successful because of the vibrations of the crystals, and I had spoken of using vibrations as a Red Indian healer. Second, colours are manifested through the crystals and used to penetrate the auras. Yes, I remembered, I HAD spoken of auras during my regression, but I had not used that name. I had said that often, I could actually prevent illness before it began by looking at the person. The aura, of course, is where the illness shows up prior to its taking hold of the physical body. Third, and probably most exciting of all — the Red Indians of North America were extremely proficient at crystal healing!

I continued reading book after book on crystals, and references to the Red Indians' use of them was predominant in every one. So, I HAD used crystals before, as the clairvoyant had told me, but I had simply called them 'vibrations'. Naturally, I began to read extensively on colours and sounds — it's a long and complicated process, and considering that I spent many, many years studying nutrition and still don't come near to knowing everything there is to know, I realise that it will take more than a few months — but then, my 'healing clinic' will not be in operation for another three to five years, according to Yellow Sun!

A few months later, I returned to the psychic artist, hoping this time to obtain a sketch of my Egyptian. Again, I spent two days asking him to attend the sitting. Alas, I was disappointed.

98

Instead of an Egyptian, another Red Indian sat for his portrait. White Cloud!

I cannot be dogmatic about this, however. The artist had difficulty with his name. She was certain it was 'White' something, but she could not be sure what the rest of the name was. She asked me if I knew. I said I didn't. She told me the 'White' part of the name was important, but she could not quite get the rest of it. 'I'm going dead on the line!' she joked. When she decided to write 'White Sun' on the canvas, I asked if it could possibly be 'White Cloud' and she said that it could very well be, and so my 'crusty old warrior' — totally different from the drawing of the handsome young brave I originally obtained — carries the name White Cloud.

I was fascinated, but also a little disappointed. I had really wanted a portrait of my Egyptian guardian, and wondered briefly if he was not, in fact, my guardian, but a guide who had since left, as he had not responded to my invitation. During the reading, he again 'popped in'. Why? In the psychic's own words, 'Your Egyptian guardian has just popped in to let you know that he is still with you'.

Three other people I know have had spirit guide sketches done recently by the same artist. Not one has had any mention made of an Egyptian guardian. If there could be any doubt about the artist, and any suspicion that she tells everyone the same story, it is my opinion that this incident stands as proof of the origin of her messages.

I had another 'visitor' during this reading. In recent months, I had been asking for humour

— and could not deny that my request had been granted. And so, enter Hubert. Hubert, it seems, was a clown in his recent lifetime. He had worn a colourful outfit, had red frizzy hair on either side of his head, and a long face. Hubert had come recently — to teach me how to laugh at silly things!

And White Cloud's message? Basically, it was to remind me that I have a right to be here, a right to my own space, and that I should not be intimidated. 'Make them aware that as you respect their position,' he told me, 'they should also respect yours.'

If indeed this was White Cloud, then perhaps he was trying to remind me that allowing the chief to intimidate me during my last lifetime had led to my downfall, and that I should therefore learn to stand up for myself this time!

White Cloud pointed out that, although I should not force my will on any other, I must also remember that no-one has the right to force their will on me.

'There are some who would wish this,' he said through the psychic. And I knew that this was so.

Before I left, I asked the psychic if she knew my Egyptian guardian's name. She listened for a moment, then told me that it was Ra-fera-ma. This would indicate an old kingdom entity, for Ra was the name of the sun god of that era. My interest in ancient Egypt tended towards the eighteenth dynasty — thousands of years after the old kingdom. But it would only be a matter of days until, in a second-hand bookshop, I would find a book entitled The Ra Material, *and this would provide the link between the two kingdoms in such a remarkable way that it would leave absolutely no doubt in my mind that Ra-fera-ma was exerting a considerable influence on me.*

But then, that is entirely another story.

Sandy's experiences are different from mine and they probably differ from yours, too, but there are a number of things we have in common. Most notably, there is the desire to find our spiritual origins, to learn the things that give our lives a sense of order, continuity, meaning and purpose. Sandy elected to begin with regression and consultations for clairvoyant readings, in quest of clues that she could fit together to form a pattern that makes sense to her. Different people will use different methods of approach, but life is rather like a jigsaw puzzle for most of us: we look for pieces that will fit together to show us more of the overall picture. How we look and where we find the pieces will depend upon whatever comes most naturally to the individual. Sandy's way would not suit everyone, but then it doesn't have to. It only has to be suitable for Sandy. One of the advantages of New Age thinking is that it gives us so many avenues to explore, so we are free to find the ways which work best for ourselves. For instance, I was advised by my guides that it would not be good for me to undergo regression, but the method has obviously worked well for Sandy.

It is worth remarking on the attitude with which Sandy approaches her investigations, because it has a significant bearing on the results. She is open-minded but not gullible, and she does not rely only on one source for her guidance. She checks and double-checks, seeks out different sources of information, does a lot of reading, and does not resist the promptings from her inner guidance. Whether she believes those inner promptings to come from a spirit guardian, her own higher self or intuition doesn't really matter: the important thing is that she pays attention to them. It's easy to dismiss those internal 'twitches' as imagination, but to do so very often means an opportunity missed.

Quite a few people are hesitant about visiting clairvoyants and not without some justification. Clairvoyants come in all shapes and sizes: some of them are attuned to genuinely advanced sources of information, others are not so useful. A few months ago, a lady told me about having visited two clairvoyants. The first told her that she had a talent for psychic healing and would do well if she developed her attunement with crystals. She had experienced a few successes with healing on previous occasions and felt attracted to crystals, so this reading encouraged her to investigate her talents further in that area. The second clairvoyant told her that one of her relatives had been killed in a car accident some years earlier, a close friend was going to be killed in a car accident within a few months, and her husband would be killed, again in a car accident, at the age of fifty-four.

One of this woman's relatives had indeed been killed in a car accident several years previously, and the details provided by the clairvoyant were quite correct. A few months later, the friend was also involved in a car accident, but the circumstances differed from the details given by the clairvoyant and the person was injured not killed.

'What do you think about the second clairvoyant?' asked my companion.

'Well,' I mused, 'she seems to have quite a thing about people being killed in car accidents.'

She bit her lip, looking distressed. 'Do you think I should be worried about my husband?'

'No, I certainly do not! The clairvoyant has only told you about a *possibility*, not a certainty. She also seems to be much better at reading the past than predicting the future. She was wrong about your friend, wasn't she? The further into the future a possibility may lie, the more likelihood that she will be wrong about it.'

'She told me that she runs classes in psychic development and that there is a vacancy for me if I want it. I do want to develop; do you think it would be a good idea for me to join?'

'That's up to you,' I replied. 'How much more do you want to know about car accidents?'

She smiled. 'Not much.'

'Well, when a clairvoyant gives a reading, she is demonstrating her own level of knowledge and capability. It isn't fair or realistic to expect her to teach you anything she doesn't know. If you want to learn how to predict car accidents with questionable accuracy, then she would be ideally qualified. Is that what you want to learn?'

'Of course not!' There was a lilt of relief in her laughter. 'What about the first one, then? She runs classes too, but she lives a lot further away.'

'Same process of reasoning applies,' I replied. 'Do you feel that she gave you anything of value?'

'Oh, yes!' she breathed. 'She was wonderful. I'd drive for hours to see her.'

'It seems to me that you have just answered your own question,' I remarked, with a smile.

When clairvoyants give information that proves useful, there is obvious value in the contribution they make, but it is not a good idea to be heavily influenced by what someone else tells you just because that person claims to be clairvoyant and charges money for a reading. Some give excellent advice, others are a waste of time and money. Sandy finds value in what she was told because it is substantiated by information she has received from other sources. If every book she read about Red Indians had told her that Apaches never lived anywhere near the Canadian border, I doubt she would have given much credence to the information that emerged in her regression, and she may then have believed that the psychic who 'saw' her Red Indian companion was simply reading an image from Sandy's own mind. It is because she was able to validate a substantial amount of the information that she readily applies it to the lessons she is aiming to learn.

Sandy also makes the significant observation that spirit guides are not necessarily all-wise or all-knowing, and should not be given unquestioning acceptance as the ultimate arbiters of cosmic truth. My guides have made the same assertion, always emphasising the need to check, test and recheck everything we're told in order to be sure of the truth. Consequently I see reason to be wary of any claims that a particular guide or guru has reached the ultimate degree of enlightenment, especially if the 'Wise One' in question encourages that belief. It has been observed that in general, the more highly advanced an entity may be, the more unassuming their attitudes tend to be. It is advisable to collect information from as many sources as is feasible, and sift it to find where there is mutual substantiation and where it is supported by the evidence of your own experience and observations.

The purpose for which a person seeks information is just as important as the messages received. Sandy is endeavouring to gain a greater understanding of the events that shape her destiny, the lessons she is here to learn, why she needs to learn them, and how she can apply her knowledge and abilities for the benefit of others besides herself. To this end, she is willing to undertake years of intensive study in which she invests a considerable amount of energy and concentration. While she acknowledges that a message telling her it's time to wear some nicer clothes may have some relevance, she does not let it persuade her to go out and buy a wardrobe full of glamorous new outfits. To her, such a message is merely an indication that the psychic's messages come from sources that have relevance to her: a trivial detail can be a useful form of confirmation. It does not, however, occupy a great amount of Sandy's attention, because her mind is focused on to more substantial matters. She is only minimally concerned with worldly undertakings and ambitions, and primarily concerned with the establishment of her spiritual identity. If she were seeking advice about her career or her love-life, most of the information she has quoted would have been irrelevant to her and would therefore have served no useful purpose in her eyes.

While she has a keen interest in spiritual matters and boundless enthusiasm for her studies in this area, Sandy is anything but an airy-fairy eccentric. She is competent, intelligent and down-to-earth, with an irrepressible sense of humour, which occasionally borders on the outrageous. Whether it comes from the spirit clown Hubert or bubbles up from within Sandy herself, she does have the ability to laugh at silly things and to make silly remarks that bring the gift of laughter to others, something she has often done for me.

She doesn't claim to be anyone special, nor does she think of herself as being particularly psychic, but she knows how to go with the flow. The fact that her psychic faculties don't appear to be especially active doesn't mean they are not operational, but rather that she has no need for startling evidence of psychic activity. Her quest is for knowledge, not psychic experiences just for the sake of having them. Spirituality does involve psychic activity to some degree, which varies from person to person, but psychic activity in itself is not a prerequisite for spirituality. It is only an aspect.

The laws that govern the function of psychic energy remain the same, irrespective of whether the psychic uses it for a spiritual purpose or some form of material gain. Energy is energy. The dynamics do not change, only the outcome varies, depending on how the energy is employed. It is apparent from Sandy's life experiences that she had a strong focus on healing long before she developed a conscious interest in having contact with spiritual beings. The law of attraction causes like energies to attract, therefore Sandy tends to attract entities who are attuned to the healing frequencies.

Even the clown Hubert has a healing purpose, because laughter is essential for good health and generates potent healing energies, not only psychologically but physically as well. Like all truths, the saying that laughter is the best medicine has become something of a cliché, but it is no less true for all that. Get ready, here comes a personal anecdote to illustrate the point.

A few months ago, Craig and I travelled to Queensland for his brother's wedding. Because I lived in Queensland for a number of years, I have some very close and loving friends there, whom I hadn't seen for two years. They were delighted to know we would be visiting and eager to meet the man who had restored the light to my heart and put the smile in my voice. We planned to stay in Queensland for several weeks: what we did *not* plan was that I would fall and break my leg only a week before we were due to leave. Nor did we foresee the bizarre misadventures that would befall me in transit!

Honestly now, does it make any sense to put a spring-loaded swinging door on a *disabled* toilet facility ... or to make the spring so strong that an able-bodied man needs to exert a noticeable amount of muscle to hold it open? That, my friends, is what the city fathers (or whoever is responsible for such things) decided to do when the Devonport Air Terminal was constructed. It should not take a monumental degree of psychic perception to figure out that whoever designed that terminal building had never tried holding a spring-loaded door open with one shoulder while balancing uncertainly on one foot and a pair of crutches, and attempting to make forward progress at the same time! That door has a mind of its own and, I seriously suspect, a personality disorder of some magnitude. Why else would it blandly allow itself to be shouldered open by a lady on crutches and wait until she has manoeuvred herself half-way through, with a certain amount of difficulty, then with impeccable timing, just as her weight is balanced somewhat unevenly on the crutches while she swings her *good* leg forward, decide to swing itself shut with enough force to bat her off balance? In that situation, the lady can either fall in a sprawling, undignified heap on the floor, or instinctively catch all of her weight on the broken leg. I did not fall. My left foot (the one at the end of the broken leg) hit the floor, I yelped and lurched drunkenly into the toilet cubicle and the door swished to a close, no doubt chuckling evilly to itself!

At Sydney Airport, where we had to change to another aircraft, I was taken everywhere in a wheelchair, with great courtesy and consideration, in the care of a porter. Like most large airports, the Sydney terminal building has those protruding tunnel walkways that nose up to the aircraft doors and disgorge passengers into, and out of, the aircraft. At least, that is what they are *meant* to do and, if all goes well, they usually do it very efficiently... except when a manic wheelchair extricates itself from the porter's grasp on the downward slope. There I was, plaster-encased leg resting almost comfortably on a board stuck straight out in front, rolling sedately down the ramp, when from the porter there issued a horrified gasp and a cry of 'Oh no! The brakes...'

I continued to roll, somewhat less sedately, straight for the side of the aircraft. My progress came to an abrupt halt as my foot (yes, the one at the end of the broken leg!) met the aircraft fuselage with a dull thud.

Two days later, while I was recuperating at the home of a friend, we received a visit from another friend, Alan. It would be nice if I could say that I greeted him with bright-eyed enthusiasm, but since it isn't nice to tell lies, I won't. Recently broken legs, villainous swinging doors and kamikaze wheelchairs do not exactly combine to make anyone feel like dancing a tango. I had awoken feeling stiff, uncomfortable and out of sorts, and my leg was mounting a vehement, if somewhat belated, protest. It hurt. A lot. In fact, it hurt with stubborn ferocity, and it obstinately refused to stop hurting, even when I spoke to it nicely.

I don't like pain. It doesn't do nice things for my disposition and, besides, it hurts. Whenever I am in pain, I could easily be convinced that God is not only a female, but that She suffers from chronic and severe bouts of PMT! On that particular morning, I had grown extremely tired of wearing a brave smile. I had progressed through annoyed impatience to the swamps of depression. I had been crying. I felt sorry for myself. I was not enjoying my holiday. I was severely displeased with my guardian angel. And my leg *still* hurt! By the time Alan made his appearance, I was tear-streaked, dishevelled and thoroughly miserable.

Seeing my wretched expression, Alan asked me what was wrong. I indicated the offending limb. 'My leg is broken, Alan,' I pointed out, somewhat unnecessarily. 'And it hurts. As a matter of fact, it hurts like hell. It feels like it's been hurting for-ever... and I've had enough. I can't *stand* it!' My words ended in a wretched wail and I subsided into a chair, sniffling dolefully into a handful of tissues.

'Oh, dear!' Alan seated himself facing me and gazed with consternation first at the injured leg, then at me. 'What did the doctor tell you?'

'Which doctor?'

'The one you saw when this first happened.'

'What was he supposed to tell me? He said it's broken, he gave me some painkillers... which are not working... and told me to keep my weight off it until it heals.'

'Nothing else?'

'What else *could* he tell me?'

A slight frown creased Alan's brow as he rubbed his chin pensively, as though considering the best way to deliver some grave news. 'I'm really sorry to hear that,' he remarked. 'There is something very important that he has apparently neglected to tell you. It's not exactly pleasant, but you obviously have a need to know.'

'What is it?' I asked, not entirely sure that I wanted to hear the answer.

'Promise you'll be brave?'

I nodded. Alan took a deep breath and leaned forward, eyeing me with an expression of careful solicitude.

'Broken legs hurt,' he said.

I waited for him to say something else. He sat back in his chair, wearing an expression of supremely innocent candour. Then the penny dropped.

'You *beast*, Alan!' I chuckled. 'I thought you were going to tell me something really serious.'

'I know,' he agreed, nodding his head like a sage. I dissolved into a fit of helpless giggles.

'Good on you, mate!' cheered Craig. 'You've got her laughing!'

Between the pair of them, Craig and Alan kept me laughing for the next two hours. They clowned around with each other and kept up a stream of banter that had me bubbling over with laughter. Somewhere in the midst of the merriment, my leg stopped hurting, but I hardly even noticed. The bone didn't heal instantaneously (although it did heal several weeks earlier than the doctor expected) but it never seemed to hurt as much from that time on. I can't prove with scientific certitude that the laughter did the trick, but it certainly helped things along. If Sandy's spirit clown has a similar effect on the people with whom she comes into contact, no doubt she will be a magnificent healer!

A lot of the people who write to me have expressed the concern that because they do not experience any noticeable manifestations of psychic ability, they may not be able to make very much progress with spiritual development. In fact, most people are more psychic than they realise, and because their guidance comes in the form of subtle inner promptings and fortuitous 'coincidences', they don't always recognise the significance of those events. Powerful and dramatic psychic experiences can actually impede the process of spiritual development in some instances, because people can become so fascinated by the phenomena that they overlook the central purpose.

Sandy's account of her experiences offers a clear demonstration that anyone who is sufficiently motivated to explore their spiritual potential can do so without the need for startling demonstrations of psychic phenomena. You need only have an interest, an open mind and a willingness to pay attention to your inner promptings. Once you invest the energy that gives impetus to your quest, the universe has a way of keeping things in motion. Chance encounters lead to people who share your interest and can offer helpful advice, books that answer the questions you've been asking find their way into your hands... all kinds of wonderful things can happen, and frequently do. It helps if you maintain a certain amount of common sense, and of course there is another sense that constitutes a vital ingredient... your sense of humour!

Spirituality has its serious aspects, and there is no doubt that it is a matter of personal importance to those in quest of enlightenment, but there is no reason why it should be a dreary process. We are told that humour has the effect of raising our vibrations, so it actually helps to draw us closer to the spiritual spheres. Read profusely, study with care and meditate on everything you learn along the way, and while you're doing it, remember:

The angels rejoice to hear your laughter.

CHAPTER FIVE

Karmic common sense

Most people are aware that karma is a system of balance which returns to us the consequences of our actions, thoughts and words, but in letters and conversations with readers, I am often asked questions which seem to indicate a number of misconceptions about the ways in which this system operates. The confusion is illustrated in questions like the following, quoted from letters I have received, which represent questions that I encounter most commonly on this subject.

'I have been told and have read a couple of books that suggest that whatever you do will also happen to you, e.g. if a person is murdered, then that person had actually murdered someone, too, in another life.'

'Having been sent to, and loved, a convent school, I was taught as a child that to genuinely repent my "sins" meant forgiveness by my Creator. What has me puzzled now is whether the law of karma allows one to repent. Would I still receive a "zap" from karma whether I am genuinely sorry or not? Or will I be forgiven entirely with no ill effect returning to me?'

'If a spirit is evil, committing atrocities against other living beings, and then somehow comes to a realisation that what they are doing is wrong and

112

seeks to change this, would they then have to start repaying the karmic bill they'd mounted and therefore continue to have horrible things happen to them? In payment for the hurts that they have caused, would they then experience pain etc., for a period of time until that debt was cleared? If so, there doesn't seem to be much incentive to stop being nasty if your situation doesn't change. Or is God so forgiving that the slate would be wiped clean and the "born again" (!) patted on the back?'

Karma is not administered by a deity seated on his throne, making individual judgements and handing out punishments or rewards. This is not to imply that the Creator has nothing to do with karma at all, simply that it is not a matter of some cosmic personality making case-by-case decisions. If a craftsman constructs a machine that is self-propelled, he does not need to push it along himself in order to make it move. In this sense, karma is self-fulfilling. We frequently refer to it as the *law* of karma, which sometimes causes it to be misconstrued as a commandment, but in reality it is a principle of energy, like the law of gravity, for instance.

Under natural law, if you hold your head under water and inhale, your lungs will fill with water and you will drown. That is not a punishment inflicted by some deity, it is simply a natural consequence of your actions. Karma is also a natural law in this sense: karmic events are simply natural consequences. Karma is a law of cause and effect, not of punishment and retribution.

All energy moves in a cycle that will ultimately return it to its point of origin, along with the effects of the chain reactions set into operation by that energy. To use a physical analogy, if you leave your car parked on a hill, facing downwards, in neutral gear and with the handbrake off, the likelihood is that it will roll down the hill. If it encounters no obstruction until it rolls off the road to end up nose-down in a ditch, the karmic result of your carelessness will probably be a car with a bent nose and maybe some mechanical damage, which will cost you a certain amount of money for repairs. On the other hand, if the car crashes through someone's front fence, flattens a glasshouse containing a collection of prize orchids, cripples a champion racehorse, careers back on to the road and glances off several parked vehicles before smashing through a car showroom window to collide head-on with a brand-new Rolls Royce, the karmic consequences for you will be considerably more serious.

My spirit teachers have repeatedly emphasised the necessity to exercise great caution with the energies we set into motion because of the karmic principle governing the returning cycles of energy.

'Before you release an energy,' warns David, 'make certain that you can maintain control of that energy, and its effects, as it traverses a complete cycle. If, at any point in the cycle, the energy passes out of your control, you have no knowledge of the effects that it may cause, but you are still responsible for those effects. It is to you that the consequences shall return when the energy completes its cycle, for you are the point of origin.'

Applying this teaching to our analogy; if you are aware that your car could cause damage should it roll down a hill, you take precautions to ensure that it will not roll. It is your car, and you are responsible for keeping it under safe control at all times.

Although the principle of karma is incorporated in the Christian religion ('whatsoever a man soweth, that shall he also reap' 'all they that take the sword shall perish with the sword') the New Age concept of karma is based more heavily on the Hindu religion. Hindus believe that one's present status and condition is the result of a previous existence, thus if a person commits acts of violence and cruelty in one life, that person must suffer violence and cruelty at the hands of others in the next incarnation. Modern spirit teachers, however, have pointed out a basic misconception in that interpretation of karma.

Since it is our purpose to learn and grow in spiritual wisdom, and part of that process consists of learning from the consequences of our actions, it stands to reason that we need to know what those actions have been, and we must be able to perceive the link between actions and consequences. If we must wait for the next life before we can experience the consequences of our actions in this one, how can we see those links and know what errors on our part have caused any unpleasant consequences that we experience in that life? Without knowing what past acts one is being punished for, how can one repent and improve? There is logic and order in the function of cosmic energy principles such as karma: unfortunately the same logic and order is not always reflected in human reasoning.

One legacy of the Hindu concept of karma is fatalism, in the form of believing that misfortunes in this life have been earned in a previous incarnation, and are therefore deserved and must be accepted with resignation. I don't know how many times I have heard people say, 'Oh, it must be karma for something I did in a previous life' when they suffer some misfortune which can be clearly seen by an observer as the result of some *present* action or attitude on the part of the sufferer.

I knew a lady some years ago who had been involved in several disastrous relationships with men who used her without any consideration for her feelings, then dumped her without compassion when they tired of her and/or a new attraction came their way. Her reaction was to say, 'Well, I must have done the wrong thing by them in a past life, so they have to do it to me now to even the score'. Believing there was nothing she could do to avoid her 'karma' did not ease the heartbreak that she felt. It also prevented her from looking realistically at the options that were available to help her change the situation, and there were several options that were clearly apparent to all of her friends. Because she believed that she could do nothing to change her 'fate', she held on to a mental pattern that kept attracting her to the same type of men.

This lady had a heart of gold, was always ready to give anyone a helping hand, and didn't have an unkind bone in her body. Her many friends kept trying to help her see that she deserved better treatment, and more than a few kind and caring gentlemen would have welcomed a chance to be closer to her, but she ran from those men like a frightened fawn.

'I'm not good enough for him,' she would explain. 'And if he got any closer to me, he'd soon see that and he'd start despising me. I could fall for him so easily . . . I'd get too badly hurt.' Thus she held herself bound to a cycle of heartache and pain. There was karma involved, to be sure, but it was the result of *the mental pattern that she was broadcasting,* not misdeeds from a former life.

Thought creates reality, and the thought energy this lady emanated said, 'I am not good enough to be loved by a really nice man. I always get hurt.' She based her actions on that thought pattern, too, when she ran from the kind of men who could have given her the love that she ached for, needed and deserved. The reality that came to her in the form of her personal experiences was the karmic result of the thought patterns that she radiated. Her thought energy kept cycling back to her, bringing its consequences with it.

At the spiritual level, we are the sum of every life we've ever lived, but we start each new physical life with a clean slate, which is indicated by the fact that we do not retain a conscious memory of our past lives. The circumstances into which we are born are determined in accordance with the lessons that we need to learn and the qualities we need to develop for our growth. It is not a case of being punished or rewarded for the long-ago, forgotten deeds of past incarnations, it is simply another phase in the learning process.

Karma is one of life's ways of bringing us opportunities to learn. If people think the kind of thoughts that lead them to cause pain for others, they will keep creating pain for themselves until they learn to *change the way they think*. Action . . . and reaction . . . follow thought: it is not the other way around.

Accepting misfortune as punishment for 'past-life' misdeeds is, according to one of the spirit teachers with whom I have spoken, a form of 'psychic masochism'. It is also an impediment to spiritual growth.

When human spirits, incarnate or discarnate, undergo a change in thinking, there is no need for 'punishment' to even any scores. The souls will *seek* to redress the balance because they feel a motivation to do so, willingly, and because they *want* to.

In discussions on karma, I frequently hear people conjecturing on how much pain and torment someone like Adolf Hitler would have to suffer in order to pay for the suffering he caused to others.

117

Who is to say that the spirit of Attila the Hun didn't reach a change in thinking and decide to reincarnate as Mahatma Gandhi in order to balance his past evils with a greater amount of good? Or that Queen Mary Tudor, England's 'Bloody Mary', might not have come back in the person of someone like Mother Teresa? Shocking thought? Perhaps, but that doesn't mean it isn't possible. Restoring the balance for past misdeeds doesn't have to mean enduring torture; it could just as well involve working hard in the service of others, to bring love and healing where once that soul inflicted hate and injury.

Taking up the example of Adolf Hitler, I suppose that I have read, and been told, as much about that personality as most other people in my culture and generation. There was a time when I also wondered what awful karmic punishments that soul must have to suffer, but lately, other questions have been occurring to me.

From all that I have heard and read about Adolf Hitler, this man was a soul *already in torment*. Professionals in the field of mental health have agreed that mentally and psychologically, Hitler was a very sick man. He was consumed with fears, phobias and feelings of persecution: he was suffering from a very profound personality disorder. He was also potentially a powerful psychic. Under the influence of clever people whose zeal is not for a cause or an ideal, but for power and the fulfilment of their own desires, such a personality is easy to manipulate.

It is worth bearing in mind that although Hitler was always intense and unbalanced, he was a failure and a nonentity until after he had served in the German Army during World War I, and was noticed by his superiors for his mystical intensity, political cunning and powerful charisma. After the war, he was enrolled for duty in the 'political' department of the Army, posted to the Press and Information Bureau, which was actually involved with covert operations in espionage, propaganda and terrorism. From there, he was drawn to the attention of Dietrich Eckart, one of the founding members of the Nazi Party, an adept at black magic, and a central figure in the sinister Thule Group, a powerful and widespread circle of occultists. Under the patronage of Eckart and others, Hitler was carefully moulded for the role he was later to play. His rise to power was guided and directed by members of the Thule Group, which included police-chiefs, barristers, judges, leading industrialists and members of the aristocracy. It was expertly stage-managed from the beginning by people without whose support Hitler might have amounted to nothing more than an outcast raving lunatic.

People tend to make sweeping statements like, 'Hitler was responsible for the murder of millions in concentration camps, and a host of other atrocities', and he certainly carried no small degree of that responsibility, but he could not have done it all by himself. He had a lot of help, and every person who played a role in those activities was personally responsible for their own actions. Hitler was responsible for *his* actions, but if he had not had powerful supporters and advisors, along with millions of followers who carried out his orders, he could have achieved none of it.

I could get up on a soapbox in some city square and exhort everyone within hearing distance to follow some crusading vision of my own imagining and, if I were doing it alone and unaided, the most likely consequence would be men in white coats arriving to take me away. Without his influential mentors and supporters, the result might have been similar for Hitler. Can he be held responsible for the decisions and actions of those people?

Among members of the peace movement today, there is a popular saying: 'What if they gave a war and nobody came?' The soldier on the battlefield may protest that he is 'only following orders', but the man who gives those orders in the first place is not the man whose finger pulls the trigger of the gun. The man who aims and fires the gun is directly responsible for every person he kills or maims with it, and for every widow and orphan he creates as a result.

Hitler certainly carried an enormous karmic responsibility, but no one, not even Hitler, is responsible for the choices made by other people.

There are other questions to be considered also: for instance, what influences in Hitler's environment and conditioning caused him to be so unbalanced, and who was responsible for those? What influences within their society caused millions of people to follow the Fuehrer's call, and who perpetrated those influences? Just how many people were involved in creating the conditions that spawned and nurtured the Nazi movement?

Look at the picture from this perspective and it can be seen that millions and millions of people contributed to the events for which Hitler stands as the figurehead. There is also the fact that the man was psychologically unhinged and already suffering inner torment. Would more suffering improve his way of thinking and make him disposed to work with Light and Love for the highest good of all concerned, or would it push him further into the depths of insanity? Is it more important to punish that soul and 'make him pay' or to heal the conditions that caused him to become what he was? Was Hitler a cause, or was he an effect? Or both?

If we do not have the answers to all of the questions I have raised, we are not in possession of all the facts and, therefore, we are in no position to make realistic and balanced judgements. Lack of data is no basis on which to form a conclusion.

I have a young penfriend named Mark who has been an inmate of Her Majesty's prisons on more than one occasion for crimes of quite a serious nature. Our penal systems in Australia are conducted under the auspices of the Department of Corrective Services, but Mark has been writing to me regularly since he first went to prison at the age of eighteen, and during those years I have seen no evidence that the department has done anything to *correct* the problems that caused Mark to commit the acts that got him sent to prison. Mark doesn't *want* to be a criminal, and he tries very hard to overcome his problems, but he gets confused sometimes, and he doesn't have much faith in himself. In fact, he sees himself as being amongst the scum of the Earth. He seeks the Light, but he doesn't believe, deep down, that he deserves to find it.

Mark is also psychic, and although he wants to follow a spiritual pathway and there is evidence of the presence of highly advanced spirit beings who are doing their utmost to help him, he is unsure of the voices that he hears in his mind. He can't quite bring himself to trust them, because he has no trust in himself and it's difficult for him to believe that any highly advanced spirits would think him worthy of the slightest attention, much less any efforts to help him save himself.

Every time he goes to prison, Mark is immersed in a psychic atmosphere that is saturated with negative energies. He has had numerous heavy encounters with malevolent entities and he feels the pressure they exert to destroy any self-control he may have. Prison is profoundly distressing and damaging for Mark, but if his inner conflicts are

121

not resolved and his energies remain out of balance, he'll get sent to prison again and again... and each time it happens, he will find it more difficult to withstand the influence of the malevolent beings that infest such places.

Would you declare that Mark should be left to suffer for his past misdeeds? Would you say that he must have earned bad karma in a former life? I would not. In Mark, I see a lost, confused and frightened soul who is suffering a tremendous load of pain and is crying out for help. We live in different states and our only contact is through letters: I try to encourage him to recognise the good things about himself, but it's an uphill battle for the two of us because Mark finds it hard to see anything good in himself at all. He is too full of shame and self-disgust. In his most recent letter to me, he wrote, 'You say in your letters that there has to be something very good in me. Excuse my bluntness but I am yet to find one solitary thing.'

Think back to the lady I mentioned earlier, who kept being hurt in her love affairs, and the mental patterns that created that reality for her. Apply the same energy principles to Mark's situation, bearing in mind that he sees himself with so much self-loathing, and think of the conditions this mental pattern must create in his life. In spite of all this, he keeps trying to improve himself and is earnestly seeking the Light. If he doesn't give way to despair and succumb to malevolent influences, he'll find it, too. He tries so hard! Within Mark, there is a beautiful soul struggling to get out, but he needs help and healing. Sometimes he also needs a comforting hand to hold, but he doesn't believe he's a fit person to mix with decent people.

Why should the Creator want to hurt Mark any more? What good would it do? How much better might it be if everyone who knew of his plight were to think of him as being surrounded constantly with Light and Love, thereby projecting those energies to help and to heal? Don't you think Mark would joyfully work his heart out to achieve something good if only he could find the way? I *know* he would.

Punishment has not improved Mark's condition, nor has it done anything to identify and correct the problems that got him into trouble. If he could be taken to a place of healing, where the atmosphere is peaceful and harmonious, if he could be helped to recognise and develop his most positive qualities, and if he could be taught to understand how to correct the mental patterns that lead him astray, wouldn't the result be more beneficial for all concerned? As it is, Mark is afraid that if he loses control again, 'I might really hurt somebody'. Physically, he is big and strongly built, he knows what kind of harm he could do if he lost control and became violent, and he doesn't *want* to do it. If ordinary people like you and me can see that more pain and abuse will not help Mark to make the changes he needs to make, I sincerely doubt that a cosmic intelligence, capable of creating and sustaining all life in the universe, could fail to be aware of it also.

If there is pain and confusion in the mind, there will be pain and confusion in the physical life. Thought creates reality: the physical reality that we live is a consequence of the way we think. Not a punishment, or a reward; simply a consequence. If you change your way of thinking, for good or ill, there will be corresponding changes in your life. There have to be; as above, so below is a cosmic law. When we experience pain and distress, karma isn't saying, 'This will teach you a lesson, you loathsome creature!' It is simply saying, 'Attention please, there is an error in the programming of

123

your computer'. No blame, no guilt, just a simple error, to be corrected.

I really think we humans are often too hard on ourselves. People in this world have been submitting to pain, abuse and torment for thousands of years, and what has resulted from it except more pain, abuse and torment? There are people who teach that human suffering is 'God's will', and must be borne as a punishment for our sinful condition. What each person believes is a matter of personal choice, but more and more people today are becoming open to the awareness that pain and misery are *unnatural* conditions which can and should be corrected for the highest good of all concerned. In this sense for us, karma is a teacher. When we experience joy and a sense of well-being, 'good' karma is telling us that our energies are well-balanced and we are moving smoothly within the flow of life. Unhappiness and pain, or 'bad' karma, says, 'Back to the drawing board!' We are taught that there are no punishments or rewards, only consequences. To me, these teachings make sense.

I am no psychologist, but it seems to me that the idea of being afflicted with torments by a wrathful deity, who builds imperfections into us and then punishes us for being imperfect, carries strong overtones of sado-masochism. Likewise, to have one's conscious memory of past lives wiped out at birth or soon afterwards, then to be punished in this life for misdeeds committed in previous lives that we can't remember, doesn't make a great deal of sense. If you don't know what you are being punished for, how can you possibly learn anything worthwhile from the punishment? It is feasible that a spirit may carry unbalanced thought patterns through more than one life and therefore continue to create 'bad' karma until it learns to

124

correct the balance, but this represents a *continued pattern* of behaviour and attitudes, not an accumulated debt.

Mature, balanced and healthy spirits do not indulge in depravity, nor do they commit atrocities, and they don't see any worthwhile advantages to be gained through greed and corruption. Spirits who do indulge in such things are therefore seen as immature, unbalanced and unhealthy; all conditions which can be corrected, given the right kind of knowledge and understanding. In order to correct a problem, it is best to identify the cause and set the balance right at that level. When the cause has been set right, the problem ceases to exist.

Let us imagine that there is a person suffering some sort of chemical imbalance in the body, and that every time the amount of vitamin C in his bloodstream drops below a certain level he starts punching people. What would be the best way of correcting this problem? To keep punching him in retaliation? Or to teach him how to monitor his blood levels and provide him with all the vitamin C that his body requires? If he refuses to take the vitamin C and keeps on punching people, his choice will very likely create a reality in which he gets punched a lot, and he can develop an unpleasant physical disease called scurvy. He has the power, and the freedom, to choose whether to keep suffering unpleasant consequences, or take the vitamin supplement that his body requires and live a happier, healthier life. Either way, his life experiences will be the consequences of his choice, and in that sense they can be said to be karmic.

If the chemical imbalance in this man's body is not detected and treated when it manifests at the 'psychological' level, i.e. when he has fits of violence, it will progress until it manifests in a physical way and he develops scurvy. Spiritually, the traditionalists might say, the disease is a punishment for his outbreaks of violence. In reality, the disease is only another manifestation of the same imbalance that triggered the violence, and through the manifestation of the disease, the cause of the violent outbreaks will be made known and it can be corrected, so it can really be seen as a blessing in the long term. When the man is given enough vitamin C to correct the physical disorder, the 'psychological' disorder will be treated also.

When unpleasant things happen to us, they indicate that something in our energy pattern isn't flowing as it should, not that we are wicked people who need to be punished. The more we learn to understand about life energies and the natural laws by which they are governed, the greater becomes our ability to analyse and identify the imbalances that cause 'bad' karma, and to correct the balance so that the unpleasant events do not recur. Karma is simply a word we use to describe the cycle of life energy output and feedback, or cause and effect. We *directly* control the nature of our karma by choosing the nature of the energies we generate through our thoughts, words and deeds.

If we look no further than the physical, and regard the spiritual or 'supernatural' as a mystery beyond our comprehension, we deprive ourselves of the means by which we can understand and regulate the cycles of our own life energies. We also accept that our lives are influenced by external forces over which we can have no control, and we submit to a lot of unnecessary woes and afflictions.

There is no dividing line between the physical and the spiritual; each exists within the other. At ground level, when you look at a rainbow, you see an arc, half a circle. If you fly up high into the sky and look at the same rainbow, you can see it as a full circle. The rainbow doesn't alter; you simply change your level of perspective. In the same way, when you add the perspective of spiritual understanding to your observation of the events and experiences in your physical life, you can see the full circle, or the cycles of energy flowing through physical and spiritual. If we take away false images, such as guilt and blame, to see the cycles of energy for what they are, we can learn to work with them, adjusting the pattern within ourselves as and where necessary in order to produce desired effects in our daily lives right here in the present.

A mechanic doesn't blame himself if something goes wrong with his car, nor does he accept that he must put up with driving a malfunctioning vehicle as a punishment for his 'guilt'. He checks the engine, locates the problem and fixes it. If the same malfunction recurs, he knows that he didn't fix the problem completely or that there is some other factor he didn't notice first time around. He will check the engine again and continue working on it until it keeps running smoothly. If we use the same attitude in working with our life energies, without guilt or blame, but with the methodical approach of a technician, we can not only make things simpler for ourselves, we can achieve more effective results. This, I believe, is why it is considered so important in the overall scheme of life for us to have an understanding of spiritual energy principles: not because of any moral standards set by theological doctrines, but simply to give us the understanding we need in order to *make our lives work* for our own sakes. It is not a matter of obeying arbitrary rules to please a deity, but rather of applying an understanding of energy principles to keep the machinery of life running smoothly.

When it is viewed from this perspective, karma can be seen as a part of the mechanism that allows us to measure how effectively we are using our energies. 'Bad' karma tells us that the engine isn't running at optimum efficiency. If we keep checking the engine and adjusting it but the bad karma continues, we need to learn more about how the engine works, that is all.

Learning to analyse karmic feedback, reading what it tells us about the way we are using our energies, and applying that input to adjusting our actions and attitudes appropriately, is not a facility that can be developed overnight. It takes practice, perseverance and concentration, and no matter how good our intentions may be, we won't get it right first time every time. Making mistakes is part of the learning process: if we already knew all there is to know, we would not be incarnated here. Guilt and blame are programmed emotional reactions that have little to do with accepting responsibility and correcting mistakes: they only get in the way and confuse the issue. We all make mistakes, and when it happens we feel bad about it, but from that point we have a choice: wallow in the mires of guilt, crying, 'Oh, wretched, worthless me!' or try to find out where we went amiss and correct the situation. One choice will keep us bogged down; the other helps us to learn and grow.

Karma can be a relentless burden, or it can be a valuable asset to our progress; the difference is only a matter of attitude. Just because it is a cosmic energy principle, it doesn't have to overwhelm us or make us feel that we are helpless against its force. We can learn to understand how it works, and work with it to our own advantage if we choose to do so. It isn't a matter of vice or virtue, only cause and effect. Karma doesn't judge or blame, it simply functions in accordance with natural laws. Learning to understand those laws and apply them to the improvement of our own life conditions is simply a matter of common sense.

128

CHAPTER SIX

Be kind to yourself — Kay's legacy

It is natural that we feel concerned about the state of the world... the preservation of wildlife... the environment... the peace movement... and caring for the Earth in general. We *need* to be concerned with those matters; our survival depends on it; however, it is possible to be so concerned with world issues and the welfare of others that you neglect to consider yourself. To be most effective in whichever cause you may choose to serve, you need to be in a condition of optimum balance, clearly focused and energised. It takes work to establish that condition within yourself, and more work to maintain it, but if you are in a condition of balance and upliftment, that will be the influence you radiate into the environment around you. If you are serene, there will be serenity around you. Like attracts like: this is cosmic law. That thought creates reality is also cosmic law.

Of the many thousands of people who write to me, I know of none who do not wish to be of help to others in some way. What many people seem to overlook, however, is that in order to give unto others, you first need to give to yourself. We all get burdened with a lot of hangups when it comes to our own needs. We can even feel guilty about wanting to enjoy our own lives; we have learned to believe that considering others before ourselves is the right thing to do, and in some cases it is, but there is a line of balance to be considered, also. Unselfishness is one thing: self-sacrifice is something entirely different. Conditioning leads us to believe that, in order to fulfil our spiritual potential, we must sacrifice any desire for physical happiness, but that idea is a distortion of the truth. There is nothing holy about sacrifice.

Like many others, I believe in a loving divinity. Questions relating to the names by which that divinity may be known are incidental as far as I am concerned. The issue of central importance to me is learning to understand more about what the divinity *is*, what it represents, what it does, how and why. I want to *know* it, not just put labels on it, and because of that wanting to know, I have spent many, many years in a quest for deeper and more profound levels of understanding. I've learned many things about the divinity in that time, and there is an infinity yet to be learned, but one thing I know as a certainty: a LOVING divinity asks for no sacrifices of any kind, not even self-sacrifice.

Most Christians know the story about Jesus driving the merchants from the temple with a whip, overturning their tables of trade and accusing them and the priests of making the temple into a den of thieves. The orthodox version of that story focuses on Christ's objection to the use of a House of God as a place of commerce, which is reasonable enough, but the Aquarian Gospel gives more detail. According to the Aquarian account, it is not only the act of trading in the temple that angered Jesus, it was also the goods in which the merchants were trading. They were selling lambs and doves to be slaughtered in blood sacrifice, and the priests were aiding them by teaching that blood sacrifice was required as tribute by God. To Jesus, according to the Aquarian account, that teaching was blasphemy and the ritual slaughter an act of sacrilege.

The Christian Bible tells of how Jesus confounded the priests in the temple with his wisdom when he was only ten or twelve years old. The Aquarian Gospel mentions some of the ways in which he confounded them. In one instance, the boy Jesus appeals to Hillel, chief of the Sanhedrin, drawing his attention to the pathetic cries of the lambs and doves being slaughtered in ritual sacrifice, and declaring that any god who took pleasure in sacrifice and burning flesh could not be his Father — God.

In the episode years later, when Jesus drove the merchants from the temple, the Aquarian Gospel records that in addition to driving the merchants out, overturning their tables and scattering their money, he also *opened the cages to set free the captive birds, and cut the bonds that had imprisoned the sacrificial lambs* . Of course, it could be argued that this was blood sacrifice, and self-sacrifice isn't the same thing; but isn't it? Blood, says the Bible, is the life-force of the physical body: what is self-sacrifice if not a surrender of the *spiritual* life-force? Is the body more sacred than the spirit? I do not think the Aquarian Christ would say so.

You are put into this world to blossom and grow, not to be withered to death with a burden of futile sacrifice. You can give generously of yourself in service to others, but if you wear yourself out in the effort, you deprive yourself of your own life energy. If you do not see to it that the battery in your car is charged, there is petrol in the tank, water in the radiator and oil in the engine, and you

131

keep on driving it, what will happen to the car? How much better will that motor vehicle serve you if you take care to ensure that it has all its needs attended to before you take it on to the road? If you really want to be of the greatest possible service to others, give yourself the same consideration that responsible drivers give to their motor cars. See to it that your own needs are fulfilled, then you will have more that you can give to others, and what you give will be of the highest quality.

You have as much right to be happy as anyone else. Furthermore, you cannot give others anything that you don't have, so if you aren't truly happy, you can't give real happiness to others. It is a cosmic impossibility. You may give others what they want, and satisfy some of their desires, but you can't give happiness if you don't have it.

I'm not saying that we shouldn't give of ourselves at all or that we should grasp everything for ourselves. It is a question of balance, with a touch of cosmic common sense thrown in for good measure. Since there is a limitless sea of energy from which we can all draw to satisfy our needs without ever depleting the supply, why flatten our batteries? I find it difficult to believe that any deity with a modicum of common sense, let alone omniscient wisdom, would see any value in that kind of waste. We may do it with the best intentions in the world, and for the most loving of motives, but if we sacrifice ourselves on the altar of giving to others, it is still a tragic and unnecessary waste of precious life energy.

We tend to our physical needs with food, exercise and shelter, and to our spiritual needs with prayer, meditation, communion with the divinity, but we have other needs, too. We need to feel loved and we need to be happy, for instance. We have minds, emotions, inner feelings of many kinds, and all of these need sustenance also.

132

The only sure way of creating a happy world is to fill it with happy people, and since we can't give happiness unless we've got it, it seems only common sense to find happiness for ourselves. If your emotions are hurting, every other level of your being will be affected, from the physical through to the spiritual and beyond. Your energy levels will be low, your mood depressed, your body tired and sore. Your spiritual energies will drop also, placing your vibrationary wavelength at a low level, at which your clarity of communication with the higher levels of spiritual existence will be impeded and you will be vulnerable to negative influences. How can you possibly give of your best in a state like that?

Puritanical conditioning in our culture deems it wicked to pursue personal happiness but, with that kind of attitude, the puritans don't appear to know the difference between true happiness and hedonistic pleasure-seeking. Hedonists are not happy people: their pleasure-seeking represents a *search* for happiness, but because they're looking in the wrong places they don't find it, which is why they keep on seeking more pleasure. In this sense, the hedonist and the puritan have something in common: neither of them knows the difference between happiness and pleasure. Pleasure is ephemeral, it comes from without and it passes. Happiness is something deep and abiding, it comes from within and it stays. Happy people will certainly experience a great deal of pleasure in their lives, but pleasure is not the same as happiness.

The law of karma represents a learning process, not a system of punishment: happiness and pain are ways of letting you know when you are on the right track in your life, and when you're not. If you experience unpleasantness and distress, you aren't where you need to be; you've wandered off the track. When you are happy and your life is running well, you're getting things right. It is written that we should love others as we love ourselves: 'as' means in the same quantity and in the same way, so that teaching does not say that we shouldn't love ourselves. It describes a condition of balance which says nothing about giving to others anything that you do not give to yourself. If you do not treat yourself with equal care and consideration, the situation is not a balanced one, therefore the ongoing effects will not be positive. This is *your* life, and you are here primarily for your own benefit . . . you are the most important person in your universe, and if you allow service to others to come before attention to your own needs, you aren't being fair to yourself.

Let me introduce you to Kay, one of the most caring, loving and giving people I have ever met. On one of my infrequent visits to a capital city one of my friends told me that she would like me to meet Kay. 'She has cancer, and she's dreadfully ill, but she's full of love,' said Judith. 'She's such a beautiful soul and I can't help feeling that she has something of value to tell that will benefit your readers.'

Judith herself is quite an amazing lady, who is always helping others for the sheer joy of doing it, and whenever she has seen a way in which she can lend assistance to me, she has done it without a further thought. Her spiritual work is done in a different area, in different ways from mine, but we share the same pathway. In the course of her work, Judith moves around and meets a lot of people. One of her many talents is psychic healing, and it was as a healer that she was first drawn to Kay, who was bedridden with multiple melanomas, but as she made further visits, the two also became friends.

I used to be a nurse and I have worked with a

number of cancer patients so, when I met Kay, her emaciated appearance was not a surprise to me. It was when I took her outstretched hand in mine that I felt something I hadn't encountered before. It was the *lightness* of her. It wasn't just the fragility of her wasted body that I felt; that was expected and not unfamiliar, but there was another quality of lightness which was not of the body. As soon as I felt it, something told me that I could feel a spirit preparing for flight. Across the bed, my eyes sent a message to Judith, who gave an almost imperceptible nod. 'Yes,' answered her eyes. 'I know.'

Kay smiled in a gentle, languid way, remarking that she felt privileged to have me as her guest. I shook my head and laid a hand against her cheek. 'Privilege has nothing to do with it,' I smiled in return. 'I am here because I want to be, and for me it's a pleasure.'

Judith had previously told Kay that I was gathering research material for a book and that I would be pleased if Kay wished to share her story, for this purpose. Kay was happy to oblige, but a little bewildered about why anyone would be particularly interested in her.

'What do you want me to say?' she asked, as I settled myself beside her and slipped a cassette into the tape-recorder.

'It isn't for me to tell you what to say,' I replied. 'I'd like you to ignore the tape-recorder and just talk to me as a friend. Speak to me about the kind of things you'd say to the people who are going to read this book. If you could meet those people in person, what would you want to tell them? What do *you* want to say?' Kay considered for a few moments, then she nodded.

'When I first discovered that I had melanoma,' she began, 'I was surprised and disappointed, but I wasn't shocked. Why wasn't I shocked? Because I wasn't *happy*, and I hadn't been happy for a long time, but I hadn't done anything about it, so in one way it was inevitable that something was bound to give. The melanoma was the thing that came to me.

'My melanomas... the first one I got in the eye, and they took the eye out. The second one I had came up in my head and they took that out. The third one came up in my liver, at which they said, "There's no way we can do anything for your liver". So that was it. They could do no more for me, other than give me drugs, painkillers, and help me in those ways. But I had to start thinking, and there have been a lot of things that I've done, trying to get my body back into better health...

'About my happiness. I spent a long time married. I had two children who are eight years old now, and I'm thirty, so I was just twenty-two when I had the children, and that was a big shock for me because they were undiagnosed twins. I found it very hard emotionally when my husband went to college from 9a.m. to 9p.m. This was in Brisbane, and in those days I didn't have a car, no money to spend, so I tried to amuse myself. The kids cried a lot, cried a lot, cried a lot, and that really got to me... and not long after that, I got the melanoma.

'I hadn't been happy in my marriage for a long time. I guess it was... one personality was much stronger than the other and I felt stifled. When I tried to get out, it hurt the other person so badly that I couldn't stand hurting him, so I kept going back, saying, "Oh, we'll be all right," and things like that. There was never any beer or alcohol involved, bashing or money problems... it was just a chemistry problem, where he was stronger, yet he always seemed so open and friendly. With a lot of other people, I can be me. You could say something and I could say, "No, I don't agree with that", but with my husband I couldn't be bothered. I used to just think, oh, what's the use?

'I came over here to Hobart for a holiday. This is where I was born. I was looking down a barrel and I decided, well if I die, I don't want to die here, so I came home. We got a house, just down here across the road (when I spoke with her, Kay had been living with her parents for some time) and everything should have been right, everything was there. I should have felt good and enjoyed it, but nothing was ever quiet. I couldn't rest.

'At the beginning of last year, around Christmas, I got very sick, and I went to the doctor... I felt very much more for the alternative side of healing, but I hadn't shut out the Western side where they could help me, either. Well, the doctor told me, "This is it", and I felt desperate then. I felt that I had to get away, to get well again. One thing I've learned... life *is* worth living. I'll get better...' her voice trailed off as a wistful expression filled her eyes.

'In this whole time,' she continued, 'I had never, ever told anybody, for twelve years, that I wasn't happy. Oh, I did tell my brother and he offered to help me leave, but it didn't seem the right way to go. We had discussed it, but when I told my husband, he was so upset, so I went weak at the knees again. Then when they told me I wasn't going to get better, that frightened me, because I wanted to get better. So I broke down one night and spoke to Mum. I told her, "Mum, I've got to get out', so we talked and she said, "Yes, I know, I've seen it coming for a long time".

'I feel sad for my husband, because he really loves me. I find that hard, but to be staying with him and not loving him in the way a man should be loved... it would have been a sin to stay. It's

137

taken cancer to give me the strength to get out of
my marriage. That's a big statement and it's one
that I don't like saying, but it has taught me a lot. If
I hadn't had this experience, I wouldn't be where I
am now, as far as spiritual, personal growth go . . .
I feel that I've got a lot more strength now than I
had before.

'Now I've got this lightness about me. Very
bright . . . now it's all happening. People are coming around to be with me, I've been finding out
how much they care. Like this lovely lady,' she
smiled, indicating to Judith. 'I tried to track her
down a couple of weeks ago. I thought I wouldn't
have the energy to follow it up and then my sister
rang me and said, "Judi would like to see you
tonight, to visit and do some healing for you". I
was just so rapt!'

Kay told me that until just a few weeks previously, she had been controlling her pain with
Panadol (Paracetamol) and had only begun to
need morphine two weeks before; even then, she
was taking the lowest dose for that drug, a half
tablet each day . . . and this woman had over fifty
melanomas in her body! It was her belief that the
psychic healing she was being given controlled the
majority of her pain. Her only reason for giving in
to the need for morphine was because 'I realise that
I can't do anything that is worthwhile if I'm in
pain all the time. If I'm in pain, I only do things
half, and I don't enjoy it while I'm doing it. It's
just an effort.' She was practising meditations for
healing and relaxation, but the pain had been
interfering with her concentration: still, she maintained that she fully intended to 'beat this cancer'. I
studied the soft, unearthly glow around her and
thought, 'You'll beat it, Kay, but not at the physical level.' But I said nothing of my thoughts; this
time was for Kay, to speak as she wished.

138

Throughout her message, she repeated her belief that the cancer has resulted from the unhappiness she had bottled up for years and that, in some ways, it had been a good thing, because it had made her break free from what was for her a prison of unhappiness. More than this, it had brought so many loving people to her. She was resting in the bosom of her tenderly caring family, and discovering just how many people really cared for her. In her company, it was easy for me to understand why so many people cared; she gave off such an aura of love, it would have been impossible for anyone with a heart not to feel love in return. Love and caring were what she inspired, and it had taken cancer to make it possible for her to see that. She bathed in the love, she exuded it, and although it may seem difficult to comprehend, she was enjoying her life.

'Now I'm free to just kick my heels up, and say, "To hell with the rest, I'm doing all right!"' she smiled. 'I'm looked after by my mother and sister, I have wonderful people coming to visit me. I enjoy the company. I've found Me... no, Me was always in there. I never really lost Me. If I die today, I'll die happy, because I've discovered all this love. I *feel* so loved.'

I asked Kay what she would like to say to anyone else who might be dealing with cancer, and she replied, 'Have faith. Don't freak out. I've never freaked out, I feel I'm guided by a spiritual force. I've never blamed... I've often cried, you know, feeling sorry for myself, but whatever happens, I have faith that it will all come out right in the end.'

Finally, I asked Kay what was the most important message that she would like to give to others.

'Balance,' she said. 'You need to live for yourself, not only for others.'

Then, seeing that she showed signs of weariness,

we decided to take our leave, and let Kay rest. Although she bravely insisted that she was happy for us to stay, we all knew it was time to go.

A few days later, Judith telephoned to let me know that Kay had finally defeated the cancer. It had been consigned to the dust with her wasted little body, and the beautiful spirit that is Kay was set free to fly.

The legacy that Kay gave to me is in her words. She said that her illness had been inevitable *because she had neglected her own happiness*. Physically, the cause of her death was malignant cancer, but in Kay's own words, it was unhappiness that killed her.

Kay's story, and the way she told it, made me do some very deep thinking. The way she described her former life struck deep chords in me, for she was also describing the way I had once lived my own life; only the superficial details were different. I have also had cancer, although mine was caught in the nick of time, just before it reached the stage where the cancer cells would have begun to invade other areas of my body. My carcinoma was found in the reproductive system and, during one of our consultations, I asked my specialist how many of his women patients who developed cancer in the reproductive system had negative attitudes to their own sexuality. His answer was, 'You've hit the nail on the head. One hundred per cent of them.' I was raped as a teenager and I had not been fortunate in my sexual relationships with men since that time, with the result that I had a lot of hang-ups in that area of my life.

Louise L. Hay, author of *You Can Heal Your Life*, also had cancer, from which she recovered. She says that cancer is linked to longstanding feelings of deep resentment which literally gnaw at the body from within. As a healer and metaphysi-

cal counsellor, she understood that mental patterns create conditions for disease, and that if she
accepted orthodox treatment but did nothing to
alter her mental patterns, she would just keep
having operation after operation until there was
nothing left of her to be operated on. She worked
on altering her mental patterns, engaged the help
of a good nutritionist, and recovered.

Ian Gawler, author of *You Can Conquer
Cancer*, also writes from personal experience as a
cancer patient. Like Louise Hay, he focused on
nutrition and on positive mental programming
through meditation. He also confounded the doctor's prediction, about ten years ago, that he only
had a few months to live. He writes that cancer is a
'multi-factorial' condition, which can have a
number of causes. One of the major contributing
factors that he describes is the personality profile.
Characteristically, he writes, cancer patients are
people who repress their own needs in the effort to
please others. These people bottle up their feelings, rather than risk hurting or offending someone else.

Both Louise Hay and Ian Gawler are well
known for their work in the field of health. Both
have successfully defeated cancer, and both say
that our mental attitudes play a large role in
creating the conditions in which cancer can grow.
According to quantum physics, consciousness has
an essential role to play in the creation of physical
reality. Cosmic law says that thought creates reality. All of this, put together, does appear to indicate that our feelings and our mental patterns play
an essential role in the creation of our life conditions, and as such they require as much care and
consideration as the body and the spirit.

If you keep the tyres on your car in good condition, fill the tank with petrol, ensure that the

battery is charged and the radiator filled with water, but neglect to put oil in the engine, the engine will inevitably seize up. No matter how well you have attended to its other needs, the car will break down and be unable to fulfil its purpose as a vehicle. The same principle is true of your personal, spiritual well-being,

As above, so below. On Earth as it is in Heaven. A cosmic energy principle is as true in the material reality as in the spiritual realms. What applies to a motor vehicle can be applied to the spirit also, except that instead of engines, batteries and gear-boxes, we speak of emotions, feelings and thoughts. Universal law is precisely that: universal. The comparison of spirituality with the mechanisms of a motor vehicle is discussed in an entertaining and enlightening narrative by Robert M. Pirsig in his book *Zen And The Art Of Motor Cycle Maintenance*. I don't know how to make a motor-cycle work, I'm not even brave enough to learn how to ride one, and if you put a spanner in my hand I'd probably use it as a paperweight, but I had no difficulty with understanding the relationships, as Mr Pirsig explains them. The world is full of living parables.

Kay's life in this world, and her departure from it, also represent a parable, and I know how dearly she wanted others to be helped by what she had learned from her experience. How much it would delight her now to know that her wish is being fulfilled, as it can be if other people are willing to fulfil it. Her message was that we should live for ourselves, not only for others. She didn't say not to live for others at all; she knew the blessings of giving and receiving much too well for that. She kept saying to me that we should live for ourselves *also*.

Whatever considerations other people deserve

from us, we deserve from ourselves as well. It is not the responsibility of anyone else in this world to make you happy, nor is it your responsibility to make anyone else happy, but we can all help to create conditions in which *everyone* can find happiness. Your primary responsibility in this life is to your Self, and a part of that responsibility is to see that you do not impede the happiness of others, but that doesn't mean that others have the right to be happy at your expense. If you are happy within yourself, you will radiate happiness. Consequently, you will create an atmosphere that generates feelings of happiness and upliftment in others wherever you go. You will just naturally want to do the kind of things that bring happiness to others, but it will not be a sacrifice, any more than it is a sacrifice when a flower gives out a beautiful fragrance. When you give in that way, you will enrich others as well as yourself. Remember, you have a *right* to be happy as much as anyone else.

Kay's story should not be taken to indicate that anyone who lives an unhappy life will die of cancer. Unhappy people can die of old age, too. As Ian Gawler has said, cancer is a multi-factorial disease: many different things can cause it, but unhappiness creates ideal conditions in which it can grow. It creates the same conditions for any number of other diseases, too. Unhappiness itself is a condition of dis-ease, and dis-ease within the spirit leads to disease in the body. There are many different diseases, and many different ways to die. You can, for instance, be so unhappy that you feel yourself dying on the inside, yet be comparatively healthy in your body. Sooner or later, however, the effect of the inner condition will manifest itself in the body, unless something is done to prevent it.

Physical pain tells you that, somewhere in your body, some thing has gone wrong. Emotional and

143

psychological pain indicate something similar; a condition of dis-ease within your psychic energy field. If the imbalance is corrected at the psychic level, there will not be an extension of that dis-ease into the body. Have you ever noticed that happy people have a vibrancy about them, and they don't seem to suffer as much illness as unhappy people? Something else can be seen about truly happy people: they are people who are happy with *themselves*. They don't claim to be perfect, nor do they stop seeking to improve themselves, but they don't put themselves down, either. They give themselves love and approval.

Do you need to love yourself? Yes, you do, but unless you've had a very fortunate upbringing, you've probably absorbed the idea that loving yourself is an expression of conceit and egocentricity. 'She loves herself' is an expression that has become synonymous with 'She thinks she's better than anyone else: she's on an ego trip'.

I wonder how people got the idea that real love has anything to do with egotism? Egotism constantly seeks to take from others; love is a giving thing. The energies are at opposite poles. Thinking that everyone else ought to love you could be defined as egotism. Loving yourself demands nothing from anyone, not even that they return the love you give out. There is an apparent paradox here, however, for when you love yourself as you should, you get lots of love from other people anyway.

There's another important factor to be considered: what you get out of loving yourself is what it enables you to *give*.

I don't know any New Age person who would not be delighted to manifest a gift for spiritual healing, being able to relieve distress and suffering with the touch of a hand. Or better still, with a

144

thought. If you only knew how, you'd channel enough healing energy to cure the whole world of its ills, wouldn't you? Here's another question: what is the most potent healing force in the entire universe?

If love is the answer you give, go to the top of the class! If you radiate love, you are radiating healing energy, and that's not only going to make the people around you feel good; it feels pretty good for you, too. There are millions of people who will gladly throw every ounce of their energy into the effort to heal this world and everything in it, and many of them are already doing their best. If every one of these people loves themselves as much as they love and care for others, the energy they can give will be boundless. There will be no limits to the happiness it can create or the hurts that it can heal.

If you do not have love for yourself, you do not have enough love to give others. You may give of yourself, your emotions, your time and your energy until you wear yourself to death, but you cannot give another soul a feeling of being loved if there is no feeling of being loved within you. If you do not love yourself, a vital ingredient is lacking. Without it, you can never feel completely loved.

These are fairly persuasive reasons why it is necessary to love yourself: it means dissolving some barriers, like guilt and doubt, but you really don't need those in any case. They only get in the way and block the flow. Maybe you've done a few awful things in your lifetime, and sometimes you make silly mistakes. Do you know of anyone who wouldn't admit to the same if the truth were told? Making mistakes doesn't mean you need to be loved any less; everyone needs love and we all deserve to have it. Love is our birthright, and it is the greatest power for good that we can extend to others. All we need to do is claim the birthright of love, and we'll have enough to heal the whole world and make it into a paradise if we want to. If you are devoting yourself to the service of others but do not have love for yourself, you are putting the cart before the horse.

In the Christian Bible, it is written: 'Make love your great quest: then desire spiritual gifts . . . ' (1 Corinthians 14:1). That message seems clear enough; fill yourself with love, then seek to manifest your spirituality. Love comes first; it is the essence of spirituality. But . . . and there are often 'buts' in this life . . . people don't find it easy to love themselves. How do we overcome the programmed-in barriers that make it difficult to love ourselves? Ah, now we approach a whole new chapter!

CHAPTER SEVEN

Hayley's challenge

> If we could read the secret history of our
> enemies, we should find in each man's
> life sorrow and suffering enough to dis-
> arm all hostility.
>   LONGFELLOW: *DRIFTWOOD*

I have a lovely young friend named Hayley, who
first wrote to me about eight years ago when she
was fifteen years old and stricken with grief after
the death of her first love in an accident. A very
special and beautiful friendship grew through our
letters to each other, and we have maintained it
through the years. Hayley is now in her early
twenties, a young wife, and very much in love with
her husband. In one of her most recent letters, she
told me of a problem she has at her place of work; a
problem that, I am sure, many other people will
recognise all too well.

*I have a great job, good wage, fringe benefits
and a lovely atmosphere, but over the years that
I've been here, the quality of staff relationships
has deteriorated, to an extent that it's now
backstabbing, everyone for themselves, but on
the surface, oh, so friendly!*

I have tried to do everything that I think is right in each situation, only to be seen as malicious and 'out to get people', which is utterly ridiculous. I found out that the guy one above me in the hierarchy has been telling the other employees that I must be 'watched' and 'be very careful with Hayley, don't tell her anything, she'll use it against you. She's malicious and evil!' I was stunned; then I was furious! He had pretended to be so sweet to me all this time, so I confronted him — rationally but very firmly — and demanded reasons and apologies for his behaviour — which I got from a shaking, quivering man who was so embarrassed about having been caught that he almost cried. We agreed that we'd probably never be best friends, but perhaps we could respect each other and leave each other alone. I stuck to my part, but this guy has continued to express his hatred of me to all and sundry, which, knowing the laws of the universe, of course rubs off on those he's ranting to: they in turn agree with him and have a wonderful time together, then come to me and say the same things about him!

I feel like I'm going insane. It's so unbelievably childish and petty, and it ends up catching everybody up in its foul wave. The trouble is, all I can think of is that I have obviously caused this to happen through karma and I keep thinking, 'Well, they must be right. If they all think it, then I must be a horrible person'. But, Dawn, I know I'm not! It really gets me down, and it affects my balance and sense of self-esteem, and everything compounds itself.

I've heard it said (I'm not sure if it was by

148

you) that 'you can tell the purity of a person's soul by their surroundings. Look at their friends and the people who surround them, because all these things are the mirrors of their souls'. My God! I must be awful!

My dearest wish is one day to study and become a natural healer (homeopath, naturopath, iridologist etc.,) but I doubt my own purity because of my rationalising about the way I'm seen by the people at work. How can I channel pure healing energy and give the right advice to other people when my own energy system is impure?'

How many times have you found yourself in a situation like Hayley's? People tend to think such things are 'physical hassles' that have nothing to do with matters of the spirit, but that is not the case. This kind of situation *affects* the spirit! There are very damaging and painful effects on anyone who gets caught up in it, and those effects can be serious and long-term. In her work environment, Hayley has become a target in a psychological battlefield. At the spiritual level, she is being subjected to a barrage of malicious, harmful energies that can cause serious injury to her life-energy field, and we have a name for that kind of thing: we call it psychic attack.

Thought is energy; so is emotion, and at the psychic levels, these energies have tangible effects which influence the physical reality sooner or later; often sooner than later. It is not only the words being said that are injuring Hayley, it's the negative energies being projected at her on the psychic levels. The people who project those energies probably don't understand what they are doing, but they are harming Hayley and them-selves as surely as if they were putting poison in the drinking water. Those malevolent thoughts and emotions are poisoning the *psychic* atmosphere, and this will have a detrimental effect on anyone who enters that workplace. Since it is a commer-cial establishment that is open to the public, this means that any customer who enters the place will be affected in some way, so it is not only a problem for the staff. I cannot speak of the other staff members because I do not know them, but the harmful effects on Hayley are beginning to show. Her personality is being undermined, she is doubt-ing herself and beginning to believe that in some way, although she doesn't understand how, she must deserve this kind of treatment. I've known Hayley for quite a long time and she tells me her innermost thoughts and feelings; I know that she doesn't deserve to be treated that way. Very few people do, but in this world it happens, and I think we'd all like to see it stop happening, to anyone.

I know a woman who stayed with a husband who abused her mentally, emotionally, psycho-logically, physically and spiritually for years, and she submitted to that treatment because she believed him when he told her that she deserved it. Somewhere, way back in the past, Anna had, like Hayley, started listening to the voices of self-hatred. Like Hayley, Anna also thought, 'I can't be right and everyone else wrong. If everybody is saying these things, I must be a terrible person', and so, whenever bad things happened to her, she took it as punishment for being a bad person. Thus with every hurt she suffered, her negative self-image was reinforced.

It was a gradual, insidious process over a period of years, listening to those voices that ate away at Anna's soul. At first she tried to protest, crying,

'No, it isn't true! That isn't me, not the way I really am.' But the voices of self-hatred told her that she was deluding herself with wishful fantasy, and she heard no voices of reassurance, so her cries of protest grew progressively weaker and weaker. She didn't know anything about psychic energy back then, so she could not prevent her aura from absorbing the corrosive poisons created by negative thoughts and emotions in the atmosphere, either. Inexorably, her resistance at all levels was eroded and she came to believe that, whenever anything went wrong, it was always her fault. Even the fact that she was talented and successful in her career did nothing to enhance her self-image: professional success, she reasoned, was something she *did*, not something she *was*. On the surface, she was a normal, competent human being, but on the inside she had become a lost soul.

In public, Anna's husband took pains to be charming and attentive. Privately, he subjected her to scornful criticism and humiliation. His affairs with other women were flaunted at her, even to the extent that he often brought a girlfriend home for dinner, demanding that Anna be a perfect hostess and 'disciplining' her in front of any of his mistresses in whose presence she ventured to say a word out of place. He subjected her to debauched sexual practices, and physically beat her whenever she dared argue with him.

He told her that he was criticising her for her own good, to help her improve herself. He insisted that if she were to satisfy him in the way a good wife should satisfy her husband, he wouldn't need sexual affairs with other women. She saw his desire for 'healthy sexual fun' as degrading and depraved, he said, only because she was too prim, narrow-minded and sanctimonious. When he hit her, he shouted that it was her fault for being such a trial to him that she drove him into rages in which he 'couldn't help himself'. She bore it all because she believed him when he told her it was all her fault.

Why shouldn't she have believed him? He was only reinforcing what all the other voices of self-hatred had been telling her for years. Voices like the ones Hayley has been hearing lately.

Under natural law, whatever affects the spirit will affect the body also, and vice versa, and in addition to her physical pains, Anna was being subjected to a continuous barrage of negative and destructive psychic energies. She suffered continually from ill-health, chronic and at times life-threatening. She had cancer, which was successfully removed, but as soon as one disorder was healed, another would take its place. Anna had a few close encounters with the Angel of Release and no doubt she would have continued to suffer repeated bouts of illness until one of them succeeded in putting her out of her misery if something hadn't happened to reverse the process. Fortunately for Anna, something did happen, and she has since been reclaiming her life.

'Anna', of course, is not her real name. For obvious reasons, she does not wish her identity to be made public, but her story is important because it is not unique: Anna could be almost any abused person. She has broken free from her torment, and I'm sure a lot of people would like to know how she did it.

Anna had a belief in New Age philosophy, and although her husband derided her for it and forbade her to join 'any of those hocus-pocus psychic groups', she read widely on the subject and did her best to meditate and develop her spiritual awareness alone, whenever she had the time to herself. Like many other people, however, she made the mistake of believing that the brutal treatment she suffered from her husband must be some kind of karmic punishment for misdeeds committed in some other life. Given the mental conditioning she had received in her present life, this is hardly surprising. It was automatic for her to believe that anything hurtful must be her own fault. What she did not recognise at that time is the way in which other cosmic forces were at work in her life.

Thought creates reality. Like attracts like. The second of those laws can be misinterpreted by someone like Anna, who assumed that she was attracting bad experiences because she was a bad person. In fact, as she was later to discover, she attracted those experiences only because she *believed* herself to be a bad person. What Anna thought about herself and her life became a reality for her, and because she believed herself to be unworthy, she attracted conditions and people who reflected and reinforced that belief. Karma was involved, to the extent that the energies we give out are returned to us, magnified, and Anna continually broadcast thoughts and emotions that said 'I attract hurtful conditions because I deserve them'. That was the reality she created with her beliefs, therefore it was the reality she experienced.

It is possible that Anna's feelings of unworthiness may have been 'carried over' from other lives, in which she received the same kind of mental conditioning. People have been conditioned to think of themselves as worthless sinners for hundreds of generations in our history. It is also likely that she did commit a few misdeeds in other lifetimes: given human conditions and tendencies, it would be surprising if she had not, but wrong deeds are the results of wrong thinking, and karma is not a punishment, merely a law of balance that can, if applied appropriately, show us areas in which our thinking is wrong. Action follows thought; it is not the other way around. Strictly speaking, it was wrong for Anna to submit to the maltreatment she received from her husband, but she did so because her thinking was wrong. Not bad or evil, just wrong, as in erroneous and mistaken.

One day, after what had seemed like an eternity of praying for guidance to help her see and correct her mistakes, Anna decided that she'd had enough.

'Living by myself was a lonely prospect to face,' she writes. 'But I came to the decision that no matter how lonely it might be, it had to be better than the life I was living. The more I thought about it, the more convinced I became that I would rather live alone than continue living with my husband.'

After her marriage ended, Anna felt relief, but also guilt. She still believed that she had to be at fault in some way for the failure of the marriage. She also felt guilty because her husband's response to her action had been a display of heartbreak over her 'callous' treatment of him. Not surprisingly, she became unwell again. Her menses had always been painful and difficult for her, but now she suffered a mysterious bleeding ailment for which medical tests and exploratory surgery could find no organic cause.

She had been meeting and making friends with other New Age people and, eventually, one of them remarked on her state of health. 'There has to be a reason for it,' said the friend. 'And if medical science can't find the cause, it's probably outside the scope of conventional medicine. I know a wonderful homeopath who also reads auras to help him diagnose and treat health problems. Maybe he can help.'

Anna consulted the homeopath who told her

that, indeed, the cause of her health problem was a psychic disorder, not a physical condition. Her aura had been battered by destructive energies for a very long time and had suffered extensive damage. It had also absorbed horrific amounts of negative energies, which poisoned her whole life system, and the bleeding was part of her system's efforts to rid itself of the poisonous energies. Her life energy system had reached a critical state of imbalance and, although the physical assaults from her husband had ceased, the psychic harm done to her over the years was still affecting her physical body.

She was given a homeopathic elixir and advised on herbal teas and tablets that would stimulate the liver and kidneys to assist with the cleansing of toxins from her body, plus vitamins and minerals to strengthen her system generally. She was advised to obtain certain crystals and to use them to help the healing process. Amethyst to help cleanse and energise the blood, cut through illusion and give a calming influence. Chrysoprase to ease depression, help balance the body, mind and emotions and give insight into personal problems. Kunzite to assist the balancing process and to heal the heart and enhance self-esteem. Rose quartz to aid the blood, clear bottled-up resentment, fear and guilt, reduce stress and enhance self-confidence. She was advised to perform White Light Meditations at least twice each day to cleanse negative energies from her aura, and she was given a cassette tape by Louise L. Hay, and asked to work with it.

The tape was entitled *Cancer: Discovering Your Healing Power*, which puzzled Anna somewhat, since she did not have cancer at that time. When she listened to the tape, however, she understood: while it is designed to help people who have cancer, that is not its only purpose. Louise Hay

155

aims to help people clear the mental patterns that create conditions in which diseases like cancer can grow, and those mental patterns specifically involve negative self-images.

'The first few times that I listened to that tape,' says Anna, 'I cried all the way through, but it felt good, as though I was crying away years of pain and despair.'

Having listened to several of Louise Hay's tapes, including the one given to Anna, I can understand why it made her cry, why it brought her such a sense of relief, and why she now credits Louise Hay with playing a substantial role in her self-healing process. Louise explains that what we choose to believe about ourselves and our lives becomes true for us, and although we have unlimited choices about what we can think, the process of thinking negatively is a habit that begins forming when we are very little, while we are learning how to feel about ourselves, and about life, influenced by the attitudes of the adults around us.

If you grew up with people who did not love themselves, it would be an impossibility for those people to have taught you how to love yourself. They could only pass on the mistaken ideas that *they* learned as children. The thoughts we think, the emotions we feel, and the words we speak all create our experiences to match our beliefs, but as Louise says, we are only ever dealing with a *thought*, and thoughts can be changed. Even when you hate yourself, you are really only hating something that you think about yourself. Think of how often people refuse to think positive thoughts about themselves: they could just as easily refuse to think negative things about themselves.

Wherever there is self-hatred and guilt, explains Louise, the bottom line is always a belief that 'I'm not good enough'. That statement struck a very strong chord in me when I heard it, and I have yet to meet a person who does not feel a similar response. We are all exposed to the idea that we are 'not good enough', but have you ever asked, not good enough for whom, and by whose standards of comparison? If you think about it, we are taught to think that we aren't 'good enough' by people who believe *they* aren't good enough either ... it's like a contagious disease, and does as much damage as any plague. Like other New Age healers, Louise Hay maintains that love is the healing force, and in order to heal ourselves, we must love and approve of ourselves and if we wait until we attain perfection before we love ourselves, we will be wasting our lives.

On one side of the tape Anna was given, Louise explains all of these principles in some depth, and on the reverse side, she gives a guided meditation, designed to assist with the healing of all the negative thought patterns that create conditions of disease.

I don't make a habit of recommending anything that I haven't tried for myself, even when other people tell me it has been good for them. I have listened to the tape Anna used, and I have undertaken the guided meditation, as Louise recommends. It did a lot of good for me, too. I doubt that any one of us doesn't have some old, negative ideas about ourselves that are best dissolved, so that we can live a more positive, happy and effective life, and I do recommend that tape to anyone who has problems with a negative self-image, or to anyone who simply feels like doing some mental and emotional spring-cleaning.

It is necessary to bear in mind that while everything given to Anna *assisted* in her healing process, external aids could not have done it all for her. The most important factor was Anna's willingness to work *with* the healers and to change her ways of thinking. Having taken the responsibility for all the bad things that had happened in her past, she began taking responsibility for making good things happen, and it worked. After a while, she met another man, who gives her the kind of love she has always needed, but had once believed that she could never deserve. Before that happened, though, Anna had to learn how to love *herself*, and it was when she radiated the positive energies that said 'I am worth loving' that she attracted real love from someone else. The damage to her physical health was a result of many years of abuse, and Anna knows she still has work to do in order to correct that, but she is happy, she is loved, and she doesn't take any notice of the voices of self-hatred any more, except to pity those who speak them.

The challenge Hayley faces now is to overcome any 'not good enough' feelings that reinforce a negative self-image and give greater power to the voices which try to drag her down. To do this most effectively, there should be a holistic approach to the problem. It isn't just a problem for Hayley; it's a problem for the people she works with also, because in truth they are really projecting their own self-hatred on to her. Ideally, it would be wonderful if Hayley could not only overcome her own pain and distress, but help the other staff members to overcome theirs as well. In time, perhaps she may be able to help them, but her first responsibility is to herself. She is not responsible for the fact that other people have been taught to have contempt for themselves, and she cannot help anyone who isn't ready to be helped, but she needs to give help to herself before the situation reaches chronic proportions. It may seem like a selfish statement to make, but the burden of other people's problems is not Hayley's to bear: she is responsible only for seeing to it that she does not *add* to those problems for other people. She can, and will, do her best to project positive, healing energy to those other people, but if they repel that kind of energy and persist in their negativity, she is not responsible.

For Anna, it was necessary to end her marriage. Hayley could leave her job, but as she points out, 'Until I stick it out and clear up whatever it is that's causing my problems at work, these problems will follow me wherever I go'. She is quite right: there are voices of self-hatred almost everywhere, and wherever Hayley goes in this life, she is going to come into contact with other people like those she must deal with at her present place of work. She cannot make other people change their ways of thinking, but she can make changes within herself, so that negative words and energies do not hurt her, and the methods available to her can be equally effective for anyone else who wishes to work with them. She does not need to go to the extent that was necessary for Anna, because her problem is still at an early stage and she is young and healthy, but she does need to strengthen her psychic defences and work on removing any mental patterns that create or reinforce a negative self-image in her.

Psychic self-defence is necessary to deflect and neutralise harmful energies in the atmosphere around her, but if Hayley concentrates on the psychic techniques and does nothing to adjust her self-image, she will weaken her own defences. Likewise, if she concentrates on building a more positive self-image but does nothing to defend herself from the psychic venom, her efforts will be undermined. She also needs to maintain her physical vitality: stress at the psychic, mental and emotional levels takes a toll on physical stamina, and if she loses energy physically, the other levels of her being will be weakened also.

Hayley (and anyone else in a similar situation) needs to recognise that she is not suffering any form of retribution for being a bad person. She is, in fact, being given an opportunity to strengthen and develop the qualities that will be of particular benefit in her spiritual development, particularly in the area of healing. Too many healers neglect to strengthen their resistance to psychic contamination, and as a result their auras absorb impurities which can build up and ruin their own health. This applies to health workers in any field, but I think the New Age needs to make more progress in terms of credibility and community acceptance before we have doctors, nurses and health workers of every kind cleansing and shielding their auras as routinely as they now wash their hands and practise aseptic techniques.

If Hayley decides to see this situation as an opportunity to strengthen the capacities she wishes to develop in order to achieve her long-term ambitions, instead of taking it as a personal indictment against her character, she will turn a negative condition into a positive one, which is a vital step in itself. She also needs to remind herself regularly that denigrating statements made about her by others do not reflect anything that is true about her; they only reflect a *thought* that she has about herself, and thoughts can be changed.

Hayley might not even have consciously realised that she had any negative self-images until the people at work brought them to the surface of her mind. It's a bit like having a cut finger: once the initial pain has eased, you can forget that you have hurt the finger, until you bump it and the instant pain that you feel reminds you that you've suffered an injury. We absorb many ideas about ourselves, and about life, at a subconscious level, and the process begins in early childhood. We might not be consciously aware that we are acting out negative beliefs about ourselves, because it is programmed into the subconscious mind so insidiously. By raising these images in Hayley and forcing her to confront them, her detractors may even be doing her a favour, provided that she recognises what is being shown to her and responds by eliminating her own self-critical thought patterns.

Where do the voices of self-hatred come from? They come from people who inwardly hate themselves, and those people learned it from others in childhood. People who inflict hurt and suffering upon others are also lost souls, and they are hurting, too, but they don't know any better way to react than to strike out at others. That is what they have learned to do because it is what their conditioning has taught them. Understanding this makes it possible to see that there is really no one to blame. Blame in any form is a barrier to understanding, and to spiritual freedom and growth. There is no blame, only situations to be resolved, negative mental patterns to be melted away and lessons to be learned. People who love and approve of themselves feel no need to cut others down with hurtful words, and when others try doing it to them, they are able to rise above it and not allow it to affect them. People who know how to cleanse and shield their auras against penetration by damaging psychic energies have an even greater advantage, because they are protecting themselves on both levels.

The power to do all of this, and more, rests within the human mind — *every* human mind. There is no person who is too dull, too stupid or too ordinary to use that power effectively and with wisdom.

Thought creates reality. What you think about yourself is reality for you. How do you feel towards the person you see in the mirror? Do you love and approve of that person, wholeheartedly and unconditionally? Or do you see a collection of faults and flaws? If you do not feel that whole-hearted, unconditional love and approval for yourself, something is wrong with your self-image. This is an indication that there are negative thought patterns that need to be resolved: starting *now*, not after you've finished attending to everyone else. Help yourself first, then you will be better able to help others.

In the Christian Bible, Jesus is quoted as telling people to remove the planks from their own eyes before they try to take a splinter out of someone else's eye. In the biblical account, Jesus is reprimanding a group of religious hypocrites, but the principle expressed can be applied in other ways. 'Remove the plank from your own eye...' could easily be rendered as 'Relieve yourself of your own burdens before you try to lighten the load for others'. In other words, tend to your own needs first. That is not a doctrine of selfishness: the more you help yourself in loving ways, the more help you will be able to give others. Helping yourself in the right ways will *increase* your capacity to give, not diminish it.

Self-defence at the spiritual levels is not some form of psychic martial art. There is no wrestling with adversaries or competitions of strength in which someone has to emerge as a winner. Psychic self-defence is exactly what the term implies: defence, protecting and shielding yourself from harm. To understand how it works, it is necessary to have a knowledge of the human life-energy field. This may already be familiar territory for you, but other readers may be new to the subject, and unless this basic information is given, it can be difficult for a newcomer to understand how and why the methods work. Even if it is already familiar to you, some revision of the basics never does any harm, so please bear with me.

As spiritual beings, we have a life-energy field that includes the body, but also extends beyond it. We call this energy field the aura, and because the substance from which it is composed is finer in density than physical matter, it is not normally visible to physical eyesight, but it has an intrinsic relationship to the body, as well as the mind and emotions. In a sense, the aura 'breathes', drawing in energies from the surrounding atmosphere and giving out energies that are generated within our life systems. If the psychic atmosphere around you is filled with noxious energies, this contamination will be absorbed through the aura and, if permitted to remain, will afflict the mind, emotions and physical health. We are all quite well aware of the dire consequences of ingesting foul air and toxic substances in food and water, but because there has not been an awareness of *psychic* influences in our culture, people are not taught that what applies to physical matter applies on other levels also, nor to understand that thoughts and emotions are energies that have real and tangible effects, like electricity. Malevolent thoughts and emotions can harm us, while their benevolent counterparts can increase our well-being at all levels. We are aware of this to a certain extent, but it goes further than many people suspect.

Quite a few years ago, when I was only beginning to learn about the functions of psychic energy and knew very little about its projection, I did something that caused me to think very carefully

163

about what can be done with thoughts and emotions, and to exercise a lot more caution with respect to the control of my own energies from that time onward.

With my former husband, I was attending a Christmas party at his place of work. He was dancing with a friend on the other side of the room, about five metres from where I was sitting, when I noticed a voluptuous young woman, wearing a slinky, revealing dress, who was making some flirtatious moves in my husband's direction. I saw her catch his eye, I saw him begin to gravitate towards her, and I have to confess that my reaction bore no resemblance to benevolent Christmas cheer or goodwill towards men. I neither moved nor spoke, but my thoughts turned to vitriol and I shot a savage glare at my husband, mentally hissing, 'Don't you *dare*!'

He was facing away from me and could not possibly have seen my facial expression (which was probably thunderous), but at the instant that I shot my ferocious thoughts in his direction, my husband jerked as though he had received an electric shock. Leaving his bewildered dance-partner standing, he strode angrily across the room to me.

'That *hurt*!' he declared indignantly. 'What did you do to me?'

'I didn't do anything,' I protested, in genuine surprise.

'Don't give me that!' he snapped. 'I know about your little psychic tricks, and whatever you did, it feels like I've been lashed with a whip. I'm still stinging! I repeat, *what did you do*!'

'I don't know! I just saw you heading towards that . . . that vamp in the black dress, and I didn't like what I was seeing. All I did was think . . . '

'Then do me a favour, and *don't* think!' was his acid reply. 'Your thoughts are dangerous.'

I suppose I could have retorted that if he didn't want me to think dangerous thoughts, he'd be wise to avoid playing dangerous games, but I was too stunned by the revelation that my anger had struck with such tangible force clear across the room. At that time, I hadn't learned what I now understand about thought energy. The physical pain I had inflicted on my husband was not intentional on my part; I didn't even understand what I was doing, but I had caused him physical pain nonetheless. The fact that I was ignorant of the effects of my thoughts and emotions did not make them less potent, or less hurtful. The jealous wife in me might secretly have thought it served him right for the kind of thoughts that *he* had obviously been thinking, but the incident really doesn't stand in my credit. We all make some mistakes in the process of learning and that was one of mine. My purpose in relating the incident is not to heap retrospective blame upon myself, but to demonstrate a little about the very real effects of thought energy. If one person can cause lashing pain from a distance of five metres with a single angry thought, can you imagine the effect as it is multiplied by the number of people who are firing those energies into the atmosphere every minute each day? Or the effect of a group of people in the workplace, projecting malicious thoughts at Hayley . . . or anyone, anywhere else, for that matter? It may be 'only a thought', but thoughts have power, and that power needs to be controlled.

We can't make other people change their ways of thinking, but we can use our own thought energy to counter the effects of injurious influences in the atmosphere, and the best way is to start from within. If you are not already cleansing your aura on a daily basis, have you any idea how much stored up contamination you may be carrying, or how much damage it is doing to your physical health and your ability to function clearly at the mental and emotional levels? Furthermore, since like attracts like, if there is negative energy in your aura, more will be attracted to weigh you down even further. We cannot effectively shield our auras against negativity if we do not also remove from the aura any energies that attract negativity, so the first stage in self-defence must perform the double function of cleansing and shielding. The simplest and most effective method I have found is known as the White Light Meditation. This is based on the principle of spiritual Light, which emanates from the Source of All Life. Many people think of 'the Light' as a metaphor that represents spiritual qualities, but it is much more than mere allegory. This Light really does exist, and it is a potent, living force. I could write many pages, describing the Light and its effects, but understanding comes more readily from experience. When you have felt the effects for yourself, description becomes superfluous.

Whether or not you are facing a challenge like Hayley's, and even if you do not wish to become 'too involved' with psychic activity, the White Light Meditation can still be of benefit to you. Think of all the fear, hatred and hostility that is discharged into the atmosphere, every moment of every day, by billions of people who have no idea of what they are doing, to themselves and to others. Do you really want to be infested with all that psychic toxicity?

Some people find, in the first stages of a White Light Meditation programme, that they are inclined to become tearful at times. If this happens to you, don't be dismayed. Tears are a natural release that proves useful in the cleansing process and, as you continue with your meditations, this phase will pass. It is recommended that you perform the meditation twice daily as a minimum. Some people like to do it more often, which is fine; others can only find the time to do it once daily, which is better than not doing it at all, but it is important to do it regularly, each day. A haphazard approach, doing it some days but not maintaining it regularly, will not produce satisfactory results.

The White Light Meditation uses the power of thought to draw on a cosmic energy stream and pass it through the aura, where it cleanses and revitalises your energy pattern at every level of your being. It uses the law of attraction by generating an energy which attracts the Light into your aura. It may sound a bit simplistic if you have never done it before, but remember, thought does create your reality. A lot of meditation techniques focus on visualisation: trying to inwardly 'see' the effects you wish to produce. If that comes easily for you, use that method, but some people find it difficult. Not everybody thinks in pictures, and if you try forcing yourself to see mental pictures when it does not come naturally to you, the likelihood is that you will create inner tensions that defeat the whole exercise. If you have difficulty with visualisation, try focusing instead on the feelings that you wish to produce. It is your focus and intention that produces the effects, not the mental form in which you generate them.

White Light Meditation

Sit or lie down in a comfortable position. You can link your fingers together if that feels comfortable, but your arms and legs should not be crossed, and your spine should be straight but not rigid. The idea is to become as relaxed as it is possible to be, without actually falling asleep, so take some time to relax your body. Allow your muscles to become limp. Take two or three slow, deep breaths and, as you exhale, imagine that you are breathing out all of the tensions that have accumulated inside you. Breathe in, and feel a relaxing energy flowing through you, smoothing out any knots of tension and relaxing you more and more.

Close your eyes to shut out external distractions, and allow your breathing to become regular and even, the way people breathe when they are sleeping. Just relax and *let* it happen; you are doing this to feel good.

Now, become conscious of your body being surrounded by the aura, and yourself as the living entity that inhabits the entire energy field. You could imagine yourself as something like a large cell, with your body as the nucleus and the surrounding sphere of protoplasm being the aura, but remember, you are the *complete* cell, not just the body in the centre. Take as much time as you need to create this attunement within your mind.

When you are ready, begin to imagine a flow of crystal-pure White Light streaming over you and through your entire organism, aura, body, mind and emotions. Perhaps you can see this flow of sparkling Light, or maybe you can feel it as a warm, tingling glow. However you perceive it to be, or even if you have no sensations at first, know that it is there, drawn to you and through you as you link your thoughts to the cosmic mind.

Allow the Light to penetrate every particle of your life energy, cleansing, uplifting, energising and purifying everywhere it touches, raising your spiritual energies and drawing you closer into the warm, pure, loving presence of your Creator.

Let yourself enjoy a warm, lifting, tingling sensation, as this pure, loving Light energy effervesces through every part of you. Feel it flow into your mind, clearing it and lighting it up: imagine that inside your head is a dusty old attic and the windows have been flung open to the Light, allowing a heavenly breeze to blow all the dust and shadows away. Feel a mental calmness, a crystal clarity and quiet confidence. Let the muscles in your scalp relax.

As this wonderful, cleansing Light penetrates further, let the muscles in your face relax. Feel all the expression leaving your face as tension dissolves and warm, purifying Light flows downwards, cleansing and relaxing, and filling you with a feeling of comfort and upliftment.

Feel the muscles in your neck relax and glow as the Light reaches further through you. Now the shoulders, upper arms, forearms, hands and fingers.

The relaxing Light energy moves through your chest, abdomen and back, down through the buttocks, thighs, lower legs, feet and toes. Your body is now cleansed and glowing with pure Light, which builds and grows, welling up inside you and radiating out to fill your auric field. You are being transformed into a being of pure Light, radiating white brilliance through every pore and particle of your being.

Still feeling the warm, purifying flow of Light filling your entire being, now imagine that your aura has been enclosed within a sphere of one-way glass. From inside, you can see out quite clearly, but on the outside, the sphere is a mirror, reflecting away from you any energies that do not belong within your auric field. The positive energies that you wish to attract will penetrate easily, drawn to you in the universal stream of White Light, but the reflective mirror surface around your aura and the powerful radiance of Light energy that streams out from you repels any form of negativity. Your aura is now clean, bright, glowing and sealed, shielded from all harm.

In your mind, be aware that the Light now coursing through you is the living energy of your Creator, the Giver of Life, who loves you more completely and more tenderly than the most wonderful physical parent. Mentally, repeat to yourself these words: 'I am filled with divine Light, and where there is Light, darkness cannot enter'.

Bask for a while in the living, loving glow of Light energy. Enjoy the feelings that it brings to you.

Now ... *hold the awareness of all this Light in your mind* and bring the sensations back with you, as you gradually and gently allow the focus of your consciousness to return to your physical surroundings. Let it happen naturally and gently then, when you are ready, take a deep breath, open your eyes and relax.

When you are accustomed to performing this meditation, it takes only a few minutes, although at first, while getting used to it, you may find that it takes a little longer. Although some people begin to feel the effects right away, not all do, so don't feel discouraged if you don't feel significant results for a while. Remember that it took a long time for the negative energies to build up in you, and while overnight miracles do happen sometimes, it is unrealistic to expect them. If you keep persevering, you *will* achieve results, and it won't take years to happen.

Once you are familiar with the basic White Light technique, it can be adapted for other beneficial purposes. In Hayley's case, the Light can be projected to her place of work, to 'lighten' the atmosphere and surround all who enter there with more positive and uplifting energies than currently operate in that location. At first, it can be difficult to project this energy while she is actually at work and the negative atmosphere is strongly oppressive, but fortunately time and distance present no barriers at the psychic level. At first it is better to work on the projection of Light at a time when she is away from the stress and negativity, preferably at home, in surroundings where she can feel comfortable and secure. The method given for Hayley to use can be equally effective for anyone who faces similar problems in any area of their life.

First, perform the White Light Meditation to cleanse, uplift and brighten your own energy field. When you have completed this, focus your mind on the place where all the stress and conflict is occurring. Don't try to mentally put yourself there, just focus your mind on the place; imagine that you can see it, if mental pictures come easily to you. When you have that focus established, imagine a stream of White Light cascading down over the place, and through it, penetrating every corner, suffusing every atom of furniture and equipment, and lighting up the atmosphere within and around that location. As the cleansing, healing Light does its work, mentally ask the Creator to keep the Light flowing through that area at all times, and to uplift the spirits of all who enter there.

After you have focused on that flow for a few minutes, turn your mind to the people who cause you hurt and perplexity. One by one, imagine each of them standing in a beautiful flow of pure White Light. Perhaps you may like to imagine each person, one after the other, standing on a stage, with a spotlight shining down on them. Imagine that person smiling, healthy, happy and full of positive energy, with all cares washed away, and as each one is bathed in the Light, say to that person in your mind, 'I forgive and release you. May peace be with you.'

Not an easy thing to do for someone who has been giving you such a hard time? That is precisely why you *need* to do it. Any feelings of resentment, blame or negativity of any kind that you hold towards that person will bind you to the person and to the negative situation. The price of freedom in cosmic law is freedom. If you really want to be released from all negativity generated between you and another person, you must forgive, release and give that person lots of loving Light. It is by doing this that you release *yourself* from the situation that causes you pain and distress. What you do unto others in this respect *is* what you do for yourself.

When you are actually in the workplace, or wherever it is that you have encountered an antagonistic atmosphere, radiate as much Light as you can whenever you get the opportunity. Don't worry if you find it difficult at first, just do your best when the chance arises. In moments of conflict, when you are confronted with someone who is trying to nettle you or draw you into more negativity, even if it is directed at the person who causes you the most trouble, don't be manipulated. Take a slow, deep breath and say to yourself in your mind, 'This does not touch me. It has no part in my reality.' Even if it doesn't feel 'real', keep saying those words mentally: the aim is to programme your subconscious mind to such an extent that the thought *becomes* real. You are using your thoughts to create your reality, and one day, before too long, someone will try their old tricks on you and you will discover that it is *not* touching you.

Wherever there is psychic attack in any form, there is always some link that allows the negative energies coming from the other person (or persons) to penetrate your energy field. You do not need to know exactly what the link is in order to sever it; all you need to do is release all negative feelings from your own energy field, and techniques such as those I have given here will achieve that purpose. There are other forms of meditation that can achieve the same effects; the meditation given in the Louise Hay tape that Anna found so helpful is an excellent one, for example. If you find that it helps to use different techniques, don't hesitate to do so. The aim is to set you free from negative conditioning and allow you to function happily and effectively, as it is your birthright to do. By forgiving those who hurt you, this release is facilitated. It has nothing to do with excusing the other person's behaviour or surrendering to their treatment of you, it is simply letting go, letting yourself be free of the ties that bind you to negative thoughts and emotions that can only drag you down. If you look up the meaning of forgiveness in a good dictionary, you will find that it means giving up, not as a form of capitulation, but as releasing, disengaging.

When you hold on to feelings of resentment, judgement, blame and criticism, whether your own or others', you are holding on to the chains that bind *you* to negative and destructive situations, and thus you play an active role in contributing to your own imprisonment in the lower realms of life, stifling your spirit and preventing it from growing and expanding, as it is meant to do. Letting go of negative feelings towards others sets you free, so that your spirit can rise and you can find in this life the happiness and fulfilment that is your birthright.

It is also your birthright to be loved, and this means loving yourself. If you think of yourself as a horrible, wretched person who isn't worthy to be loved, you are not loving yourself, and if you don't love yourself, you emanate a message to others, which says that you aren't worthy of their love either. At all times, and in every way, the process of spiritual upliftment starts from within, and your *real* progress starts when you learn that it is okay to love yourself. Real love has nothing to do with ego, and it doesn't have to be earned. If you find it difficult to love yourself, then somewhere inside you a voice from the past is saying 'Not good enough'... and it is telling you lies. You don't have to be 'good' to be loved, you only have to be prepared to accept love, and when you can love yourself, you have a vast and limitless reservoir of loving energy that you can give to everyone else who needs it, and don't we all?

'Not good enough' means that you are feeling guilt and blame for mistakes you have made in the past, but we all make mistakes in the process of learning. That isn't a crime, it's a natural human tendency, and we learn as much from our mistakes as we do from our successes; sometimes more. The past is over, it can't be changed, but it *is* past. Your life exists in the present moment, and what you do with your thought energy right now will create the conditions for your future, so let go of the past. Take all of the mistakes, all of the hurts, all the wrongs you have ever done and all the wrongs that have ever been done to you, wrap them up in a parcel, tie it with a pretty pink bow, and *let it go*... imagine it floating away into the distance until it disappears completely. Then concentrate on making each moment of your life as positive and as loving as it can possibly be. You don't need the guilt, the blame and the hangups: you've been carrying them around for years, and what good has it done you? Let them all go, you'll feel much

174

better without them and other people will feel better in your company. This is what Anna did, and when she succeeded in letting go of it all, she found the freedom and the happiness that she had always craved. She found something else, too.

For quite a long time after they separated, Anna's husband repeatedly called her on the phone, still trying to manipulate her emotions and make her feel guilty for 'letting him down' . . . and for some time he succeeded in making her feel guilty, but she kept on with her 'treatment' and one day when he rang, she was intrigued to find that she felt nothing at all.

There was no guilt, no shame, not even resentment or a feeling of triumph at having 'defeated' him. Her only reaction was a recognition that this man was no longer a part of her life and that his thoughts and opinions had no place in her reality.

'When I put down the receiver, the first thing I felt was a sense of puzzlement,' she writes. 'It was as though I should be feeling something, but there was nothing there, and it took me a little while to analyse the sensation. It's a bit like the feeling when you have a tooth pulled. Your mouth is numb and you're feeling no pain, but there's an odd, funny-feeling gap where there used to be an aching tooth. You can feel it when you probe with your tongue. It took me a little while to realise that the 'aching tooth' that had been removed was the guilt that I had been carrying for so long it had become a part of me. It felt quite strange at first, but I'm glad it's gone, and from now on, I'm not going to let it back in. Who needs it?'

Who needs it indeed? Not Anna, nor Hayley, and not you, either. Guilt achieves nothing but to cause pain and make you easy for others to manipulate. When you let go of the guilt and replace it with love, you take control of your own life, and that is how it's meant to be. There is a saying that I quoted in one of my previous books, in a section about New Age children. I called it the 'mother's motto' then, but since that time, I've had letters from people who tell me it makes a good motto for everyone, in just about any situation. So, whenever you are facing trouble and adversity, or when you simply need to give your spirits a lift, adopt the 'mother's motto' and give yourself this message:

LOVE IS THE ANSWER, WHAT WAS THE QUESTION?

CHAPTER EIGHT

Pixies in the bush

When I was a very little girl, I used to believe in pixies. I held many animated conversations with them, and with the tree-people who lived in the bushland near my home. Maybe saying that I believed in them isn't quite appropriate, since it wasn't really a case of believing as though there were an element of choice in the process. They were just... there, like the wind and the sunshine. I didn't see them the way I see physical objects, I saw them in my mind, I felt their presence and they talked to me silently, in thoughts and feelings. It didn't occur to me that their existence was a matter of question; you don't question the existence of something that's *there*, not when you're very little, anyway.

I knew that grownups didn't believe in pixies and tree-people, even though they didn't come right out and say so. I could tell by the false brightness in their smiles, the knowing looks they exchanged and the way they humoured me when I talked about my invisible friends. Grownups are dumb sometimes!

'They've forgotten,' whispered the voices from the trees. 'They don't remember...'

The tree-people seemed very sad about that. I felt sadness too, though I didn't quite understand why.

177

Despite the obvious obtuseness of grownups with respect to such things, I presumed that other children, or at least some of them would know about the pixies and the tree-people. After all, lots of other youngsters played in the bush also and, although they usually managed to alarm the birds and the bush creatures with their boisterous, exuberant games of cowboys and Indians, I assumed, because they spent so much time in the bush, that they must have encountered the tree-people at some time or another. It seemed a logical assumption to make and, on that basis, I made a few casual references to the invisible bush inhabitants at school, only to discover that other children differed from the grownups only in their lack of diplomacy.

'Dawn believes in *fairies*!' they howled, dancing with scornful glee. 'She's a *baby*!'

Others enthusiastically picked up the refrain, 'Baby, baby, baby . . . ', while I clutched my hands over my ears in a vain attempt to shut out the mockery and ran, seeking some hidden corner where I could allow the hot tears of humiliation to gush forth in secret. When you're six years old, it's extremely demoralising to be called a baby!

I learned very quickly not to speak about invisible sprites in the company of other people, and, as time went by, I came to regard such beings as the products of childish fantasy. If you see things that nobody else seems to see, and if every voice you hear keeps saying that you cannot possibly see those things because they do not exist, pretty soon you stop seeing them, or if they do infringe upon the edges of your perception, they are brushed aside with the implacable word 'imagination'. The world without pixies and tree-people was nowhere near as pleasant as it was with them, nor as much fun, but everyone insisted that it was 'reality', and so I learned to accept it, even if I didn't like it very much.

Many years later, as I began to explore the subject of mysticism, I found repeated references to beings known as devas, or nature spirits. These, I learned, are the spirits who inhabit the world of nature, and whose existence gave rise, in old times, to the legends of fairies, elves, pixies, goblins and all manner of 'mythical' creatures that our society relegates to the sphere of fantasy. In earlier days, when our ancestors had a more intuitive alignment with the forces of nature, they were aware of the nature spirits, as naturally as they were aware of the ebb and flow of tides and seasons. The advent of orthodox Christianity, the growth of huge cities and the industrial revolution all played a role in suppressing this attunement with nature and, with it, the affinity with the spirit beings who exist within its sphere; but the fact that we lost our ability to perceive them does not mean they ceased to exist.

There is infinite variety among devic entities, just as there is unlimited variety in nature itself. As a human spirit can incarnate in a physical body, so can devic spirits, but they take on the forms of nature; animals, birds, trees and so on. These spirits have awareness, but it is of a different kind from ours. They exist in a condition of unity, in harmony with the flow of life's energy streams, not possessing the quality of *self*-awareness that makes people see themselves as individuals, separate and distinct from all other forms of life. As with human spirits, devas exist on a multitude of levels, ranging from the most primitive forms of mindless energy, the elementals, to the most advanced levels of development. The qualities and values of devic intelligence are different from, but not inferior to, that of human spirits.

179

In addition to the spirits who take physical form, there are other devic entities who function in a caring capacity for their physical kindred, in much the same way as our spirit guardians care for us. These spirits, visible to clairvoyant sight, take forms which resemble the physical life-form they attend. Thus the spirit of a gum-tree will look gum-treeish and quite distinct from a wattle-spirit or the spirit that watches over a daffodil, or a dog. In the light of this revelation, it seemed likely to me that the tree-people with whom I dallied as a child were of such as these.

There are devic spirits forming the elements of earth (gnomes), air (sylphs), water (undines), fire (salamanders), and other elements beyond the perception of our physical senses, such as akasha. It is possible to communicate with these beings, and to invoke them for specific purposes, but it is never wise to do so without an understanding of their essential characteristics, and dangerous to invoke them at all in their elemental forms. They are not necessarily hostile, although some don't like us very much, which is scarcely surprising. If you were a tree-spirit, is it likely that you would look with favour upon a species that hacks and burns whole tracts of forest in its greed for economic wealth? Would an undine feel kindly disposed towards a race that dumps lethal cocktails of toxic waste into rivers and oceans, turning pure water into poison? If ever the forces of nature were to turn upon us en masse and wipe us off the face of the planet, it would not be possible to say that we didn't ask for it in the light of our track record as a species, would it? The elementals aren't so much hostile, however, as indifferent. As energy forms, they operate within the laws that govern all energy, but at those lower levels they neither reason nor argue, they simply do what it is their nature to do. We can stimulate them to act, but we cannot control them, which is where the danger arises. We do not know enough about the laws of nature.

There is so much to be learned about the deva kingdom; a whole series of books could be written on that subject alone. It is not a subject I could undertake, however, as my knowledge of such things is far from comprehensive. For me, it was gratifying to learn that my earlier contacts with invisible friends in the bush were more than just a product of childish fantasy, but for quite a few years my interest remained abstract and chiefly intellectual. The immediacy and vividness of my childhood awareness had diminished and, however much I may have liked to, I seemed unable to recapture it. Until I went to Sherbrooke Forest.

Sherbrooke Forest is in the Dandenong Ranges, not far from the outskirts of Melbourne. I visited the forest with Roland in 1984 during the filming of a video documentary. We had been asked along to function in the role of interested observers while Ian and Sue Gordon recounted a supernatural experience they had encountered some time earlier in a clearing at the edge of a picnic area. It was autumn and the weather was chilly, with a continuous misty drizzle that lightly shrouded the atmosphere, making it ideal as a background for the topic under discussion, but not very comfortable for us.

Film work, we learned, involves a lot of standing around during breaks while the film crew load cameras, check light meters, discuss the composition of scenes and carry out various other technical tasks understood only by themselves. At such times, the rest of us were required to do little more than keep out of the way. During one of these breaks, Roland called me to a wooded area at the

181

side of the clearing, where he had been standing for some time. As I approached, he indicated a place where drooping branches formed a graceful alcove under the trees, no higher than my shoulders and about a metre wide.

'Something's odd about that space,' he told me. 'If you put your hands in there, you can feel a noticeable difference in the air temperature. Check it out.'

I stepped forward and extended my hands into the leafy opening. Immediately I could feel a current of soft warmth; and there was something else, a gentle, barely perceptible tingle in the downturned palms of my hands. I glanced at Roland.

'Did you feel anything other than warmth?' I asked.

He shook his head. 'No, why? What else is there?'

'There's a tingle. Feel it yourself.'

Roland thrust his hands forward, close to mine, and waited. Then he frowned and shook his head. 'No, I can't feel anything but warmth. But if you say there's a tingle, I guess there's a tingle. What do you think is causing it?'

'I'm not sure. There's a feeling of life, but I don't think it comes from the trees. I'll take a closer look.'

When I want to use the faculty of clairvoyance with maximum efficiency, I close my eyes to shut out physical distractions. It isn't necessary to do this, but it makes the process easier. The most commonly experienced form of clairvoyance is not to see supernatural manifestations with the 'naked' eye as though they were solid physical matter; it is much more common to see mental pictures, as though watching images cast on to a screen behind the eyes. It isn't difficult to watch the clairvoyant images while also viewing the physical surroundings, but it can be distracting.

Still holding my hands outstretched and letting my consciousness be centred on the tingling warmth, I closed my eyes... and gasped with surprised delight. Each of my hands rested lightly on the head of a merrily smiling pixie! Two of them, identical in appearance, clad in green and brown, they resembled nothing more closely than the image of Peter Pan as depicted in the Disney movie. They were small rather than tiny, just under a metre in height and light of build, with pointed ears, gamin features and eyes that slanted upwards at the corners. Heads cocked slightly to one side, hands clasped behind backs and eyes alight with amusement, they smiled up at me and in my mind I felt their cheerful greeting.

'Oh... hello,' I answered softly, wrapped in wonder.

'What did you say?'

Startled by the sound of Roland's voice, I jumped, eyes snapping open.

'Pardon?' I blinked.

'You said something just now,' he pointed out.

'Oh, yes... I was talking to the pixies...'

'Talking to *what*?'

'Pixies. In there. You can see them if you close your eyes.'

'You're joking!'

'No I'm not, see for yourself.'

Roland eyed me suspiciously for a few moments, then shrugged and stretched his hands to the warmth. He waited. Then he opened his eyes. 'I can't see anything.'

'They are there, two of them. Wait a moment, I'll get Sue. She's good with clairvoyance.'

Buzzing with elation, I went skipping back to where the others stood.

'Sue!' I called. 'Sue, come and look at the pixies!'

'The *what*?' echoed a startled cameraman.

'Pixies!' I repeated. Was everyone afflicted with

hearing problems? 'Pixies. Over there, under the trees. Come and look.'

In my excitement, I had temporarily forgotten that the film crew had not been exposed to psychically active people before, and they were being paid to film a documentary, not to believe in the supernatural. While they were open-minded enough to accept the possibility of psychic communication, I doubt that anything had prepared them for the sight of a fully grown woman warbling joyfully about pixies in the woods. Under the circumstances they coped rather well, joining Sue and Ian as they accompanied me to where Roland waited. After we had related the circumstances of our discovery, everyone took turns putting their hands into the alcove, but while they all felt the difference in temperature and agreed that there was no 'logical' explanation, nobody else saw the pixies.

Sue waited until last and I watched hopefully as she focused on the source of warmth, but she shook her head and my heart sank. Then she smiled and said, 'But I *can* see my spirit guide. He says the pixies are there, but no one else can see them because they only came for Dawn.'

At least there was confirmation, but I felt a pang of disappointment all the same. It would have been lovely to share the sight with someone else, I thought, as we made our way back to the clearing.

Later that afternoon, back at Ian and Sue's home, I watched the filming of an interview with a psychic artist. She was explaining that unlike many other psychic artists, whose hands are guided in a process similar to automatic writing, she had formerly been trained in Fine Art and used the facility of clairvoyance. As the interview progressed, she began sketching lightly with a pencil on a drawing pad that rested on her knees. It had been arranged previously that she would do this if she happened to 'see' anything of interest while the interview was in progress. When she was asked what she was drawing, an expression of puzzlement crossed her face.

'It appears to be some kind of nature spirit,' she replied. 'But it isn't like any of the nature spirits I've seen before. Those have always looked like animated plant forms. This is... it's like something from a child's book of fairy tales.'

Tingling from head to toe, I managed to restrain myself until the interview concluded. Then I hurried across to the artist.

'May I see your drawing?' I asked her.

'Sure.' She handed me the pad. There, in an exquisitely rendered sketch, was the smiling face of one of my pixies, just as I had seen it in the forest.

The artist had not been present with us in the forest, nor had she been told of the encounter with the pixies. She had quite simply drawn what she saw and, in doing so, answered my wish. Now I could share my vision of the pixies. When I told her about my meeting in the forest, she gave me the picture, which has been carefully preserved in a photograph album ever since.

Not very long ago, on the first day of a weekend seminar, one of the audience members asked if I believed in fairies. At first I hesitated, but a voice in my head said, 'Tell the truth. You are what you are, don't pretend otherwise.' So I nodded and related my encounters with pixies and tree-people during my childhood, then told of the adventure with the pixies in Sherbrooke Forest. When I mentioned the artist's drawing, several people asked if I would bring it with me on the following day.

Next day, I laid the album on a table, opened it

185

to the page that holds the sketch and invited the audience members to take a look. At once, people clustered around the table, and the room was filled with a chorus of 'Oohs' and 'Ahs', and remarks like, 'Oh, isn't he *gorgeous*?'

I listened to the exclamations, watched the faces beaming with delight, and learned something I hadn't known before...

Grownups aren't so dumb after all. *Lots* of us believe in pixies!

CHAPTER NINE

For the love of Christ!

One Saturday morning not long ago, I answered a knock at my front door, to be greeted by two bright-eyed teenagers, beaming huge smiles and announcing, 'We've come to share the love of Christ with you!'

'Well, thank you,' I smiled, slightly bemused. 'But I have enough of my own, already.'

'Oh really?' they chorused, in too-eager voices. 'Tell us about it.'

'I shouldn't need to, should I? Don't you think you should be sharing what you have with someone who hasn't got enough?'

'Oh, no,' they insisted. 'We want to hear about *yours*!'

I have learned to recognise Jehovah's Witnesses by their little briefcases full of religious tracts, and Mormons by their gleaming white shirts and neat-as-a-pin suits (not to mention the American accents) but these two youngsters were of neither faith. Dressed neatly but casually in jeans, coloured shirts and sneakers, neither carried so much as a Bible.

'Please tell us,' repeated the girl. 'We really want to know.'

What they really wanted was to preach their particular brand of religion to me, and I knew it,

187

but I was curious. By this time, I had guessed what that brand of religion would be and it intrigued me, because it was the first time I had seen members of that faith preaching door-to-door.

'You're Born Again Christians, aren't you?' The question was really a statement, and both youngsters nodded their confirmation. 'Then you will understand when I tell you that I was baptised in full immersion, in a Pentecostal church, over twenty-five years ago,' I remarked. They nodded again, brimming with enthusiasm. 'And I was told that after the water baptism, I would receive a gift of the spirit, such as healing with the laying on of hands . . . '

'Yes, we've got that in our church,' lilted the girl.

' . . . the gift of speaking in tongues . . . '

'Yes, yes, that too!'

' . . . and the gift of interpretation.'

'That's right!' Their faces positively glowed.

'The only problem,' I continued, in a pensive tone, 'is that nobody warned me about premonitions.'

The smiles disappeared as if by magic, their eyes went cold, and the girl's lip began curling into a sneer. 'Oh!' she declared, with palpable disdain, 'you've mixed it with *witchcraft*!'

'Do you think so?' My voice remained neutral. 'What do you know about witches?'

'I used to *be* one before I was saved by Jesus!' she retorted, all scorn and defiance.

'Really? Then define witchcraft for me.'

'Indoctrination, manipulation and domination,' she recited, parrot-fashion.

'For what purpose?' I persisted.

She hesitated, momentarily nonplussed. 'Uh . . . to control people's minds for the powers of evil,' came her answer, after a few moments.

188

I shook my head. 'Sweetheart, you were never a genuine witch,' I told her. 'For a start, you don't know the difference between witchcraft and Satanism. Secondly, had you been a member of that faith, you would have been able to tell me that 'witch' is a *Christian* word. The correct term is Wicca, and in any case, I am not a witch...'

'Premonitions come from *SATAN*!' Her voice was savage.

'Then what does it mean,' I asked quietly, 'to prophesy?'

'Prophesying isn't really foretelling the future,' she countered.

'In that case,' I answered smoothly, 'there are an awful lot of lies in the Bible, aren't there?'

Outraged in the extreme, the girl could only make incoherent noises, and her male companion decided it was time to intervene.

'If you were baptised with the Holy Spirit, you would understand the words of Christ,' he announced.

'Young man, I was baptised in spirit years before you were born, and I understand the word of Christ quite well. In fact, I talk to him all the time.'

'So do I!' cut in the girl, quivering with indignation.

'Wonderful. Does he answer you?'

'What do you mean?'

'I mean hearing the voice in your head.'

'That's not talking with Christ, it's communicating with spirits!' she protested.

'Isn't Christ a spirit? In any case, the Bible doesn't condemn communicating with spirits; it even gives instructions on how to tell the difference between the spirits that are of God and those that are not.'

'Where in the Bible does it say *that*?' she demanded, in a tone of challenging disbelief.

'1 John 4,' I answered. 'Just a moment, I'll get my Bible and show you.'

'No!'

'No?' I was genuinely puzzled. 'You want the truth, don't you?'

'Don't bother.'

'You're a Christian, and you won't use the Bible as a reference? I find that strange... ' I mused aloud.

'How about *this*?' demanded the girl, her triumphant expression indicating an unanswerable argument to come. 'Imagination, not manipulation, determines the future.'

'I see no argument with that,' I replied mildly. 'It's just another way of saying that thought creates reality. Quantum physics would agree with you, too... '

'*Science*!' she shrilled. 'That's all *mind* stuff... it's got nothing to do with God!'

'For Heaven's sake, child!' I was becoming exasperated. 'Why do you think God *gave* you a mind?'

'The mind has nothing to do with religion!' she insisted, sullenly.

'If you check your ancient Greek, you'll find that the word for "spirit" also means "mind"... '

'What's that got to do with anything?' she interrupted.

'A large part of the Bible was translated from Greek texts,' I explained as patiently as I could.

In reply, she lost her temper, shook her fist in my face and yelled, 'I haven't got any more time to talk to you! You're wasting my time, and you're wasting *God's* time... '

At this point, we noticed an older man approaching, and the girl fell silent at once. The man appeared to be in his mid-thirties and from the submissive postures immediately adopted by the two young people, it was obvious that he was their leader. He walked with a noticeable swagger and the expression on his smiling face clearly said, 'All right, children, let me deal with this troublesome housewife.'

After an initial glance, I ignored his approach and continued speaking to the girl. 'Is it the way of Christ to display extremely rude manners, to interrupt and to shout people down without listening to their point of view? You call yourself a Christian, yet you will not look at a Bible. You claim to be "Born Again", but you don't know the full meaning of the term because you do not accept the principle of reincarnation, even though Jesus himself taught it . . . '

That brought their leader in, with a flourish. 'You have your facts confused, madam,' he assured me, in a voice of oiled silk. 'Jesus never taught anything about reincarnation.'

'No?' I tilted my chin. 'Check your Bible . . . sir! In the gospel of Matthew, there are two passages in which Jesus specifically states that John the Baptist was the reincarnation of Elijah*.'

'Ah, yes, that comes from the prediction in Malachi,' he said, stroking his chin in the manner of a sage. 'But Jesus didn't actually mean that John was an incarnation of Elijah the spirit; what he meant was that John was an incarnation of the spirit of Elijah.'

'What's the difference?'

'Well . . . er . . . the spirit of Elijah doesn't mean Elijah the spirit; it means the same spirit that Elijah had, like . . . uh . . . like the spirit of Anzac that inspired our young men during the wars.'

A spirit of *war*? Saints preserve us! I refrained from remarking that any 'patriotic' spirits that drive people into frenzies of bloodletting can

*Some versions of the Bible give the name as Elias.

hardly be equated with a spirit of love, and from remarking that among supposedly 'Christian' proselytisers it seems a favoured tactic to claim that the Bible doesn't really mean what it says, while at the same time insisting that it is the only book that contains the absolute truth of God's word.

'If you would open your heart to Christ,' crooned the preacher, 'and let the Holy Spirit be your guide, you would be able to see the truth.'

'As I told your young followers here, I did that years before they were born . . . and probably while you were still in short pants,' I retorted, with some asperity. 'And the truth I see is groups of so-called Christians, pointing to other groups of Christians, saying, "They're all going to Hell because they aren't like us" . . . *despite* what Jesus taught about a house divided within itself being unable to stand.'

'Oh, *that's* not Christianity,' he replied airily, 'that's denominationalism, and I have no part of that. It is *my* mission to prepare people for the second coming of Christ.'

'Christ never left,' I said.

'Christ died on the cross, at Calvary,' the preacher spoke slowly, as though addressing a backward child.

'The body of *Jesus of Nazareth* died on the cross,' I replied, imitating the preacher's tones. 'The spirit known as Christ is immortal and cannot die. That spirit has never left, and can be contacted directly by anyone who wishes to do so, without interference from so-called intermediaries.'

'Christ died on the cross!' insisted the preacher. 'Then he descended into Hell for three days, after which he rose again, to show that all who follow him can be saved from Hell through his blood. You see, God didn't create Hell for humans, he made it for Satan, but a lot of people are turning away from God and following the path to Hell.

'There are people in this world whose hearts are filled with darkness,' he continued. 'And it is my mission to reach those people with the love of Christ, before it's too late.'

'Then while you're about it, I suggest that you teach your young follower here,' I said, indicating the girl, 'that giving way to anger and yelling abuse at people is hardly the way to share the love of Christ.'

He drew himself up in a pose of righteous dignity. 'No, I won't teach her that!' he declared. 'I teach by my own example, and *I* get angry when I see people living in spiritual darkness.'

'Really?' I asked softly. 'I feel compassion for them.'

'*I* don't!' he proclaimed loftily. 'They are Godless sinners, and they deserve all the torments of Hell!'

'Isn't there a passage in the Bible that says, "Judge not, lest ye be judged"?' I murmured. 'Besides, what if a person has been raised from childhood with no religious education and has never seen a Bible? Would you condemn that person as a sinner?'

'The word of God is here, if those people want it,' he replied, pointing to himself. 'If they don't come seeking it, they are choosing damnation.'

'How are they supposed to know where to seek?' I demurred. 'How can you judge them if they don't know? I pity anyone who doesn't know where to turn.'

'I don't pity *anyone*!' he announced. 'If I saw a man in a wheelchair, unable to walk, I wouldn't say, "Oh, you poor wretch, I pity you". I would say, "You don't need that wheelchair. By the power of Christ, vested in me, I say to you Rise Up and Walk"... because I *know* that Christ moves in me.' His voice positively thundered with pride.

'What if the man in the wheelchair *can't* rise and walk after you've done your thing?' I enquired.

'Then he is obviously cursed by God and must be a sinner.'

'You believe you have the authority to make such judgements?'

'Of course! It is my ministry to spread the word of Christ in this Godless society, and I know the servants of Satan are fighting hard to stop me. Do you realise that there are people in our town who forcibly keep their children locked up at home, to physically prevent them from coming to our Bible meetings?'

I glanced at his two young disciples, but refrained from remarking that, seeing the results of his influence, I was not surprised that parents wanted to keep their children away from him. I simply remarked that I know of people who are locked away in worse circumstances, confined to psychiatric hospitals because they hear the voices of demons tormenting them.

'It's a pity that you can't do something to help people like that,' I commented.

'If they consort with demons, they *deserve* to be locked away!' he declared.

'Even when they have done nothing to invite it, and are crying out for help?'

'Yes. They have obviously committed some crime against God, and the demons are their punishment.'

'I'm sorry,' I told him, 'but I don't hear the love of Christ in your words. I hear something arrogant, fanatical and dangerous.'

'Then we have no further grounds for discussion,' he grated.

'It seems that way,' I agreed. Then as they turned

194

to leave, I added (with only the slightest hint of mischief), 'Peace be with you.'

I have not recounted this incident merely to provide some entertaining repartee: spirituality is far too important to be treated so lightly. What I saw and heard that day was not what I know as spirituality, nor was it in keeping with what I understand of Christ's teachings. It was nothing short of fanaticism, brainwashing and egotism: none of which, if I have studied the Bible correctly, are qualities generated under the influence of Christ. The preacher displayed unmistakable pride and an inflated sense of power and importance, while his young followers were obviously in his thrall. To show a reasonable amount of respect for a teacher is one thing, but the immediate submission, heads bowed, hands clasped behind backs and eyes downcast, spoke to me more of domination than respect. The youngsters seemed incapable of independent thought, and they spoke in jargon, using key phrases and slogans which, so far as I could discern, had little connection with the teachings of Christ, but indicated very well washed brains.

I have heard it said, of 'Christians' like these that they are 'the kind of Christians who make atheists out of other people'. It is the negative view of Christianity, as portrayed by the fanatics, the hypocrites and the narrow-minded, that causes most New Age people to turn their backs on that religious structure. This saddens me greatly, partly because of the barriers it creates, but also because there is some wonderful spiritual potential in the 'Born Again' movement and, tragically, too much is going to waste or being diverted because of people like the preacher. The two young people who called at my door were sincere seekers of the Light, and they were fired with heartfelt enthusiasm, but it was being twisted in a negative direction. That man was not helping them to become vessels for the love of Christ: he was turning them into fanatics.

A quotation from *The Fall of Hyperion* (John Keats) says:

Fanatics have their dreams, wherewith they weave
A paradise for a sect.

Sectarianism is aligned with schism. It divides people, breeding into its adherents an elitist attitude; a belief that they are the members of a superior class and that all outsiders are virtually subhuman or outcast in some way. To this way of thinking, what happens to outcasts doesn't matter; in fact they are seen as *deserving* to suffer. 'Let Armageddon come: let all the sinners and unbelievers burn in Hell. We of the chosen will be with our Master, in Paradise.' Sadly, this kind of thinking has become prevalent in the fundamentalist movement that permeates many world religions, including Christianity. The same pattern of thinking was also the breeding-ground in which the Third Reich flourished. If you care to read Neville Drury's book *The Occult Experience*, you will find the same kind of thinking described as a characteristic of Satanism. It has nothing to do with the love of Christ, or with true en-Light-enment.

Before I had my first conscious psychic experience at the age of eighteen, I was a Born Again Christian, although if the term 'Born Again' was in use in those days (the early 1960s) I had yet to hear it. We were known as Pentecostals, or Full Gospel Christians. I took vows in which I dedicated my life to Christ, and I was baptised into that faith. I would not have made such a deep commitment if I had not believed profoundly that it was the right thing for me to do, but I made that commitment to *Christ*, and to everything Christ stands for: I did not dedicate myself to a religion.

There came a day when our pastor told me that all Roman Catholics were damned to Hell eternal, with no hope of salvation.

'But if a Catholic came to you as I did, repenting and wanting to be raised in Christ, couldn't she be saved then?' I asked in dismay.

No, I was told, Catholics are not admitted to our faith. There spoke the voice of élitism, and it did not sound like the voice of a loving Christian to me. I felt myself confronted with a choice: the Christ *I* believed in, or the church. I left the church.

For me, there isn't enough 'Christ' in any form of Christianity that preaches intolerance. According to a teaching from the Christian Bible, 'The Spirit's fruition is love, joy, peace, forbearance, kindness, generosity, fidelity, gentleness, self-control' . . . (Galatians 5:22,23), and in the same passage (Galatians 5:25,26) 'If we live by the Spirit, let us also be directed by the Spirit; let us not become vainglorious so as to compete with each other and to envy one another.' I do not see the fruitage of that kind of Spirit in any form of religious intolerance or élitism.

What saddens me most about the fundamentalist Born Again movement is the stifled potential. The teachings that support the basic principles of that movement are sound, but limited. For instance, as I mentioned earlier, Born Again Christians believe that the 'Baptism of the Holy Spirit' brings to the baptised person certain spiritual gifts: the gift of healing, the gift of speaking in tongues or the gift of interpretation (of tongues). That belief is based on a passage in 1 Corinthians 12, but it does not include the other spiritual gifts listed in the same chapter, nor the teaching that all

197

of the gifts listed are bestowed and energised *by the same Spirit*. Those gifts include wisdom, knowledge, faith, prophecy, discernment of spirits and the ability to work miracles, in addition to the gifts officially sanctioned by the Born Again movement. No wonder the preacher discourages his young followers from allowing anyone else to open a Bible to them. They might learn things he doesn't want them to know; like the fact that they don't *need* his intervention, to bring them to Christ. All they need is a group of two or more people to gather in the name of Christ, and Christ is quite happy to come to *them*. Where would the preacher's power-base be tomorrow if his followers were to gain that kind of knowledge today?

It seems to me that there are Christians who preach, and there are Christians who practise, but the two don't necessarily coincide. In addition, there are many other people who live by the principles on which the teachings of Christ are based, but who do not call themselves Christians, yet in their actions, attitudes and ideals, they demonstrate the Light of Spirit.

There are people in the New Age movement who believe it isn't possible to be an enlightened New Ager and a Christian at the same time. That isn't true, and it also carries warning overtones of élitist thinking. There is a need to take care against prejudice in any form. There are some New Age thinkers who started out as Christians and some who did not. Of those who did, some have left the church, others choose to stay. I get a lot of letters from people who have trouble reconciling their New Age experiences and awareness with the doctrines they were taught as Christians, and this conflict is no trivial matter. These people can go through agonies of doubt and confusion.

Dear Dawn

I have just finished reading your book Reaching for the Other Side *and found it very interesting and moving. The knowledge in it fitted in with other likeminded books I've read of late, by people like Shirley MacLaine, and books speaking of the reincarnation teachings that were part of the Catholic Church before the Council of Nicea (325 AD) banned them and replaced them with myths about Hell and eternal damnation.*

My problem is that until about six weeks ago I was a practising Roman Catholic who went to mass every Sunday. I no longer believe in the modern church — I think it has changed too many things from the original teachings of Christ. I can see from history how wrong it has been in a lot of what it has taught for the past two thousand years. My main worry, though, is that a lot of questions are starting to plague me now. Questions like, am I better off with no religion — no philosophy and rules to set my standards by? Who is going to teach my children about Christ and his teachings, and about God? I'm no theologian. How far do I go in abandoning what I've been brought up to believe — e.g. sex only in marriage, and other issues that I've always agreed with?

When I look around me and see people who have no religion, I see bed-hopping, drugs and crime gradually becoming less and less wrong to them. I don't want to live a life with no limits. I know I probably sound prudish, but I've seen so many friends who've lived with no limits and totally stuffed up their lives.

I'd love to get involved with the type of thing

199

you're involved with, but like you said in the book, it's dangerous to rush into this type of thing, and there are conmen around. I don't want to stagnate spiritually. I'm worried about where I go from here. What replaces what I've given up? I think I've made the right choice, leaving the church, but I feel as though I should be taking up something 'better', to justify giving up my only 'link' with God so far.

You must get a lot of letters and I can understand that you only have twenty-four hours in a day, but I would be truly grateful if you would write and give me your opinion or suggestions.

Yours faithfully
Cheryl

The question, 'Am I better off with no religion?', as Cheryl asks it, is difficult to answer, since it seems to imply that either a person subscribes to an orthodox system of theological doctrine, or that person has no philosophy or rules by which to set her standards in life, which is not the case at all. Many New Age thinkers prefer not to be involved with formal religious structures, but that doesn't mean they have no philosophy or system of standards: in fact, it is often because they have such deep beliefs that they turn away from religious organisations which, in their eyes, do not fulfil those standards. For instance, the New Age people whom I know all believe that it is wrong to kill. In this belief, they are quite in accord with the commandment 'Do not kill' which is part of the Christian teachings, but they disagree emphatically with the 'Christian' churches which, *in spite* of that commandment, send their priests into battlefields to bless the guns and tell the soldiers that

'God is on our side'. New Agers have no difficulty in accepting the teaching from Christ that we should 'Love one another', but they do not see that love made manifest in religious prejudice and intolerance towards any who are 'not of the faith'. They also recognise that spiritual truths are universal. When I was told, quite a few years ago, that the philosophy in one of my books was 'pure Christian' the speaker wondered why I couldn't suppress a giggle of amusement, until I told him that only a few days earlier some Hindu friends had commented to me that the same philosophy was 'pure Vedanta'.

In discussions pertaining to religion, I use Christianity as my frame of reference, because that is the faith in which I was raised, therefore I am able to speak from a background of personal experience. I am always reluctant to speak on subjects in which I lack this personal experience, and while I have read about different religions and discussed spiritual principles with people who come from some of those other religious backgrounds, I do not feel qualified to use their frames of reference, for the simple reason that I do not know enough about them. It is obvious to all of us that every major world religion has its share of sects and fanatics: the same can be said with respect to the enlightened thinkers who come from a wide variety of religious backgrounds. No religion has the franchise on truth, and no religion is immune to falsehood and fanaticism. It suits me best to have no particular religious affiliations, but when I speak in a religious context, my terminology is unavoidably derived from my Christian upbringing. That doesn't present a problem for me; when I want to call on the Lord of Light, I use the name of Christ, but I am fully aware that the same Being answers to many other names, in other languages and systems of belief. Nevertheless, while my terms of reference may be Christian in origin, I am not a member of the Christian religion and therefore I will not attempt to speak as one. To present the most balanced picture possible, however, I want to include a message from someone who can speak from the viewpoint of a New Age thinker *and* as a practising Christian.

I have known Yuana for many years, and although she generally prefers to maintain a certain degree of comfortable anonymity, she is not afraid to speak her mind when it feels right for her to do so. When I told her about this chapter, and of my wish to present an unbiased discussion on the subject, she readily agreed to write of her beliefs. At first she seemed a little awed at the prospect of 'writing for a book', so I suggested that, like some of my other friends, she could express her views in the form of a letter. She felt comfortable about doing it that way, and eventually presented me with the following:

Dear Dawn

You have asked me to write down for you my philosophy on life — and the moment I begin, I come up against one of the greatest difficulties this life presents: terminology. I am convinced that this means of self-expression is the greatest cause of conflict, division, crosspurpose — even war — that this world has ever known.

For example, I am a Christian, a psychic, a medium, and a New Age thinker. I worship God, the Lord Jesus Christ, His son, and I pray to Mary, the Mother of God (oh yes, I'm also Catholic!). I was once the medium for a Christian psychic group, and while in trance, I was the instrument for Istari, an ancient (pre-history) Earth goddess, who in her time ruled under the guidance of one Michael, who later on came to Earth as Jesus Christ. She used His teaching, and His guidance made her rule a golden age of the distant past.

This might sound to most people like the most preposterous statement of conflicting philosophies one could gather together, but I have no difficulty whatsoever with my faith. The difficulties arise when people start to put labels on their beliefs and put them into little boxes marked 'never to be changed'. One group I have attended would express 'shock-horror' if I used the word medium or psychic, but in meetings, after we pray and call on the Lord to protect us from all that is not His will, I speak out the message He has given me to speak, and I have been thanked and told I am 'spiritually aware'. I have tranced in a psychic group and, through these trances, spirit teachers have given the members the same kind of message, and I'm thanked and told I am 'very psychic'. I have visited a third group and done exactly the same thing, and have been complimented on my 'cosmic consciousness'.

Now, I am exactly the same person, doing my own thing in all three of these situations. The messages are similar, the presentation is similar, the content exactly the same. But if I used the term 'cosmic consciousness' to the first group, they would throw me out — or at least express profound concern for my soul — because the terminology is alien to them. But the message is exactly the same, and it is the message that is important, not the messenger.

The message is being disregarded and

discarded, because sometimes the messenger wears different symbols and uses different terminology, and this is the tragedy of all ages. It is what *we say*, not *the voice which says it*, that is the essence, yet over and over again, society has made an idol of the messenger and overlooked crucial realities within the message.

Some very good friends of mine, sound, sincere Christians (in fact, the husband was a Methodist minister) discovered that the wife had psychic gifts. They prayed and agonised over the difference between their prayerful experience and what their particular Protestant denomination thought of such things. The gifts deepened and developed. They managed to strike a working balance, but prejudice and bigotry within the church first forced the husband to resign his post as minister to a small parish. They continued their Christian life and dedicated the wife's psychic gifts to God. They founded a small but vibrant group which meets regularly, prays constantly, conducts healing prayer therapy, rescues lost souls and provides teaching and guidance to all who seek it. They have been persecuted, slandered and vilified by those so-called godly members of their former church. Who, in this instance, would you call Christian?

About forty years ago, when I first became aware of my psychic gifts, namely automatic writing and trance mediumship, I was very nervous. I was not at all sure of it, so I did what I always do in times of doubt — I went into the church and prayed about it. 'Dear Father,' I prayed earnestly — I was never more sincere! 'if these gifts are not of you, then I want nothing

204

to do with them. Please clear them from my being.'

When I pray and get answers, I never rationalise them away, and after I had prayed with all my heart a couple of times, the gifts developed and deepened. So I dedicated them to Jesus and went on with it.

The mind of God is infinite, the mind of man is finite; so it stands to reason that the limitations of our human-ness sees us able to grasp a truth (and for different people, different truths) of all that is God. This does not negate other truths, or render them untrue; they are simply different areas of a mighty truth that we are unable to grasp in its entirety.

For example, I have heard many New Age people refer to 'Father-Mother-God', since they cannot relate to an all-male, father-figure deity. I have no difficulty with that, although I suppose having had the male image presented to me all my life, I usually preface my prayers with 'Father in Heaven', which is the manner in which Jesus presented God to the world. There are religions in the world, and throughout history, which present the female side of the Deity and insist that God is Mother. To counteract this, the Church of Rome in past times cleverly stressed the presence of Mary, both to balance the all-male image and to make Christianity more acceptable in societies where the Deity was worshipped as female. After all, Jesus was from the Jewish, male-dominated society, and there is no way the Jews would have tolerated a female God! Jesus presented a loving, caring, wise Father image, His church added a Mother image. I don't think it matters a great deal how we perceive this aspect of the Deity — it can be whichever we are comfortable with, just so long as it helps us to relate to the Divinity.

In my own mind, I believe that ultimately, the God figure is neither male nor female; that the concept of male/female cuts out where the human ability to comprehend cuts out. An Infinite Being who is eternal, unchanging and constant has no need of sexual reproduction, since It is already All That Is, and never changes. Sex or gender is only required on levels where 'Being' has to be renewed and reproduced in a physical way. Where this form of reproduction is unnecessary, the gender factor becomes irrelevant. The Infinite God, containing all the elements necessary for ongoing wholeness, has no need of separation into genders. The Infinite just IS.

Most of us on the human level find this wholeness a bit intimidating and, because of our human-ness, are able to relate better to the Infinite if we conceptualise it into a superhuman image of Fatherhood or Motherhood — and that's okay. A three-month-old infant can have no possible concept of the complex individual who is its parent, and it doesn't need to. All that child needs is the love, the care, the cuddles, the security, the strength and the comforting warmth of the parent. That is how it is for us as spiritual babes — we'll learn the rest as we grow.

It's enough for me right now; I guess as a spiritual being, I'm the equivalent of that babe! And the teachings of Jesus are enough for me — after all, there is so much developing for me to do to attain the level He set!

One of the ways I might express my faith is to say, 'Keep it simple'. Jesus did not bring a complex message to us. When mankind began to lose its closeness with God, Jesus came to teach us the way back. He brought the message — and we worship the messenger! His claim was, 'I have come so that you may know God'. He didn't say 'Worship Me', He said, 'Worship He who sent me'. He said, 'I am in the Father and the Father is in Me' and 'The Kingdom of Heaven is within you'. Within YOU ... not out there on some unattainable pinnacle!

If we had the courage to grasp the idea, we would know then that in our daily lives and our search for Truth, and our sincere effort to live better lives, we have no need of spirit guides or angelic messengers, although they are a help along the way in our spiritual infancy. We've been told over and over again all that we need and what to do, and it's so simple, we seem to say to ourselves, 'There must be more than that'. Mankind seems to think that everything in life must be immeasurably hard or terribly complicated. Yet Jesus said, simply 'Love one another, as I have loved you'.

Who could commit atrocities if they lived by this rule? Who could deprive others of their natural environment if they lived by this rule? Who would steal from someone they loved? Who could kill, rape, maim or intimidate one they truly loved, as Jesus loved? Who could destroy the environment mankind depends on if they loved all mankind and not just their own clique? Would there be homeless youth? Would there be domestic violence? Would we need drugs? Would we need atomic weapons?

I think I relate best to the Catholic Church because throughout its history, even to the present day, it has had a succession of mystics, people who had visions, talked to angels, and believed in the power within some sacred places. As long as I remember my terminology, use terms like spiritual and mystic, and don't use words like psychic and clairvoyant, I don't have much trouble with the church in which I choose to live out my Christian faith.

What worries me, within all denominations, is the number of people who are 'Churchian' instead of Christian. They are good, well-intentioned people who live out a set of worthy humanistic rules that they call their faith. Really, as far as spiritual content goes, they might just as well join the Rotary Club, Apex or the Red Cross. In fact, many of them do, and there isn't much difference between their activities in their organisations, and in their church. Please don't misunderstand me — I don't mean to denigrate their works or their motives. On the physical and social level, they can show me a thing or two! They show wonderful concern for the earthly condition of their fellow humans, but where is the spiritual in all this?

Oh, I know the prayer, 'Oh Lord, protect me from the man who is so Heavenly-minded, he's no earthly good', but it seems to me that many people who call themselves Christian are no such thing; they are humanitarian with a dash of Paul. Where in all this is the Christ who walked on water, fed five thousand people from a few bread rolls and a couple of small fish, turned water into wine, talked with angels, healed incurable illnesses, gave sight to the blind, drove demons out of those who were possessed, and brought the dead back to life?

John and Peter saw Him talking with Moses and Elijah, who had surely been dead for hundreds of years. Care for His fellow man, He certainly did, but He did so much more as well, on a mystic and spiritual level. People will say, 'Oh yes, but He was the Son of God and He was exceptional.' Why then did He say, 'That which I have done, you will do also, and better than I have done'? Why did He say of Mary, sister of Martha, that she took the better path when she sat at His feet to learn of spiritual things while her sister rushed around ministering unto human needs?

There are people who say to me that 'psychic' and 'occult' practices are of the devil. These are people who never looked up the meaning of the words in a dictionary. Psychic gifts are part of the human condition, and if one took every story containing reference to psychic, occult, clairvoyant and clairaudient experiences out of the Bible, one would have a very thin book indeed, and certainly not one on which there could be based a religion that has survived for two thousand years. However, it's my belief that the religion won't last too much longer unless its members get their physical, mental and spiritual levels back in balance.

God is still waiting for us to get it right.

So I'll go on being a psychic, Christian Catholic and if ever my church demands that I choose — I'll no longer be a Catholic.

Yours sincerely
Yuana

Yuana provides a good illustration of the fact that, while we share beliefs in common, New Age thinkers don't all have an identical belief structure, nor should we. The capacity to accept differences and yet be in harmony in spirit is one of the healthiest characteristics of New Age thinking, and I hope we all continue in harmony, for that is the way to true spiritual enlightenment.

Superficially, Yuana's belief structure may seem different from what many people might see as the 'typical' New Age philosophy, which is precisely why her contribution here is so relevant. If we fall into the trap of believing there has to be a set pattern of expression for New Age awareness, we will simply be creating another form of sectarianism.

For someone like Cheryl, who feels insecure about stepping away from the familiar religious system in which she was raised, Yuana's story contains some valuable advice. When her psychic gifts began to manifest, Yuana turned to the spiritual source she knew, fully trusting that her God would answer. When she was reassured that gifts were sanctioned by her God, she 'committed them to Jesus and got on with it'. I did something very similar when I became aware of my own psychic faculties.

I had been taught, in my church, that the supernatural is the realm of Satan and, when I first started having premonitions, I was very much afraid that I had fallen victim to the clutches of Hell. I sought advice from a number of clergymen: some dismissed my premonitions as 'teenage hysteria', some suggested that I see a psychiatrist and some, quite frankly, didn't want to know. Eventually, however, I was advised to pray and ask God to take the burden from me if it didn't come from Him, and this I did. I prayed my heart out, every waking moment... and the experiences continued. Since I had been taught that 'If you ask your Father for bread, he will not give you a stone' I accepted that, for some reason I didn't understand, the Creator must want me to be psychic, so, like Yuana, I committed it to God, although perhaps not as formally and respectfully as in Yuana's earnest prayers. My commitment sounded more like, 'All right, God, if you want me to keep having this stuff happen to me, I suppose I'm stuck with it... but there aren't any roadmaps for this kind of territory, it's too big for me and I don't know how to handle it wisely, so you take care of it. I commit it to you, it's yours, do what you will with it... and make sure I don't get hurt!'

Fortunately, the Deity doesn't seem to have problems with terminology!

There is no need to abandon everything you believe in when you find yourself awakening to New Age awareness, in fact it would be foolish to do that. I would suggest that you start with those beliefs as your framework: you may alter some of them in time or you may not, but let them be the foundation upon which you build. In addition, *ask* to be guided by the Spirit. If your religious background is Christian, ask in the name of Christ to be protected against deception and guided in Love, Light and Truth. If you come from a different religious background, make the same request, addressing it to whichever Being represents the ultimate power for good in your faith. You don't need any special prayers or invocations, just ask in your own words. Then, at the human level, do the best you can to live up to what you believe to be good and true. No more than that is expected of you.

Maybe it sounds simplistic, but as Yuana has remarked, we humans tend to make things unnecessarily complex for ourselves. Her advice to 'Keep it simple' is a suggestion with which I heartily agree. It *is* simple: and it works, not only for practising Christians like Yuana, but for anyone who asks.

It doesn't matter what your religious background may be, or even whether you have any religious beliefs at all, nor does it matter how you conceptualise the ultimate power for good. Work on a framework of understanding that is familiar to you, ask for help from the highest spiritual source of love and truth that you personally believe in, and do your best with what you have at the physical level. It works for Yuana, it works for me and it works for many, many other people from all walks of life and all philosophies. It will work for you, too. Try it!

CHAPTER TEN
The Lady

In previous books, I have written of my association with the spirit teacher David, who initially made contact with me through the trance mediumship of my former husband, Roland. I have written of David's teachings and some of the adventures experienced during the earlier stages of my psychic/spiritual education with David and several other spirit entities. These spirits were all male in essence, and many people have asked me since if spirit guides must always be male and whether I have any female spirit companions.

No, spirit guides are not always masculine, and yes, I do have feminine companions in spirit. One, in particular, has been with me for many years, and in recent times her presence has been manifesting more and more frequently. I have not written about her before for the simple reason that the time has not felt right. Until now.

I have often *thought* about mentioning the Lady in my writing, but on those earlier occasions I would see her in my mind's eye, shaking her head, and with that image came the words 'Not yet. Other things must happen first.' I never had the feeling that there was any big secret about her presence, rather I was given the impression that there was a sequence of events that must unfold and that when the time was appropriate for me to write about her, I would know.

Communication with the Lady is different in its qualities from the communication I have with David. Mind-to-mind communication with David is a bit like radio: I am familiar with his 'wavelength' and, when I seek contact, I focus my mind on to that frequency and wait for his response. A similar principle operates when David calls my attention. The communication that follows is primarily cerebral, like holding a conversation in my head.

With the Lady, there is more of a feeling than a conversation, a sort of wordless knowing, a non-verbal flow of awareness. Sometimes words come into my mind but, most often, verbal communication is unnecessary, even incongruous, although it has never been difficult to translate that flow of awareness into words when it is appropriate to do so. The essence of the Lady's energy flow is distinct and different from that of 'masculine' guides; she is of the feminine affinity or 'Goddess' energy, while male entities are aligned with the masculine God-force. The two work in harmony, and ultimately both energy streams are united in the one Source, but as most of us would perceive them, their qualities and characteristics are different.

When I was a very little girl, I thought the Lady might be my fairy godmother. Later, I thought perhaps she was my guardian angel, and by the time I was ten years old, I had learned to believe that she could be nothing more than a figment of my imagination, because anything else was 'impossible'. I don't recall ever talking to anyone about my Lady, not because there was any secretiveness in her but more because she was special to me, and there are some things that little girls just like keeping to themselves. Later, I didn't talk

214

about her because I believed she couldn't be real and I didn't particularly wish to face more scorn and ridicule than I already had to deal with. I was not being over-sensitive about it, merely realistic.

I have an affinity for music and there are some songs that put my feelings into expression for me with heart-touching eloquence. One of these 'special' songs is Neil Diamond's 'Shilo', in which he sings of a childhood companion by that name, who keeps a lonely child company, the impression being that Shilo is what grownups would call an 'imaginary playmate'. The child grows to young manhood and falls in love, but his new love lets him down, leaving him alone and brokenhearted. The singer recalls how Shilo always came to ease his loneliness in childhood and the song ends with the poignant cry to Shilo, 'Come today!' The Lady was my Shilo.

To explain at a more personal level, let me speak for a time of my childhood. My family lived in a small and very isolated mining town during an era when 'divorce' was a word that people whispered behind their hands. A divorced woman was regarded as being, if not exactly a scarlet woman, one who was definitely a hot shade of pink. To be the child of a divorced woman in those days was seen in some eyes as being practically illegitimate, and to be illegitimate was to be an outcast. There were some parents who would not allow their children to play with me, treated me as though I carried some contagious and shameful disease, and taught their offspring to do the same. In today's society, where a child whose original parents are still together by the time she reaches high school is the exception rather than the norm, more couples are opting for de facto relationships and unmarried mothers abound, the attitudes held by society when I was a child might seem preposterous, but they were nonetheless real. And my mother was the only divorced woman in town.

Mum has not spoken often to me about the prejudice she faced and how it hurt her, but I can imagine. It must have been worse for her in many ways. It wasn't all horrible; Mum did have some nice friends and I had some amiable playmates, but I spent a lot of time alone . . . or wishing to be. At the age of eight, I developed bronchial asthma, which meant that I could not keep pace with the other children in their energetic games, and I also became a target for the bullies, who gathered in gangs of three or five and ambushed other children, inflicting some brutal beatings just for the fun of causing pain. I wasn't the only child who suffered that kind of persecution, but being asthmatic made it more fun for the bullies because their other victims didn't go blue in the face and collapse, choking for breath.

I preferred to avoid most people; grownups and children alike. I preferred the company of animals, who were more attuned and responsive to my feelings. I would happily roam for miles in the bush, most of which I knew like the back of my hand. Sometimes a dog or cat friend (or both) would come along with me, sometimes I wandered away by myself. I would lie happily on my tummy for hours in a patch of clover, searching for (and often finding) lucky four-leafed clovers, or stretching out on my back in the grass watching cloud-pictures weave across the sky.

At such times as these, my Lady would come and play games with me. She would also be there whenever I was hurt and lonely, crying in a corner. She was there when I lay huddled in my bed, in terror of the invisible monsters that I could feel prowling around me in the darkness. Whenever she came, the monsters fled, my tears were dried and, somehow, everything felt better. She helped me find the four-leafed clovers, she wove stories through the cloud-pictures in the sky, and in her presence the trees and flowers seemed to wave more cheerily. She was my special friend.

The Lady never really went away, but as I grew and my mind was turned to other things, I became less and less aware of her and, when she did enter my mind, I thought myself to be indulging in wishful fantasies. I learned better, of course, after I grew up and began to research the so-called supernatural, but there was a long, dark space during which I hardly ever thought about her at all.

I have my personal name for her, but I'm sure she is known by other names to many other people. Most of the time, I just think of her as 'my Lady': I have thought of her that way for as long as I can remember, and it is only in recent years that it has occurred to me to notice that 'my lady' in Latin is 'ma donna'.

She has been seen with me by a number of clairvoyants, some of whom describe her as a nun, others as a priestess or an angel. Others have simply asked, 'Who is that *beautiful* lady with you?' Her name, however, is not important: she identifies herself to me by a name I personally recognise, but like David, she has many other children in this world, and many names. What is of importance to me personally is that I know her to be of the Light in its feminine aspect.

David identifies himself primarily as a teacher, and he asked me to write as a messenger on his behalf. There is love and affection between us, as between a niece and a favourite uncle who always understands how she feels and never ever lets her down, but at a 'working' level, our exchanges of thought are predominantly cerebral, logical and intellectual. He does precisely what he claims to

217

do: he teaches, and since I write of his teachings, for maximum clarity I need to have those teachings clearly programmed into the left side of my brain. If they were not, I would not be able to express that knowledge in words. The left-brain likes to name everything and it felt right, when writing about David, to identify him by name. It doesn't feel appropriate to identify the Lady through left-brain processes, probably because her affinity is attuned to the right-brain, which doesn't need names and labels. When you come into contact with her, you *know* it, although most people would find it difficult to explain in words just exactly how they know. They just know... that's all.

Inner communication with a feminine intelligence is primarily in mental pictures, feelings and intuition. I can only describe *my* Lady as I personally perceive her, and to do that I must translate my perceptions into words, which gives a good illustration of the need to develop left-brain expression in conjunction with right-brain intuition. I needed David's help in learning how to recognise and express psychic awareness. It was necessary, in the process, for me to relearn a lot of things I had done as naturally as breathing when I was a child, but which social conditioning and mental programming had caused me to shut down, and even forget. There has been a lot of unlearning to be done as well, and the process is still continuing. It is also essential to discern the difference between feelings and emotions, and that can take quite a lot of practice!

Although there was a time when I would have been horrified by the heretical notion of a feminine divinity, I now find it quite logical. I have a biological mother as well as a father in the physical world, and there is no reason to assume that a similar principle cannot apply at the spiritual level as well. The creative source that gives life to all things contains a perfect balance of all the qualities of both masculine and feminine energy: if this divinity did not have a feminine element, there could be nothing feminine in the whole of creation. I see no reason why the Creator, having expressed this principle in female creatures at the physical level, should not give it equal expression in spiritual form also. I could never be accused of militant feminism, but I see no reason for believing that males have any franchise on divinity.

For me, the Lady personifies the highest, purest qualities and strengths of the feminine essence, as far as I am capable of understanding them. Because she operates in an inward-drawing affinity that can be difficult to define in words, I think the most effective way to relate something of her qualities is to tell of a few experiences in which she has had an active role to play. There are many to chose from, but a few should suffice. If I digress occasionally in order to provide background information, please bear with me.

If you are not familiar with the process known as psychic rescue, it has been compared with the Christian ritual of exorcism, although there are some significant differences. I have never seen a Christian exorcism, and from the accounts I have heard I don't think I'd want to, but from all reports, I gather that the process is centred on the belief that all cases of auric invasion or possession are caused by Satan's demons, who must be driven out with curses, hurled ferociously into the abyss and imprisoned there forever. Psychic rescue also works to remove the problem of possession, but it is more centred on the principle that where there is harm, there is hurt and where hurt exists, healing is needed. It incorporates the understanding that there are lost and hurting souls on both sides of 'the Veil'. Many human beings leave this life in a state of pain, fear and confusion, and can wander for ages in a nightmare wilderness, trapped between the physical world and the realms of healing, to which they need to go. These aren't demons or monsters, they are only people; lost, frightened, lonely and bewildered. The only difference between them and us is that we currently inhabit living physical bodies. Some of those lost souls are not even aware that they have 'died'. A lot of them don't know where they are and most of them are in a condition of misery.

Imagine if you were one of these souls, and you were suddenly confronted by a hostile figure in black, chanting curses and forcing you deeper and deeper into the pits of eternal pain and torment, which is how you'd see the priest if you were such a soul in the process of being exorcised. You'd think the priest himself was a demon from Hell, wouldn't you?

For those who would like a more in-depth account of the true principles of psychic rescue, I can highly recommend the books *Testimony of Light* and *The Wheel of Eternity*, both written by Helen Greaves. In brief, psychic or spiritual rescue aims to heal the hurt, wherever it may be. Lost and injured souls who blunder into mortal auras, get stuck there, and quite unknowingly cause problems for people in the physical world, do not need to be cursed with any more torment than they have already suffered. Certainly they need to be removed, but this doesn't mean they have to be hurt in the process. Psychic rescue recognises that the majority of us are or have been the victims of victims, therefore the aim is to heal at the physical *and* psychic levels, no matter who the victims are or what they have done.

Psychic rescue, as I have learned it, is a team effort, with some of the team workers being physical people and some of them spirits. Where there are lost and hurting souls in disembodied form, they are treated with the maximum care and gentleness as they are disentangled from the physical energy fields around our material world, to be shepherded into areas of rest and healing. Not all of these souls are enmeshed in the auras of physically incarnated people; some are simply trapped in the physical atmosphere, unable to set themselves free. Since the emphasis of psychic rescue *is* on rescue, the spirit helpers do not concentrate only on those who are caught up in other people's auras, but will go out in search of lost souls and gather them up, wherever they are.

There are a few genuine demons around, have no doubt, and a grim confrontation with one of those characters is no gentle encounter from my point of view, but I don't take it upon myself to exert the power needed to fend off one of those. When I have found myself confronted with that much malevolent power, I don't waste time testing my own strength: I yell for the Big Boys . . . fast! If that seems a rather casual way to describe the process, we could say that I directly invoke the Archangel Michael, but it amounts to the same thing. I have learned enough not to take reckless chances. I have a lot of Big Brothers to call on and, when I need their help, I call.

The rescue I want to relate did not involve a demon, however, nor was there any need to yell for a Big Brother. The soul brought to us for rescue in this case was an infant, it was the Mother of Mothers on whom I called for help, and it was the Lady who came in response.

I was living in Sydney at the time and hosting several meditation and psychic development groups at my home each week with the assistance of spirit entities who communicated with us through trance mediums. Sometimes Roland functioned as the medium, but he often preferred to occupy himself elsewhere and there were other mediums who worked with us. On this occasion, it was one of these other mediums, and we performed a series of rescues in one evening with me functioning as the control and the other group members helping to maintain the flow of healing energies.

Characteristically with psychic rescues, the guides told us little or nothing about the circumstances surrounding the injured spirits they brought to us, unless those circumstances required a departure from our routine procedure, as was the case on this occasion. The guide spoke first, informing us that the soul about to be brought to us was that of a baby who had died at the age of seven months. What kind of trauma could possibly have caused a soul so young to become earthbound was not explained, nor did we ask.

At first, I didn't know how to react. Our usual rescue procedure involved gently talking the lost spirits through, reassuring them of their safety, and encouraging them to look towards a light, where they would see someone they knew and trusted who would lead them Home. But a seven-month-old infant with no concept of language presents a different situation. How was I to help this one through? Before I could voice any questions, the guide withdrew and a hush fell in the room as we felt the atmosphere change. In my heart, I was calling, 'Mother of Mothers, help me! I don't know what to do'.

Within moments, I felt myself suffused with radiant mother-love and instinctively my hands came up, reaching out in the eternal gesture of motherhood, and I felt it: I *physically* felt the body

222

of a tiny infant being gently placed into my arms. If I had closed my eyes, I could readily have believed myself to be holding a physical baby, so distinct was the feeling. There was no mistaking the sensation.

'All right, little one, I've got you,' I thought as I cradled the tiny bundle in my arms. 'But what do I do with you now?'

Then, She was there. In my mind's eye I saw her, robed in white and radiating soft, clear, iridescent light as she smiled, arms outstretched towards me. Without thinking, I opened my embrace and held the baby up to her. She bent forward and for a moment I was immersed in the love of the Mother of all Mothers. Then my arms were empty, she was gone and I realised that I was crying. Nor was I alone in my emotional reaction; most of the people in the room were dabbing at moist eyes. My friend Beverley, sitting with face upturned and tears streaming down her face, opened her eyes and smiled rapturously at me. 'Oh, Dawn!' she sighed, 'it was as though I was seeing and feeling from inside you: that darling baby in your arms... and the Lady! Isn't she *beautiful*?'

In answer, I could only nod. My throat was much too full for words.

When people feel the Lady's touch, tears often flow. It's not difficult for me to understand why; I am well acquainted with that touch, and the feelings that come with it. It is as though all the tears I've ever held back, when my heart was breaking but I wouldn't let it show on the outside, suddenly burst forth and it's all right to cry. Sometimes I find myself crying like a baby and laughing with joy, both at the same time. This happens often at seminars, especially at the end, when people line up to give me a hug and thank me for reducing them to tears.

There are times, during the course of some seminars, when I feel the Lady merge her presence with mine, and her energy streaming through me and out to the audience, while I take a mental half-step backwards and let the words come as they will, directly from the heart, irrespective of anything I had formerly been planning to say. I have every reason to trust the Lady's wisdom, her insight and her sense of timing. At such gatherings, there are times when other entities make their presence felt to me also, but when it occurs I do not tell people that I am 'channelling a Higher Intelligence', for several reasons. To do that would cause people to focus on the phenomenon itself, distracting their attention from the message that the entity wishes to relay. It would also make me feel self-conscious which would alter the direction of energy-flow and disrupt the connection, thereby scrambling the message. In situations of this kind, personalities take a back seat as far as I am concerned: it is the *message* that is most important, not the messenger or the manner of delivery.

The Lady doesn't always cause tears to flow, of course; she simply touches the heart. If the heart is heavy with a burden of unshed tears, those tears will find release and the heart will be lightened. The Lady's presence brings comfort and healing, and if the release of tears is a necessary part of the healing process, tears will flow, but I have noticed that, when that happens, there are smiles, too, like the sun coming out through a summer shower. Essentially, the feminine presence is one of nurturing and loving care.

The concept of a feminine aspect of the Divinity may seem revolutionary, even heathen, to anyone raised with traditional Christian doctrines and ideals, but it is not really as alien as appearances may suggest. The fact that a body of people may lose sight of a certain reality over a period of time does not make that reality cease to exist; it simply means that people become ignorant of it.

It is widely believed that Jesus of Nazareth, the Christ, was a member of a Hebrew sect known as the Essenes. In 1936, a book entitled *The Gospel of Peace of Jesus Christ* was produced by Edmond Szekely, based on ancient texts held in the Vatican Library and translated by Szekely and Purcell Weaver from the original Aramaic. This was followed some forty years later by *The Gospel Of The Essenes*, in which further texts in Hebrew and Aramaic were translated, and both books have become classics for students of esoteric lore, particularly for people whose background is basically Christian, and who may previously have believed that the teachings of Christ allow no access to mysticism. The existence of a feminine stream of divine life is strongly advocated in the Essene gospels; like the Red Indians, the Essenes associated the Father with Heaven and the Mother with Earth, teaching that we receive our spiritual life essence from the Father and our physical being from the Mother, from whose essence our bodies are formed.

How many times, on hearing the commandment to 'Honour thy Father and thy Mother' have you heard someone ask how this commandment should be applied if the parents are cruel and abusive, having no honour within themselves? Such a question makes it difficult for quite a lot of people to accept the divine wisdom within the commandment, or to see any reason why we should be bound by it. In the Essene texts, however, there is more detail in the commandment. There, it is explained that we should honour our Mother Earth, who sustains our physical lives, and our Father in Heaven, who gives eternal life to us.

Both the Earth and the Heavens, it is explained, are given to us by 'the Law', which is defined as God.

That single commandment puts a different complexion on to the commandment as we have been accustomed to hearing it, doesn't it?

Nowhere in the Essene texts is it suggested that the Mother is inferior to or subject to the Father; rather they are given equal prominence, both being essential to our life and being. This is in perfect accord with the principle of worshipping 'in body and in spirit'. If Jesus was an Essene, then he would have accepted this belief in a divine Mother, as well as the Father in Heaven, but there is little evidence in orthodox Christian doctrine to give support to that likelihood. However, as Szekely comments, the scriptural writings on which the Christian Bible is based were not collected until several generations after the words were spoken by Jesus of Nazareth. He adds that although those words have been misunderstood, mistranslated and rewritten many times over, they have nevertheless profoundly influenced half of humanity, and all of Western civilisation. How much more powerful would these teachings have been, one wonders, had they come down to us in their original form?

Anti-female prejudice within the framework of orthodox Judaeo-Christian doctrine is well documented and still largely evident today, although thankfully we have evolved beyond the days when the mere fact of being a female placed a person in certain danger of ending her days under torture and, if she happened to live in Europe, being burned at the stake. In Christian philosophy, women are regarded as being the cause of man's downfall, ever since the first woman tempted man to eat of the forbidden fruit. One of these days, I keep promising myself, I am going to get myself a T-shirt emblazoned with the message 'Eve was framed!' As a statement, it is unorthodox and certainly unprovable, but I think it has a valid point to make. Besides, it appeals to my sense of humour!

Given the pre-conditioning received by most people in a Christian society, it is natural that there would be more inclination to accept the validity of teachings delivered by a masculine entity rather than a female, and it is probably for that reason that, so far, there has been a predominance of masculine guides. When it is necessary to open people's minds to a philosophy that often seems to be at variance with what they have been taught to believe, it might seem wiser not to ask those people to accept too many radical changes at once. When people reach a level at which they begin to perceive for themselves that the divinity manifests equally through male and female, then female spirit guides will be more readily accepted, and their teachings given as much credence as the words uttered by the masculine entities. It is not a matter of female guides being inferior or less reliable in any way, but simply a case of what we, the human recipients of those teachings, are prepared to accept, and from whom we will most readily accept it.

I don't think it is at all coincidental that, at a time when awareness and concern for the environment is on the increase, people are becoming more open to the concept of feminine aspects in divinity. One is inextricably linked with the other. Thousands of years ago, human survival was dependent on an intimate awareness and intuitive alignment with the tides and seasons of nature. This insight or awareness functioned through the faculties of the right-brain's non-verbal consciousness, and was expressed not so much in words as in symbols and images. The primary symbol, most revered of all, was that of the goddess. In archaeological sites around the world, images of the goddess have been brought forth, giving silent testimony to the goddess as the most ancient, venerated and adored of all deities. The ancient peoples who produced those images perceived the invisible forces of life beyond outward form as being very real, and they believed that co-operation with those forces was essential for maintaining a balance of life. Can we say that they were wrong simply because their symbolism was that of mythology rather than science?

The world as we know it today is very much focused into 'outer' consciousness, dominated by the perceptions of the left-brain. Our view of life is one of fixed objects separated from their surroundings, and is governed by a process of linear logic. Reality being dictated by outer form, God is considered as a power outside ourselves and nature as a kingdom to be mastered. All of these concepts have their origin in the left side of the brain which is associated, not by chance, with *masculine* characteristics. In a left-brain oriented world, God must be a male: it's axiomatic.

So-called 'goddess consciousness' is based on more intuitive modes of perception, seeing patterns, connections and relationships rather than isolated objects or events; attuned to the inner reality, the unseen forces that give form to the outer. Nature is seen as a swirl of living energies which is at one with us, and we at one with her. These are perceptions of the right-brain, which senses the divinity not as an outer force, but as a power arising from within.

The left-brain has its uses. There is value in the purposes to which it can be applied and there is no

228

doubt that its functions are essential for our well-being. The fact remains, however, that it is only half a brain.

The price we pay for centuries of left-brain domination is imbalance on a global scale, and the fruits of that imbalance are clearly seen in the world today. We are now realising that the price is too high, that if the balance is not redressed, we cannot continue to survive. Coinciding with this realisation, scientists are exploring the functions of the right-brain, recognising that it is not, as was once believed, subordinate and inferior to the left-brain, merely different in its mode of function, providing qualities and insights that the left hemisphere could never conceive. At the same time, there is the burgeoning New Age movement, with its emphasis on meditation, development of the intuitive faculties and inspirational processes, all of which are within the province of the right-brain, the feminine aspect of our consciousness. Are we to assume that all of this is happening as a result of random chance? It seems more likely to be a cycle in the evolution of consciousness, in which the feminine elements of the life-force that powers the universe are beginning to re-assert themselves.

Neo-pagans call this the re-awakening of the goddess; others might prefer a less controversial turn of phrase, but whatever we may choose to call it, the essential purpose for this re-emergence of the feminine influence appears to be that of balance, not confrontation or denial. A world dominated by right-brain processes would be different from the world we have now, but no less unbalanced. There are two great life-giving principles at work in the universe, and neither is superior to the other. There is a unity and a connection between these opposite forces, each of which is essential in the cycles of life, as day and night, birth and death, form and energy, masculine and feminine. The key is *balance*.

As we become more aware of the feminine principle and all that it represents in the world as we perceive it, so we become more open to an acceptance of that principle in its spiritual aspects. As this evolution in consciousness progresses, female guides will undoubtedly become as prominent as their masculine counterparts. There are female guides now, of course, but in general people tend to give more credence to the males, and the guides themselves work within those parameters. They will no doubt continue to do so for as long as we continue to impose those limitations on ourselves. When we witness female guides sharing equal prominence, we will know that we have made significant progress in the evolution of our own conscious processes. Bearing in mind the deeply ingrained prejudices that tend to be bred into us by our society, that represents an achievement of some considerable proportions.

The central message in the feminine principle is one of balance and harmony. We live in a world that has been dominated by male hierarchies for century after century, in which females, until quite recently, have at best been regarded as second-rate citizens, and, at worst, subjected to the vilest forms of torture and defilement, just because they are female. So far, these 'superior' male hierarchies have not done a very good job with their global housekeeping methods, to say the least, and it's hardly unfair to point out that they have had more than enough time to prove their worth. A few thousand years should be long enough for anyone! What are the fruits they have produced? Technological achievements notwithstanding, this world now teeters perilously close to the brink of disaster, either through being blown to pieces with weapons of destruction or choking to death in a relentless deluge of manmade poisons. Either we change, or we prepare for extinction; and change has to involve a correction of the balance.

The appeal of the feminine principle is by no means the exclusive province of members of the female sex. Increasingly, large numbers of men are welcoming the opportunity to cast aside stereotyped roles and express the caring, nurturing qualities in their own natures. There are plenty of men in this world who are no less strong for being gentle and sensitive. In fact, it takes a greater amount of moral courage for a person to break free from the mould of conditioning than to be carried along with the tide. A man with that kind of dynamism and fortitude can make his macho cousins look like gorillas.

I am not a member of any feminist movement and I have no particular religious or political affiliations. When I look at the world around me, I see nothing that is not equally as obvious to anyone else. I don't believe that a new religion or political system offers any real solutions either: what I have called the feminine principle is not a doctrine or a philosophy, but an experience arising from a potent inner force, not separate from the world, but in it. I don't think any of us is making it happen; I simply *see* it happening, and as it gathers strength I see the changes it is bringing. It doesn't come from any outside source; it's just there in the people I see in the world around me.

If the Lady symbolises anything for me, it is not a doctrine but the qualities that she exudes. Qualities of strength, peace, wisdom, compassion and insight. Those qualities exist in all of us and, somehow, the Lady's presence seems to call them forth. If that is her purpose, it can only be beneficial for all of us.

For me personally, the Lady is more than a

principle, and certainly much more than a symbolic experience. She is, as she has always been, one of my most special and loving friends ... and with a friend like the Lady, all sorts of wonders are possible.

CHAPTER ELEVEN

The Earth Religion and The Owl

Early in the year 1988, a few months after the publication of my second book, I received a letter from New Zealand that started radiating warmth and vibrant good humour before I even opened it. My interest was further aroused by the symbol stamped in ink on the face of the envelope; a five-pointed star within a circle, which was repeated in the letterhead design on the first page, along with the title 'Peoples Liberation Movement' and the motto 'If it harms none, do what you will', which latter told me that the writer had more than a passing acquaintance with the Earth Religion known as Wicca. I had by this time received letters from more than a few Wiccans and other neo-pagans, responding to a chapter in the newly published book in which I had referred to the error of confusing so-called witchcraft (the word which is derived from Wicca) with the anti-Christian cult of Satanism. Like the others, this letter brought words of appreciation from its writer, but there was an added dimension in my response; a warm, tingling sensation in the solar plexus, a flickering of goosebumps along my arms and a light in my heart that smiled and said 'Friend'.

This was the start of a continuing flow of

trans-Tasman correspondence that continues to this day. I would say that it was also the commencement of a very special friendship, except for my awareness, shared by my New Zealand friend, that this was no newly formed friendship but rather the renewing of a kinship that existed long before either of us entered our present life on Earth. My friend has the name Te Ruru; it comes from the Maori language and means 'The Owl'. Te Ruru is not, as one would think from his name, a member of the Maori race, but has a very deep respect for the native culture of his land, as indeed he has for the ancient cultures of any country, as shown by his use of native names in preference to those later bestowed by our colonising Anglo-Saxon forebears. His letters to me are always sent to 'Gondwana' although in consideration for harried postal workers and the possibility of his letters all disappearing into the depths of Africa, he adds the name Australia in brackets. In anyone else, such a custom might seem like an affectation, but from Te Ruru it is a genuine expression of respect.

I have received many letters from people who wish to know more about the philosophy of Wicca and I have repeatedly been asked to write in greater depth on the subject; however, to quote from the chapter on witchcraft and Satanism in *Edge of Reality*: I would not even attempt to explain all the richness and profound simplicity of the Old Religion; I leave that to those who have the wisdom of experience.

It is obvious from the number of enquiries I have received that there are many among my readers who wish me to publish more about the Earth Religion, but not being a member of that religion and not having studied its principles at length, I do not feel sufficiently informed to write about it in any real depth. I have several friends who are practising Wiccans but, in this case, intuition told me that Te Ruru was the one to whom I should turn for assistance. I explained to him my concept for this book and its title, and I asked him if he would consider writing about his spiritual faith for the benefit of the many readers who are seeking to know. He replied that it would be a pleasure and that he would write his contribution in the form of a letter, as though he were writing to me for the first time, so that he could introduce himself, through me, to you as a friend.

For quite a few months after that I heard nothing from Te Ruru, apart from a short note explaining that he was working on 'our little project' and finding it most rewarding, since it was helping him to clarify and expand his philosophy in his own consciousness. Then it arrived . . . all thirty-three closely spaced pages of it! I knew that any contribution from Te Ruru would be a generous one, but this was beyond my expectations, and it told me a number of things about my friend that I had not known before (and satisfied my curiosity about the Peoples Liberation Movement!). Although it makes a long chapter, Te Ruru's story is worth recounting in full, for it has a great deal of interest to put forward, not only to those readers specifically interested in Wicca, but to anyone who looks to the spirit for understanding. From here, Te Ruru will speak for himself.

To a dear sister in light, and her beautiful friend, in the great subcontinent Gondwana — greetings of Peace and Love! Blessed be!

My name is Te Ruru. I live in the South Pacific island country of Aotearoa; otherwise known as New Zealand. Late last year I completed a first reading of your three books:

Reaching for the Other Side, Edge of Reality *and* Lifting the Veil. *Now I wish to let you know that reading your trilogy was indeed a delightfully refreshing and educative experience. What I found particularly refreshing was your practical, ordered and common sense approach to spirituality, together with the whimsical sense of humour that flows through the pages of your books like a sparkling stream on its way to the great cosmic ocean of thought. For me, spiritual growth is the same as personal evolution; the very reason for living.*

To return a little of the love, light and wisdom you have shared through your books, I will tell you a little of my own journey. In so doing, I speak only for myself, as my experiences, my truth, my reality is unique to me. Some of my beliefs may be congruent with other people's beliefs. If so, blessed be! In fact, one of the most encouraging experiences I had reading your books was their confirmation of insights and scraps of wisdom that had already come my way. My life has turned out to be quite a chequered affair; but experience has proved to be a reliable teacher.

A few days before the spring equinox of 1946, as part of the postwar baby boom, I was born into a very traditional Roman Catholic family where discipline and religious observance were highly valued. As a child, so my parents have told me, I was a very docile and manageable little boy. Much of my time was spent dreaming, and I had a great imagination which provided the majority of my entertainment. I was very impressionable and gullible in the extreme. At the same time, like most children, life was approached with a sense of wonder. I never ceased to marvel at the beauties of nature and never thought to question what I was told by the adults who were responsible for parenting and educating me.

Into this fertile and absorbent mind flowed, unimpeded, decades of cultural conditioning and religious indoctrination. I remember having an abhorrence of violence, something that remains with me to this day. Even at the tender age of six I can remember going on a sit-down-on-the-floor strike, refusing to be punished by a nun who disciplined her little charges by belting them over the back of the legs with a leather strap. The world was for me both a fascinating and terrifying place. On the one hand there were so many wonderful things to discover and experience. Yet it also became, in terms of the Catholicism of the time, a 'vale of tears' in which I was to live out my life in fear of Hell, 'carrying my cross' under the all-seeing eye of an all-powerful God. This aspect of life was softened by an intensely pious devotion to Jesus, Mary and the saints. Evidently, as a small child I often dressed up to say a 'pretend mass'. My grandmother was heard to say on one occasion, 'One day he will be a priest'. Well, it very nearly happened.

In my life as a Catholic child, sin was never far from my mind. Somehow I was born into sin, spent a lot of time worrying about committing sin and trying to avoid the thousands of types of sins there seemed to be. My hope was, by some miracle of God's mercy, to avoid burning in the eternal fires of Hell. This was terribly guilt-inducing and contributed to a low *self-esteem. A lot of self-confidence was lost in those years. As a naturally open, imaginative and sensitive person, I retreated further and further into myself in the face of a hostile religious and cultural environment.*

As I look back, I can see how this must have been true for my parents as well. For example, my mother was an extremely religious and generous person, always helping others and sacrificing her own needs in the interests of her family and anyone else who seemed to need assistance. For a large part of her life she attended mass daily and said countless rosaries and other prayers during the day. In terms of Catholic piety, she was a living saint. Yet in conversation with her late in life, my mother confided that she thought of herself as a most unworthy person who at best might manage to scrape into purgatory: a state where, after death, souls are believed to spend a long time being painfully purged before they are allowed to see God face to face. For a wonderfully loving and beautiful woman to have such a low self-esteem was a travesty.

As a young boy I began to live a double life. To outward appearances I was a good, conforming and dutiful little son. But I also led a secretive inner life, revelling in my own thoughts and fancies while keeping very quiet about doing things I knew would not meet with approval from parents and teachers.

I enjoyed a secure home and parents who looked after their children with great care and vigilance, doing what they knew was best according to their own experience and understanding. My mother was a generous and

*loving woman who strove her utmost to bring
up her children as good Catholics, to do well
whatever occupation they chose in life. My
father was brought up during the great depression and worked hard at being a good provider
and ensuring that his children had the opportunities he never had. I salute their love and
dedication.*

*It was at a very naive and fresh-faced fifteen
that I left home to join an order of teaching
brothers known as the Irish Christian Brothers.
Three years were spent finishing college, after
which I crossed the Tasman to Sydney where I
was involved in the intense practice and study
of monastic spirituality together with teacher
training. These years served to intensify the
indoctrination of previous years, so much so
that anything I encountered which was outside
the conceptual framework of Catholicism I
considered wrong, heresy or of the devil. In
bypassing the normal years of adolescent development and personal growth, I became
severely inhibited. This was reinforced in subsequent years by the hopelessly archaic and
highly centralised authority structure within
the Brothers' communities and schools.*

*Religious life in those days was literally a 'no
man's land'. Particular friendships within the
order were frowned on because of an intense
fear of homosexuality. On the other hand,
friendships with people outside the order,
especially women, were actively discouraged
and, in fact, expressly forbidden. Women were
seen as the single biggest threat to one's vocation as a religious brother. Most of the men I
lived with were quite inadequate in their*

relationships with women. This chronic homophobia and misogyny of the order was in fact a reflection of the institutional church as a whole; a position that persists to this day.

Living a community life in that order was a contradiction. Although totally dedicated to their mission of Catholic education, the Brothers at that time paid little attention to the quality of their community life. As a result, I lived in a community yet experienced intense isolation and loneliness. So I sought friendship and affection outside the order with pupils I taught, their parents and through various extracurricular activities. It was then that I began to realise that the hours spent in prayer and meditation were only part of the picture. Holiness, or wholeness, had something to do with the quality of my personal relationships. I needed the freedom to make my own decisions, express my feelings openly, give to and receive from others love, affection, support and affirmation that I am a worthwhile and lovable person. Because of my naivety and lack of experience in personal relationships during this time, I made some blunders, especially in relationships with women. However, painful as they were at the time, they were important lessons for me. Despite the suffocating walls of religious life at that time, I was beginning to grow up. All my religious training had counselled me to 'be in the world but not of it'. Yet deep within me I loved life, felt an affinity with nature and yearned to be physically and emotionally close to others. I was to discover in years to come that one of the keys to spiritual advancement was the realisation that I was indeed 'of the world'.

About this time, I also became involved in the Catholic charismatic renewal. Initially this was a liberating experience for me. Here was a chance to give expression to my faith in an open, joyful and personal manner in close association with others. However, this movement also turned out to be dogmatic and overly judgemental.

My extracurricular activities brought me into increasing conflict with my religious superiors. Eventually, this became so irksome that I decided to leave the order and commence studies for the diocesan priesthood. It seemed to me that I would be able to serve the Catholic community more usefully as a pastor than as a teacher in a conservative order that was over-committed to perpetuating single-sex Catholic schools. This was an important transition for me as it served to ease me back into the real world. At age thirty, I was finally beginning to make my own decisions, manage money and experience life without the isolation and protection of monastic walls and rules. In short, I was taking my life in my own hands, and that seemed pretty exciting to me. Over the next few years I learned to take back responsibility for more and more of my life. It began to dawn on me that I had expected the answers to come from outside myself; I had handed over a lot of my own power to the so-called experts ... priests, doctors, politicians, teachers and technicians of every kind. Gradually, it became clear to me that I was responsible for my own destiny — I could be my own doctor, my own priest and, dare I say it, my own God. But more of that later.

It was at this point that for the first time in

my history I made a major life decision unaided by superiors or spiritual advisors. Before, important decisions that affected my life had either been made by other people or needed their approval. During one vacation I attended a mixed retreat held at the seminary. There I met a beautiful person who was to literally become the Joy of my life. Over the next twelve months, Joy and I formed a close friendship. We spent hours sharing our life experiences and developing a strong attraction for each other. So much so that I rather liked the idea of forming a partnership on a more permanent basis. Initially my mind was in quite a turmoil: would I continue the process of becoming a celibate priest, or would I walk with Joy down a different path? Marriage and priesthood are mutually exclusive in the Catholic Church. What was God's will for me in this regard? Friends, relations and parents were already looking to the day of ordination when I would be among them as their priest — the hope and pride of every Catholic family. I was held in high esteem by both students and faculty, partly because of my age and experience. I was doing well and showed great promise. But deep in my heart, which was bursting with love for Joy, I knew I would not survive the life of a sanitised celibate. I needed intimacy and affection in my life and here was a person with whom I could share so much. We had so much in common. The pain of parting would be devastating. Truly I had reached a major crossroads in my life and the big question was: 'Which way do I go?' How was I going to tell which was God's will for me?

The sun shone brilliantly on that balmy autumn afternoon in April 1978. Hardly a breath of air disturbed the browning leaves that clung to the tall oaks in the seminary grounds. As I returned from a neighbouring state school where, in conjunction with one of the Jesuit professors, I was piloting a religious education programme, light and shadow seemed to be in sharp contrast. Emerald lawns, colourful flower beds and the red brick of the seminary building took on a shimmering brilliance I had never experienced before. Suddenly a bright light flashed before my eyes, accompanied by a realisation that struck me with such force that I knew immediately what I was to do. I also sensed that Joy knew what my decision would be. After weeks of weighing up consequences, convoluted reasoning and left-brain analysis, it was as if the intuitive part of me broke through and made the decision crystal clear. At that moment I understood something of what St Paul must have felt on the road to Damascus. Fortunately though, I was not blinded — quite the opposite. Mounting the nearest motorbike, I sped across the city to ask Joy if she would walk with me. Twelve years later we are still hand in hand, and our relationship gets better every year.

Two insights grew out of that experience. Firstly, I could no longer tolerate living my life according to the beliefs and expectations of others. In the end, I was responsible for my own happiness; and what happiness and assurance I experienced having followed my heart. Secondly, I had been labouring under a delusion as to the nature of God's will. Until that day, God's will had been a guilt-inducing and controlling mechanism laid on me by other people. But here I realised that I was being confronted by two paths which both seemed pretty good choices. There was no question of right or wrong: both could equally be God's will. So all I had to do was follow my heart and conscience in this matter and whatever I decided became God's will for me. Wow! Little old me determining God's will! That was such a liberating insight. The logical extension of that, of course, was that if I could determine God's will, then I must be divine myself. But I wasn't quite ready for that yet.

Every action has its consequences; and there were plenty of those. Many of my now former friends cautioned me against such a move. People who had long admired and respected my judgement in spiritual matters suddenly saw me as some poor misled fellow who had let his heart run away with his head. The cruel part about their reactions was that Joy became cast in the role of temptress, which could not have been further from the truth. This judgemental attitude meant that Joy was seen as some sort of Jezebel. It seems to me that ever since Eve, wise and strong women have incurred anger and blame from bigots of every description.

Joy had been married before, so our private choice soon brought us into public conflict with the Catholic Church. This was a paradox to me. A church which held that the Eucharist was the fount and apex of Christian life, and that full pastoral care was to be extended to people in difficult circumstances, turned around and refused Joy and me access to the sacraments. We were deemed to be 'living in sin'.

It was the aspect of marrying a divorced person that my parents found really hard to deal with. Their dogmatic beliefs trapped them so tightly that when Joy and I finally decided to celebrate our marriage by staging a wedding, my parents refused to attend. In their eyes, what we were doing was outside the bounds of Catholicism and just too difficult to cope with; especially for my mother. I suspect that in some way my parents felt a sense of shame or failure at being unable to produce a good Catholic son.

My father in particular saw me as a failure because I never seemed to be able to stick with anything. I had failed to complete so many tasks as a child. I had failed to complete my tertiary education. I had failed to follow the vocation of a religious brother. I had failed to pursue priestly studies to ordination. And now, the ultimate failure: I had failed to remain faithful to the religion in which I had been raised from the moment of conception.

I can understand my father's disappointment. He worked very hard to ensure that his children never experienced the hardship, poverty and lack of opportunity that he had during his formative years. After very little education, he pulled himself up by his own bootstraps and, after World War II, secured a government job in which he applied himself with great determination for more than thirty-five years. He retired from a top position in his field. I admire and thank him for being such a

245

wonderful provider. However, life is not fixed; things are always changing. In fact, change can be a sign of growth: of life itself.

In a way I can understand the bewilderment and grief of my mother as well — the inevitable outcome of fixed beliefs. So entrenched were her beliefs that anything outside that belief system could not be valid. Only a month before she passed away, my mother said to me that she would die happy if she knew I had returned to the Catholic faith. That wish was never fulfilled.

It was shortly after joining forces with Joy that I decided to jump out of the 'Barque of Peter' and learn to swim for myself in the cosmic ocean of life. After an initial period of grief and anger, I began to see the institutional church from the vantage point of an outsider. What a blinkered existence I had lived for thirty years! My narrowness had kept me from benefiting from the many sources of inspiration and wisdom outside the boundaries of Catholicism and Christianity. Gradually, it dawned on me that beliefs are only beliefs. If they became inappropriate or inhibiting, then they could be discarded or changed. For me this was a really profound realisation because it meant that if I was to grow and become a more evolved person, then I would have to become open to change and explore many different paths. I have learned from this discovery that questions about the meaning of life and the nature of ultimate reality are best left open. Maximum growth and enlightenment seemed likely only if I was prepared to live with a high degree of uncertainty. That felt pretty risky at first; but it was also very exciting. Never again would I commit myself to any one tradition. To follow only one way would rob me of the experiences and lessons necessary for spiritual evolution. From that time, the only dogma I have held is 'not to have dogmas'. What had been viewed as failures now became simply changes in the direction of my life. What a positive and liberating experience I found that realisation to be.

I love mountains and have climbed a few over the years. They seem a marvellous symbol of the spiritual quest. A mountain can represent truth, beauty, goodness, even the Divine life. So when people, because of some need to label or pigeonhole me, ask what I am, I often reply that I am a 'voyager', one who draws on truth and wisdom from many different traditions. By way of explanation, I have composed a story I sometimes tell, depending on how much time people have to listen. It seems appropriate to share this story with you, Dawn.

TE MAUNGA (The Mountain)

There once was a young man who used to love standing and looking at a nearby mountain. This very beautiful mountain rose to a great height, its peak clad in a mantle of snow. Being an ancient volcano, its distant conical shape seemed almost perfectly symmetrical. Like a giant beacon, its solitary splendour dominated the surrounding terrain: a constant reference point for every traveller.

For many hours the young man would contemplate the beauty and changing moods of his mountain. Sometimes the peak would be shrouded in cloudy mystery, and it was certainly responsible for attracting much of the life-giving rain, which explained the lushness and fertility of surrounding lands. In the coolness of the early dawn, the white bluffs of this magnificent mountain would appear a pastel pink, while its western slopes glowed a fiery orange at sunset. Even slopes ascended with increasing steepness to apex in a razor sharp crater peak which stood in challenging defiance to wind, gravity, storm and climber alike — ever a peak impregnable. How the young man loved that mountain, yearning to somehow be united with its spirit.

For years he stood, his feet stuck in a mire of fixed views, and beheld his beloved mountain. Then one day in the lonely solitude of his meditation, it came to him that beautiful as his view of the mountain might be, if he were to risk travelling around a bit, he might be blessed with views of the mountain hitherto unseen. The energy and motivation of this realisation enabled the young man to free himself from the mire and prepare to journey around the mountain — and indeed it was a journey of discovery that would irrevocably change his life and beliefs.

There is no substitute for experience, and experience was to be the young man's teacher and constant travelling companion. After only a few hours of tramping, the young man was rewarded with fresh views. Each day brought spectacular mountain vistas such as he never imagined had existed. The wealth of lush bush and gigantic forest trees were a miracle to behold. This richness and variety of vegetation was matched only by the number of birds and *other animals the young man came to be familiar with as he journeyed.*

He began to draw his sustenance from the many different tree crops that he encountered. There seemed always to be adequate food and shelter as he travelled through this magic world of light and shadow. All the baggage and equipment he had thought necessary for survival began to seem cumbersome and heavy. Gradually the young man began to discard his baggage as he learned to live off the land and drink from the many different streams that flowed from the one source — the mountain.

Finally, the young man carried nothing but his own life as he followed the many paths that lay before him. Some of them turned out to be dead ends. Some of them proved too treacherous and others actually led away from the mountain. But always the mountain was there, guiding him, calling him, challenging him and forever changing its appearance as he travelled around its base, accompanied by the wind whispering through leaves and the birdsong that surrounded him. And there were always lessons to be learnt, whichever path he decided to follow.

The young man also met up with other travellers, apparently all engaged in their own journeys of discovery. Some were young and inexperienced, and with them he shared his knowledge. There were the ignorant and foolish whom he learned to avoid. But there were also wise and loving people whom he met. These he would accompany for a short time while he listened and learned from their accumulated wisdom.

The whole of life seemed to be in a state of

constant change and motion: cycles of seasons, of sun and moon, of life and death and growth. Eventually the young man completed his journey around the mountain — the first of many. Now he had a more comprehensive view of the mountain in its totality. It was then that he realised that his greatest challenge still lay ahead: to climb the mountain.

Once again there seemed to be a number of paths the young man could follow, but all held their own particular challenges and obstacles. With courage and determination the young man began his ascent, discovering the invigorating spray of many waterfalls and vividly coloured subalpine plants, the like of which he had not observed at lower altitudes. But even their freshness and vitality faded in comparison with the vision he was to behold on arriving at the summit.

There, in a rarefied alpine atmosphere where only eagles dared to fly, the young man stood atop the crater pinnacle, thousands of metres above sea level, and looked down on his sacred mountain. At one glance he could almost behold its entirety. Yet he knew there was so much that lay waiting to be explored. The young man looked out over the land with its rain forests, pasture lands, towns, rivers and, in the distance, more mountains. Surging up within him he felt a great love for Papatuanuku, the Earth Mother. This was indeed his Turangawaewae, his home — the land on which he stood. The young man felt connected with all beings and all things. He was not only in the world: he was of it. To the west, the young man looked out on the sun-sparkled

*mantle of a deep blue ocean: the womb of the
Earth Mother from which all beings proceed.
Above him, like a divine canopy, stretched
Ranganui te Matua, the Sky Father, inviting
the young man to reach out and grasp the stars,
and discover the intensity and power of his
own sun — himself. The only clouds visible
were long feathered tendrils of cirrus etched
against the brilliant azure dome of a perfect
summer sky. For one awesome moment, the
young man stood in the realisation that in his
humanity he was the meeting place and channel for both the energies of nature and the
forces of the cosmos. He heard his own inner
voice resound with utter conviction: 'I am
divine in the midst of divinity!'*

*As the young man returned to the lowlands
with joy in his heart and laughter in his step,
he realised that his mountaintop experience
had shifted his perception: he now viewed the
world through different eyes. Everything
seemed to be connected; everything shared in
the same Divine Life Force. Everything had its
own awareness and its own intrinsic value.
There was a oneness and unity about existence.
Life was sacred. Life was ever-changing. And
life was fun.*

*There would be other mountaintop expe-
riences and each would change his perception.
No longer did the young man strive to change
the world, but rather to change his perception
of the world, which was, after all, of his own
making. Never again would he allow his feet to
become stuck in the mire of fixed views, confin-
ing himself to only one view of the mountain.
As he listened to the song of the four corners,*

allowing it to blow away the inhibitions and limits he had placed upon himself, the young man realised that if, in his relentless pursuit of spiritual advancement and divine self-discovery he was going to grasp new opportunities, then he must let go of some things so that his hands were indeed free to grasp the new opportunities as they came.

In many ways, Dawn, that young man is myself. Having extracted myself from the mire of fixed beliefs, I, too, began a journey of discovery by exposing myself to different ideas and beliefs. I read avidly about all sorts of people, beliefs, cultures and religious traditions. It became clear to me that I had been living a blinkered existence: a half life. There was a wealth of wisdom to be found just for the looking. In every tradition there were shades of truth, glimmers of wisdom, maps for living and signposts indicating interesting and useful paths to explore. I began to realise there is no right or wrong way. Life is but a continuum of experience with lessons to be learned at every turn.

If this is so, then maybe it takes more than a single lifetime to experience everything there is to learn. It does not seem logical to think that one can reach perfection of realisation in one short lifetime on the physical plane. Hence I have come to believe in reincarnation; a belief that, in one form or another, pervades most religious traditions. Even the Catholic doctrine of eternal life is to me a corruption of the reincarnation theme. Reincarnation was part of the Christian belief for the first few centuries.

Now it seems to me that rather than living my life out and hoping for eternal life after physical death, I am enjoying eternal life right now. Personal and spiritual evolution becomes something like an ascending spiral along which I pass through many deaths and resurrections. As I look around the world of nature this seems to be confirmed. Why hadn't I noticed before that life is not linear — things do not develop in straight lines but in cycles? There is always death and rebirth, light and shadow and seasons. Everything is in a constant state of change. Life goes on and life always begins again.

Nature has become for me a great source of wisdom. Observation of the cycles of sun, moon, stars, winds, tides, seasons and even my own body have become significant rhythms that seem to be part of a great cosmic symphony of which I am an integral part. The extent to which I am attuned to this universal music is, I believe, directly related to the degree of harmony within myself. No wonder I am energised by bush walks, showers under waterfalls, climbing mountains and bathing in the ocean.

At about this time I was also going through a process I call 'conscience-isation'; that is, becoming acutely aware of social justice issues both globally and locally. Racism, sexism, poverty, militarism, oppression and injustice in any form became burning issues for me. As a child I had always identified with the underdog. This was heightened and led to my involvement in many social action and protest groups. I became an activist and known dissident. In much of my thinking at the time, I was influenced by the dialectical approach when analysing social systems. I had studied Marxist and other socialist philosophies, and was quite active in the union movement.

However, by the mid-1980s I began to experience some degree of burnout. Fighting the powers of oppression was quite an exhausting business. They always seemed to have formidable weapons and limitless resources to quash resistance and small popular movements. To win against such odds would require a mass movement of almost universal solidarity. In Aotearoa, we are years away from that point. It was the study and experience of various spiritual traditions that allowed me to see a different path.

One can overcome, dispel and explore the darkness by simply shining more brightly. So maybe if I was a more light-filled person, more darkness would be dispelled and more lives touched than if I was to go on angrily protesting injustice. I still think resisting injustice and oppression is necessary — lead on Greenpeace! But rather than expend my energy fighting the establishment, why not work to develop new structures, processes that will lead to a society founded on love, equality and justice? Progressively boycott all those things which oppress and disadvantage people and their environment: then the old order will eventually become obsolete and crumble. I think you're right, Dawn, when you say that, in the spiritual life, like attracts like. So rather than rousing speeches, it may be more convincing to develop my own light-filled life and share my truth with those who are attracted and want also to build a better world without dogmas, and are open to wisdom from whatever source. Onesidedness in any endeavour is bound to produce an unhealthy situation, whether that be in my diet or in my religious beliefs. A onesided religious upbringing and early adult life has left me convinced of that. Dogmatism, especially in the area of religious beliefs, produces only bigots and fanatics. This seems to be true whether it be Muslim fundamentalism, Christian bigotry or scientific dogmatism. I find it ironic that the very people who condemn idolatry, themselves treat the words of the Bible as the absolute and unalterable revelation of God, believing they possess the actual words of God in black and white. This approach, rather than being religious faith, is the adoption of fixed beliefs as if they were mathematical certainties: a sure recipe for dogmatism, bigotry and minds closed to alternatives.

This approach to spirituality has given the word 'religion' a bad name. In chapter seven of Edge of Reality, you use the subtitle 'Spirituality or Religion?' and make some interesting comments about the distinction. For many years I avoided using the word 'religion', preferring to talk of 'spirituality'. By now I think the word 'religion' — as with so many words that have been corrupted, like witch, hag, power, pagan, to mention a few — needs to be reclaimed. 'Religion' comes from a Latin word 'religare', meaning 'to connect'. Therefore religion to me is the knowledge and practice of ways of drawing on all the sources of energy, *harmony and knowledge in the universe: and they are infinite, transcending any particular tradition or set of beliefs. The essence of true religion is ageless and universal. To seek the safety of dogmas, remaining trapped within empty rituals and fixed beliefs, would be to invite sterility of mind. Rather than being strangled by dry and rigid theological rules and regulations, true religion is ever new, ever changing, ever liberating and always fun. I have the inalienable right to follow my own spiritual path. That is why I now resist any attempts to evangelise me or convert me to any one tradition or bring me 'back into the fold'. That is also why in this letter I wish only to speak for myself, as my truth is unique to me — although I am always overjoyed to find others who share my beliefs.*

In fact, it is my experience that prayer, meditation, reflection and actions for social justice, peace or conservation are most effective when done collectively. The effect of many minds tuned to the same inspiration or the same purpose is indeed a powerful force for change. Our planet has a mind of its own and I am like an individual brain cell which, united with others in thought and purpose, can achieve astounding results. One dismissive argument often quoted at activists is that there have always been the poor and there will always be poverty: or there have always been wars and there always will be wars. Besides being an erroneous statement, that is one of the reasons there is war and poverty: people believe war and poverty are part of life. I directly influence events on this planet by the way I think.

Similarly, I am limited only by my own beliefs. Sufficient numbers of people really believing and visualising peace and plenty would directly help to bring that state into existence.

I believe thoughts have an energy of their own and can be used, especially by minds in union, to effect great good. This is a very old belief: the ancient order of Essenes, for example, held that thought was both a cosmic and a cerebral function. They believed in a cosmic ocean of thought pervading all space, containing all thought which is the highest and most powerful of all the cosmic energies, never perishing, never lost. The Essenes believed that by tuning in to all positive thought currents in the universe and the thoughts of all great thinkers of the past, they could develop their ability to create powerful and harmonious thought currents, and attain intuitive knowledge and wisdom. They had a great ability to send and receive powerful thought currents.

Well, I certainly believe in the power of positive thinking and visualisation. This is most effectively done in communion with others. I am essentially a social being and called to work out my destiny and that of the planet in community. I am still learning to think positively about myself and the world and stop limiting myself. One of the effects of living a one-sided existence in my early life was spiritual and emotional isolation. I have heard it said that isolation is the darkroom in which we develop our negatives.

Learning to live in relationship has taught me so much. This is particularly true of my relationship with Joy. Until I left the seminary, *my commitment was to an organisation and its work in the field of Catholic education. Intimacy and long-term relationships were not encouraged. Living with another person and exploring the richness of friendship, intimacy, sexuality, parenthood and economic survival has broadened my outlook and stimulated personal growth to an extraordinary degree. Joy is not only lover and best friend to me, but challenger and educator as well.*

Being married to a feminist has exposed, painfully at times, my own attitudes to women. In my head, equality was important. When Joy and I decided to stage a wedding celebration, I changed my name to hers in opposition to the male-dominated traditions of name-taking in marriage. While this was a genuine gesture, it was still only a cosmetic change. Being born into a white male system and enjoying its privileges as a male, I discovered that at an unconscious level I carried many of the assumptions and sexist attitudes of that system. In subsequent years Joy has very effectively challenged and exposed those attitudes. I was also exposed to all the classic and modern works of feminist thinkers. There I discovered a rich world of spirituality, art, literature, history, music and wisdom about which I was most abysmally ignorant. The wisdom-centred and matrifocal goddess religions that cherished life, respected the Earth Mother and tried to develop communities of equality where intuition was valued, gave me a fresh view of the world. It was a view that contrasted starkly with the highly competitive, hierarchical, exploitative and male-dominated cultures that have controlled civilisation for the last few millennia, producing such one-sided societies that we are now struggling to draw back from the brink of self-destruction.

Joy also successfully challenged my emotional dependence on women. Because my personal life in the Christian Brothers was so sterile, I turned to people outside the order. My closest friends and confidantes were women; usually mothers of boys I taught or women in religious orders. As Joy did not want to carry the burden of my emotional dependence, she began to push me gently in other directions. Thus I became involved in a men's group and took an active part in the wider men's movement. I discovered that despite their privileged position in a patriarchal society, men suffer terribly from living and competing in a system which has relied almost exclusively on left-brain development. Your explanation of the split brain principle in Lifting the Veil *is most instructive, Dawn.*

I discovered that in a couple-centred society, men display intense homophobia as well. Men do not seem to share their emotional and spiritual lives with other men and are afraid of intimacy. Yet I also discovered that there are hosts of beautiful men who are discovering their own softness, vulnerability, capacity to share at a feeling level and to operate intuitively. I have been helped to understand my own father and am beginning to relate to him in a more constructive way. I have developed the courage to view things from a feminist perspective and challenge other men and the destructive systems in which they are trapped and which they help to perpetuate.

Living with Joy has also taught me about

parenting. Previously, my family, so to speak, had consisted of classes of forty eleven- and twelve-year-old boys whom I saw for a few hours during the day and on the sports field at weekends. When I teamed up with Joy, her sons Robbie and Byron were five and eight years old. I commenced a full-time relationship with these children but, like most new parents, had little preparation. The complexities of being the step-parent was something I had never considered. Well, Robbie and Byron coped very well with me and taught me heaps about myself and all the old tapes I was carrying from my own childhood and teaching days. Twelve years down the track I am pleased to say that we have developed a very high regard, respect and love for each other; but there were some painful lessons for me along the way. Robbie and Byron's education was of particular interest to me. Dissatisfaction with the local Catholic school led to the boys attending a Rudolph Steiner school for a number of years. Their approach to education of the whole person, especially through artistic expression, was the best alternative available. All your criticisms of the education system apply in this country as well. Many of your stories I could almost duplicate with regard to Robbie and Byron. Both returned to the state system in high school years. Both suffered from lack of motivation and encouragement at their schools. Education in such schools is doomed to onesidedness as it does not recognise the spiritual dimension of human life.

Over the last decade, I have benefited immensely from the knowledge of the goddess religions and feminist perspectives of history and prehistory that Joy has shared with me. Together with a comprehensive study of other religious traditions, it has helped me to realise the necessity of being open-minded in my approach to spiritual development. In Lifting the Veil, you advocate an eclectic approach. This has been so for me. I have integrated wisdom and practices from many different sources as they seem appropriate. I believe all wisdom, knowledge and truth tend to converge; so eventually we will all end up walking in the same direction. But no one individual's spiritual journey can be duplicated — what an amazing variety there is in the diversity: like spiritual fingerprints.

My particular journey has led me to discover that there are two major paths that are influencing the world today, one of which seems to be a dead end. One tradition tends to view things as unconnected. It manifests in religious sects and organisations with dogmas and fixed beliefs. Groups in this tradition tend to be rigid and patriarchal, that is, dominated by male hierarchies where power, wealth and decision-making tend to concentrate into fewer and fewer hands. This tradition works on a 'power over' basis and robs its adherents of the chance to make important decisions about their own lives. In its Christian form, the doctrine of original sin and fall-redemption theology makes it very sin-centred and focused on death. Its preoccupation with personal salvation produces a high degree of estrangement from the cosmos and nature. Its economic systems are exploitative, wasteful of resources and

261

*damaging to the environment. So estranged is
this way of perceiving reality that it can tolerate war, pursue technologies that are killing
the planet, allow mass poverty in a world of
plenty, keep people powerless and murder,
persecute or silence those who dare to be
different.*

*The second path is one based on power from
within. It tends to affirm and empower people,
encouraging them to take their lives in their
own hands. Religions in this tradition view all
beings as alive, dynamic, connected, interact-
ing, interdependent and enlivened with an
energy which is the Divine Life Force. Communities following this tradition are nonviolent and matrifocal; that is, life-giving,
nurturing and protective. The focus is usually
on the promotion, protection and celebration
of life at every opportunity. This spiritual path
encourages the development of communities
of equality in which individuals have a high
degree of responsibility.*

*Matrifocal cultures, pro-feminist groups,
environmental and peace movements, many
truly pagan religions, and the creation spirituality tradition within Christendom all tend to
develop spiritualities that follow the second
path referred to above. Communities that follow this path have their roots in very ancient
traditions which historically precede those
groupings which follow the dogmatic and patriarchal path. One of the tragedies of history in
the last few millennia is that many genuinely
liberating traditions have been subverted, corrupted, dogmatised, persecuted or destroyed by
subsequent cultures and religions. Those that*

have survived or resurfaced are often officially suppressed, regarded with suspicion or become the butt of intense prejudice. In my own country, for example, one of the most powerful spiritual traditions of Maori is still officially outlawed. This was largely the result of the ignorance and bigotry of early Christian missionaries. The first missionaries to arrive in Aotearoa had a marvellous opportunity to become open to a spirituality that was ancient and closely allied with nature. Instead they denied, repressed and outlawed it in their efforts to impose Christianity. This religious imperialism and spiritual arrogance was reflected in the colonial conquest of Maori and the merciless land acquisitions that followed. Therein lies the weakness of a dualistic way of thinking; once one considers oneself in the right, the other ways of thinking must be wrong. Ironically, obscured by centuries of dogma, deception, empty ritual and institutionalised religion, there often lie the seeds of many truly liberating ideas and beliefs. They are there for those with the eyes to see. This spiritual insight is the ability to perceive hidden wisdom.

One of the nature traditions I have rediscovered and which at present I am most aligned with is the religion of witches. I was delighted, Dawn, to read in chapter sixteen of Edge of Reality your very positive appraisal of this most wise and valuable tradition. As you pointed out, 'witch' is a word corrupted beyond recognition. This word has been absorbed into our language, folklore and modern usage with a thoroughly pejorative

263

meaning. It has become a term of scorn, prejudice and hostility. Your own early conditioning described in your book would be typical of most: it was so for me. This word's corruption is also part of the patriarchal conspiracy against women; as with the words 'hag' and 'crone'. It is a matter of history that the Catholic Church, for example, applied the word 'witch' to any woman who in word or practice criticised church policies, and proceeded to legally murder them, despite their innocence. The witch hunts promoted and authorised by the church and civic authorities resulted in the extermination of millions of women and a few men, simply because they were deemed to be witches. Yet I have found the Wiccan tradition to be an authentic religion and a liberating influence in my life.

'Wisdom' and 'wit' are words derived from the same root. A witch is a practitioner of wisdom; one who has an intimate knowledge of nature, the application of energy, and who knows and practises ways of drawing on all the sources of energy, harmony and knowledge in the universe to do good. 'Witch' is not gender specific. I was initiated into the 'craft of the wise' about ten years ago. Many hesitate to use the word 'witch' because of people's reactions. However, I do not hesitate to use the term of myself because that is a way of reclaiming the word. Witchcraft is diametrically opposed to the systems that are oppressing and impoverishing people, and ruining the planet.

In the Wiccan community one will find herbalists, musicians, gardeners, healers, arboriculturists, peace workers, teachers, poets, environmentalists, counsellors, artists and helpers of all kinds. Witchcraft excludes black magic and Satanism. Where there is any recognisable organisation, witches gather in small, independent, self-determining groups referred to as covens or circles. These groups do not belong to any institutionalised organisation and have no hierarchical structure. Covens strive to be communities of equality where differences are in function or skills utilised rather than differences in rank, dignity or value. Most witches identify with the Divine as a Mother Energy that is continually giving birth to creation, but recognise that ultimately the Divine is androgynous, encompassing God and Goddess in its fullest expression. The Wiccan tradition identifies closely with nature and uses nature's symbols in ritual and practice.

Witches strive to develop a hurtless and helpful way of living. Their philosophy is totally nonviolent, striving to avoid harming self, others or the environment. All life is considered sacred; all things and all beings — not just human life. The central ethic of witches is expressed in this couplet:

Eight words the witches creed fulfil:
If it harms none, do what you will.

It was this philosophy of nonviolence that held great attraction for me. Nonviolence is not just a philosophy, of course; it is a way of life in which I strive not to do violence to myself, to others or to the world around me. Some years ago I was looking around for a sport or form of exercise that was not so aggressive or competitive. I eventually took up the ancient Chinese

*martial art known as Tai Chi Chuan. One of
the central tenets of Tai Chi is that one never
goes against the force: one always goes with it.
Here, it seemed, was a form of exercise and self-
defence that was based on nonviolent principles. Although I use this form of exercise,
which is like a meditation in movement, for
health and relaxation, in its combative or self-
defence application the Tai Chi exponent uses
an attacker's misuse of force to unbalance and
deflect trouble. Rather than resisting, one
simply goes with the flow, manipulating force
already being used to do all the work. This
principle of Tai Chi seemed to me to operate in
all areas of life. For example, when others
express anger or hostility towards me, I have
found it far more useful and productive not to
get defensive and fight back verbally, but to
employ a communication skill known as active
listening where one tunes in to and explores
the feelings of the other person. Life and nature
have their own flow, and I am beginning to
discover that it is far healthier to go with the
flow than try to resist it. In this regard I found
one of the psychic rescues recounted in your
books significant. You were dealing with a
particularly troubled earthbound spirit.
Rather than resist the power of this individual,
you simply allowed yourself to absorb it and let
it flow on to the appropriate place with the
desired result both for your client and the lost
spirit.*

*Rituals and gatherings of the Wiccan tradi-
tion are aligned with cycles of nature: cycles of
earth, sun, moon, stars and one's own body.
There are eight major festivals during the year*

called sabbats. These are linked to the sacred wheel of the seasons, marked by winter and summer solstices, spring and autumn equinoxes, and the midpoints between these four. Many earth religions have similar cycles, such as North American Indian medicine wheels. Ironically the church, in an attempt to christianise pagan festivals, has ended up with major feasts at about the same time. However, all sabbats are seasonal feasts, and both the church and the commercial world have lost their links with nature. This is particularly so here in the Southern Hemisphere where there has been a total failure to adapt feasts to the southern seasons. For example, the festival of Samhain, the witches' New Year: this sabbat is observed on winter's eve when the themes of darkness and death are explored. Loved ones who have passed over are remembered or communicated with, and the theme of the cycle of death followed by new life is central. As with all the sabbats, it is particularly at Samhain that witches are reminded through ritual and celebration that our lives and all life, like the seasons of the year, are constantly moving and changing. By observing, meditating on and celebrating these changes, witches seek to draw closer to the natural tides of all life and move forward more effectively and easily in their own lives. Death is acknowledged and life is reaffirmed. Winter's eve is a most appropriate time to hold a celebration. Most people know this festival as Halloween, celebrated on 31 October. While this is appropriate in the Northern Hemisphere, the commercial world in the south continues to push Halloween paraphernalia in October, and the church 'down under' continues to celebrate All Souls Day at about the same time.

Perhaps an example of a particular ritual might help to explain the Wiccan modus operandi for celebrating sabbats. A recent sabbat on the Wiccan calendar was that of Mabon, the autumn equinox which this year (1990) was 21 March. This festival is sacred to Kore, Goddess of Change, female spirit of the universe and heart of the world. At this time of the year, fruits are ripe and the harvest is ready. Leaves of deciduous trees are changing colour and falling in ever-increasing numbers. On this particular date, the sun is directly over the equator so that day and night are of equal length. The Sun King is about to become Lord of the Shadows as we follow him into shorter days and longer nights. The sun's intensity is weakening, equinoctial winds are stirring and nature has taken up her paintbrush to daub many of her children in a glorious kaleidoscope of golds and reds and browns and yellows. Mabon is the witches' thanksgiving day. Those wishing to celebrate this sabbat would construct a ritual woven around themes that are appropriate to this time of the year. A ritual may incorporate one or a number of these themes.

The themes of the equinox itself might be used. At this moment, when light and dark are equal, members of a Wiccan circle may choose to focus on balance and poise, or the lack of it, in their lives. As darkness is about to increase from now to midwinter, it may be time to acknowledge the darkness and embrace it both *literally and figuratively. Women in a group may plan a public march to reclaim the night. The great wheel of the seasons is turning and that may be the focus of this celebration. The universal law of change reminds us that things are changing all the time; a new cycle is about to begin. What needs to be changed in my life? How open to the changes needed am I? Or again, the harvest may be the theme of a ritual. A group may focus on the fruit that turns to seed, encased in its hard protective shell ready for the time of winter gestation and realising that autumn's grain will be spring's seed. So it may be time for the group or individual to let go and plough the fruits of experience back into the earth. Here the sickle-shaped moon is an appropriate harvest symbol. Yet again, this occasion may be reason for a celebration of fire, one of the four elements composing the physical world we live in. As the sun's fire weakens, so the fire of the hearth comes into its own. A ritual built around the lighting of the first fire for the season or initiation of a newly installed log burner would be most appropriate. Fire destroys; but it also cleanses. Fire illuminates the darkness, warms our bodies and heats the soup. Fire in Wicca is also the symbol that represents the spiritual element in ourselves. Does the fire of the spirit energise my being or is the flame burning low? Or again, a group may choose to develop a healing and affirming ritual for someone who has reached the autumn of her/his lifetime. The mother becomes the crone and her wisdom is very impressive. Rituals to honour old and wise people, especially grandparents and their life* experiences are appropriate at this time. Perhaps it is time to tune in to the song of the four corners, the wind, and allow myself to be shaken; to shed the dead leaves of negative beliefs or inappropriate relationships. What needs to be done to turn the fruits of experience into learning? This is the time when Gaia, the Great Earth Mother, is taking a giant in-breath, ready for the gestation and hibernation of winter. Now is a time of introspection and self-analysis before moving on: life always begins again.

Having chosen a theme and prepared for the ritual by cleansing themselves and possibly fasting, Wiccan friends gather in a special place. Rituals in the Wiccan tradition are usually celebrated in circles or spirals, reflecting the circle of the universe, womb of the Mother Goddess, or the wheel of the cosmos anchored by the four corners. Witches protect themselves, making a safe place physically and psychically. Symbols such as seasonal fruits, late vegetables, flowers, leaves, grains, seeds, candles, incense, fire, earth, water and scales may adorn an altar or decorate the place of celebration. Chants, dances, invocations, meditations, sharing, absent healing, prophetic actions and the like may be part of a ritual. Energy is raised and spells for good may be cast. And always there is much laughter and feasting as well. Each Wiccan ritual is unique, flexible, active, participatory, and tailored to the needs of the group and the energy of the season.

The eight sabbats are wonderful celebrations for the renewal of life. Like the candle which burns during a ritual, we all have in common the Flame of Life which burns eternally within us. I have learned from these types of celebrations that energy can be used to effect good in the world, and in myself. What is casting spells but sending out positive thought forms to help and heal? I have learned how to put my own psychic protection in place; to relate to planet Earth and the nature forces in a personalised way; to use herbs, stones and crystals for healing; to work with my subconscious as if it were a personal friend — another inner self. The Wiccan tradition has also helped me to overcome prejudices about some of the ancient tools of guidance and self-analysis, such as the I Ching, tarot, astrology and runes.

The medium in which I 'live and move and have my being' seems to be energy. Every witch knows that energy is neither good nor bad, and whatever is sent out returns threefold. There is more to life than meets the eye, and the converging paths of science and the wisdom of the ages is highlighting the truth that I am actually a multidimensional energy field intrinsically connected to all other energy forms. By my own thought energy I shape my reality. The healthier and more positive that reality, the more my awareness is enhanced. So in the end there is not much separating the witch working her/his magic and the quantum physicist exploring the infinite realms of existence: I am but a beautiful swirl of energy spiralling my way along an ever-ascending evolutionary path of self-determination, limited only by my own beliefs. The sky is not the limit.

As a child my religious teachers, through the

repetitious and monotonous use of the Cate-chism, hammered into me the belief that 'I am made in the image and likeness of God'. But nobody seemed to really believe it, because there was so much stuff about being guilty sinners needing redemption from original sin into which we were supposed to have been born. It seems ironic that, having become a practising pagan, the truth of that Catechism answer has become clear to me. If it is true that I am made in the image and likeness of God, and that God is pure spirit, then I am essentially a spiritual being, divine in my own right. I may be here on Earth at the moment to explore the physical dimension and learn many lessons, but I am imbued with the same Life Force as the Source of all Life, and will return to one-ness with that Source. In saying that, I am not wishing to deny or undervalue the physical or my body. One of the lessons I have learnt is that being humble (Humus) means being close to the earth and delighting in sensuousness and in my sexuality. Everything is empowered by the same divine energy. I am divine in the midst of divinity: I am a spark of divine energy spiralling along the path of spiritual evolution with a Goddess-given task to discover my own creative potential to produce good and love in the universe — to be a true son of the Great Cosmic Mother.

One of the most profound effects of develop-ing a Wiccan spirituality has been the height-ened sense of the Divine as Mother. I believe that personkind's first awareness of their spirit-ual origins was a sense of the Source of all Life as Mother. The work of creation, the sustaining and nurturing of all life and the cycles of nature are very easily understood in terms of a mother energy: the continual giving birth to new life. That is why for the Wiccan tradition and, for me personally, the Divine is often thought of as the Great Mother Goddess. The logical extension of this belief is that if all life is born of the same mother, then all life is sacred and all forms of life are connected: all life has a oneness and unity which makes the universe maternally beneficent and all creation intrinsically good. Furthermore, I am a true son of the Goddess and divine in my own right. But with the inestimable birthright comes the awesome responsibility of being a co-creator with the Goddess and exercising my own motherhood; giving birth to my creative energies and preserving and nurturing all other forms of life. No longer can I think of myself as separate from nature and from other people.

Increasingly, archaeological finds are pointing to the fact that personkind's earliest religions were goddess religions. Archeosophy, the science of reconstructing the meanings of ancient world concepts with scientific accuracy and philosophical intuition from archaeological finds, also points to goddess religions being religions which had a holistic and unified world view. In fact, the further back the experts go chronologically, the fewer are the contradictions between different schools of thought. What is the cosmos but the womb of the Great Cosmic Mother? What is the universe but the welcoming arms of the Divine Mother encircling all in their ever-enveloping, embracing, inclusive and expansive way? What is nature

*but the fruits of the divine maternal creativity?
Who are other people but my dear sisters and
brothers called to exercise their own divine
creativity and motherhood?*

*Somewhere in the thrust of patriarchy
becoming the dominant cultural force in modern civilisation, the implications of God's
motherhood have been forgotten, ignored or
suppressed. Christians of the creation spirituality tradition maintain that the fear of motherhood, the suspicion of creativity and the
displeasure with birthing processes are characteristic of patriarchal culture. They also maintain that the abandonment of hierarchical
structures and return to the motherly side of
God would be a return to compassion and
wisdom as a way of life. This spirituality is
helping me to stop limiting myself and let go
of my presumptions about the need for security
and boundaries. I am learning to be more
creative, which involves the power to make
connections with the cosmos; with all beings
and all things. I can see now that true religion
empowers me to make those connections; to
become whole again. This brings me back to
the radical meaning of the word religion — 'to
connect'.*

*To live without creativity; without true reli-
gion and compassion would be to allow my
human energy to be subverted back to the
destructive and exploitative expressions so evident around the planet today. To allow this is
to accept racism, sexism, ageism, militarism,
capitalism, imperialistic socialism, poverty
and injustice. It would be to deny my divine
origins and live in a world where I see life as*

some sort of battle with nature, to see myself as fallen and in need of redemption; to see life in terms of black and white, right and wrong; to live in a dualistic world of unconnectedness with nature and the people around me. For me, one of the most appalling symbols of the worst aspects of patriarchy is a Trident submarine. By diverting billions of dollars and vast quantities of human potential, militarists have produced a genocidal monster of horrific proportions. Capable of operating at a depth of 300 metres for up to three months at a time, protected against radar, sonar and practically without emitting noise, this denizen of the deep can travel at speeds above 80 km/h. Each vessel can carry twenty-four Trident ballistic missiles, each with a range of 12 000 kilometres. Each missile can carry twelve nuclear warheads, each with a destructive power two and a half times that of the Hiroshima atom bomb. One Trident sub alone can pulverise 288 cities, industrial complexes or military targets in one firing lasting only minutes. The ultimate obscenity occurs at the launching of such a weapon: a Christian minister complete with surplice, stole and holy water, blessing such a travesty as it makes its first deathly penile intrusion into the womb of Mother Earth.

There is much creativity in the invention and construction of such a marvel of modern militarism; but what a deadly and wasteful subversion of creativity. Similarly, the nuclear power industry is an example of such subversion. This wasteful and intensely toxic industry exemplifies the worst aspects of modern technology being put to harmful uses. To use nuclear fission to produce electric current is like using a forest fire to fry an egg. After, we are left with toxic substances and decommissioned power stations that put parts of the planet off limits for thousands of years. And the story goes on.

I believe the ancient goddess religions, the re-emergence of Wicca and the current feminist movement all provide spiritualities that have retrieved, reclaimed and celebrated the symbolic meaning of motherhood and can assist me in the development of my creative and nurturing qualities, reconnecting me with earthly wisdom. As the Maori proverb suggests: 'Papatunuku to matua o te tangata' — 'Mother Earth is the parent of the people'.

There seems to be no limit to the experiences from which one can benefit. The key is being open. One of the benefits for me has been learning to rectify my own cultural onesidedness. Born into a society dominated by white people, I was also born into the prejudices and racist beliefs of that society. It was only later in life, when confronted with situations as an adult, that I realised I had absorbed a lot of misinformation through my upbringing, education and privileged place in a dominant culture. It was with some culture-shock and anger that I discovered that the prosperity and development of the land of my birth was founded on racism and white supremacy.

Initially I began to unravel my own confusion and ignorance about the original Polynesian settlers of Aotearoa by reading. At about the same time I was transferred to a Christian Brothers College at a place called Rotorua. A high proportion of the students were Maori and I became directly involved with their families and cultural events such as tangi (bereavements) and other hui (celebratory gatherings) which took place in or around maria (tribal meeting halls and their surrounds). Being a teacher, I had the good fortune to attend some educational hui where I was exposed to a vibrant spiritual and cultural heritage. I found in Maoridom many values that appealed to me: a wholesome attitude to death, strong sense of community, an identity with the land, a closeness to nature, a delightful sense of fun and a rich and ancient tradition of poetry, music, story telling, song, dance, beautiful craftwork and an understanding and utilisation of the forces of nature. These things touched me deeply.

Many of the values and practices of Maoridom have been severely eroded or shattered by the colonisation of Aotearoa by white people of English, Irish and European ancestry. The ravages of introduced diseases, alcohol, plants and animals; the insatiable land acquisitions, white cultural arrogance, Christianity and a grossly exploitative capitalist economy have devastated the Maori way of life. This process continues today with the insidious effect of modern urban life on community lifestyles, especially those of the young. Many Maori have become tenants in their own land. It is no secret that in Aotearoa a disproportionate number of poor, ill and imprisoned are Maori. The early devastation of Aotearoa by racism and white supremacy disenfranchised Maori, robbing them of their resources and economic base. *Because wisdom was passed on through oral tradition, much of the pre-European wisdom of Maoridom has been lost or suppressed by the spiritual arrogance of early Christian missionaries. Reading authentic historical accounts of reliable scientific archaeological findings, and experiencing Maori hospitality in a rich cultural environment, has opened my eyes to values that have contributed immensely to my own spiritual development: the need for a strong sense of community, closeness to nature and reverence for the Earth Mother, recognition of the spiritual dimension, non-adversarial methods of reaching consensus decisions and a sense of fun,* kotahitanga *(togetherness) and sharing. This experience has also helped me to be more culturally sensitive, not only towards Maori but also towards other groups of people of different ethnic origins from my own.*

In saying these things I do not wish to romanticise the Maori race. They had not discovered the futility of war, except for the Moriori — the indigenous Polynesians of Rekohu, known as the Chatham Islands just 870 kilometres east of Aotearoa. Although Maori were close to nature, valued its resources and knew how to manipulate its forces, they were not conservationists in the wider sense. By the time Europeans discovered Aotearoa, thirty per cent of the trees had been destroyed and several species of bird had become extinct simply through overkill.

It was partly in recognition of the fact that the primary culture of Aotearoa was brought here over a thousand years ago by the first

Polynesian settlers, probably from the Marquesas Islands, that I chose the name Te Ruru. You have probably guessed by now that Te Ruru was not the name given to me by my parents forty-three years ago. What's in a name, you may ask?

Changing my name has been for me a way of symbolising and integrating the changes I have made in my life. For some time I considered the possibility of having just one name: neither first name nor surname. The unity and simplicity of such a concept appealed to me. All my life I have had names I have inherited or that other people have given me. By this I mean no disrespect for my family or rejection of my ancestry. It was just that the prospect of finally choosing a name for myself and dropping the rest appealed to me. So in 1985 I took the bold step of effecting this change through deed poll. I had actually been using Te Ruru as a pen name for some years prior to adopting it personally.

Although I was born, baptised and raised in a Christian family, and have lived a substantial portion of my life as a Roman Catholic, I have, as you will have gathered by now — moved on and no longer profess to be a Christian. Dropping the names with which I was christened was for me like shedding the last vestiges of that religion. Now I pursue a spirituality which I feel is both vital and relevant to me as an individual with ever-expanding cosmic awareness.

I chose the name of a bird — a creature of space. Flight involves both freedom and risk; but birds always return to the Earth Mother for

279

rest and nourishment. I intend to live my life taking the risks necessary for personal growth, soaring to new heights of awareness, but always living close to nature, constantly returning to the Earth Mother who sustains me on this planet.

This bird is also a creature of the trees. I have an affinity with the bush and trees which can provide all that I need in the form of food, health, climate, economic welfare, shelter, soil conditioning and the preservation of the planet's environment. In fact, trees can be considered as the lungs of the earth. Fruit trees and forests may be regarded as the foundation of human health and society. My destiny and that of society depends on a correct symbiosis of trees and ourselves. I find it painful to see our planet being denuded at such an alarming rate. The estimate is 5000×10^6 billion cubic metres of wood annually. Less than eight per cent of that comes from plantations. Cutting down our natural life support seems to me to be a false economy.

Choosing the name of a bird helps me feel closer to nature. The choice of a bird native to Aotearoa also helps me to identify more closely with the land of my birth. However, by choosing a Maori name I do not claim any Maori heritage. Likewise, I do not lay claim to any mana that may be associated with the name Te Ruru. Using the Maori form of the name simply intensifies my feeling for Aotearoa and helps me identify with and acknowledge the indigenous culture which was established in the land of my birth over a thousand years ago.

Simply translated, Te Ruru means 'The

Owl'. The Ruru is an owl native to Aotearoa and is commonly known as the Morepork. Traditionally, the owl is associated with wisdom. It can also see well in the dark. It is my intention to develop these qualities in my personality which will enable me to bring effective insights and genuine wisdom to every life situation in which I find myself.

The owl has additional significance for me. Ruru in Maoridom is associated with the God of Peace, Rongomatane. In Taranaki, for example, this bird was traditionally venerated. Te Whiti, a great proponent of nonviolent resistance, chose the Ruru and the stalking European cat as symbols of the protagonists in the Taranaki land acquisitions. Nonviolence is a way of life I wish to develop: peace with myself, peace with nature and the environment, peace with the people with whom I live and work.

The name of my country also has great significance for me. Aotearoa is the Maori name for New Zealand, usually translated 'Land of the Long White Cloud'. It is a beautiful name, as the white cloud has rich symbolism in many cultures. But that translation is only one of several possibilities. Because 'ao' can mean 'cloud' or 'day', and 'tea' can mean 'white' or 'bright', various authorities have attempted to give the following interpretations — 'continuously clear light', 'big glaring light', 'land of abiding day', 'long white world', 'long bright world', 'long daylight', 'long lingering day', 'long bright land' and 'long bright day'. So you can see, Dawn, the richness and symbolism in the name Aotearoa. I long for the day when it can be said that New Zealand is the long bright land of peace and harmony: all of which brings me to the subject of light and darkness.

The symbolism of light and darkness is very powerful and deeply embedded in all cultures, mythologies and religions. Images of light and dark abound in the Bible, especially in the New Testament writings attributed to John. I guess this symbology is as ancient as creation itself: '... Let there be Light', and there was light. God saw that the light was good, and God divided light from darkness. God called the light 'day' and darkness he called 'night' — so the 'good book' goes. Well, I'm not so sure this symbolism that has developed with the emergence of patriarchy's dualistic thinking is so useful. I also think it is a trap for people developing the New Age spiritualities which talk a lot about being children of the light. In a dualistic way of thinking, light has become a symbol for good and darkness a symbol of evil. Fear, ignorance, violence, low life, backwardness, sin, the primitive and all the destructive forces in the world have become the forces of darkness. Light, on the other hand, has come to be associated with goodness, progress, enlightenment, understanding, knowledge, wisdom and advancement. So deeply is this dualistic thinking embedded in the collective unconscious of modern civilisation that it has unconsciously reinforced the racism of white supremacy; just as the use of 'man' as a generic term for personkind has unconsciously reinforced male chauvinism. The dark races have been considered inferior, primitive, ignorant, backward and suitable only for the more menial tasks in life. Their wisdom has been

282

ignored or relegated to the category of the quaint or amusing. Even in Wiccan circles the same error occurs. The destructive use of psychic energy is labelled the dark path or black magic. In developing a more holistic spirituality, I have discovered that this is a false dichotomy.

When I turned to nature, I saw that much of life was generated in the dark. The wonderful workings of my body are all hidden and take place in the darkness of my insides. Seeds germinate in the darkness of the soil. For nine months I grew and finally came to see the light of day from the darkness of my mother's womb. Knowledge and enlightenment grow out of the darkness of not knowing. That is why I always think of black as the colour of wisdom. The roots that anchor the forest giants are deeply embedded in the darkness of the earth. The moon only reveals her silver beauty in the darkness of night and has her own dark side as well. Even the light itself is, in a way, defined by darkness.

So developing a Wiccan spirituality has helped me to come to terms with my own fear of the darkness. I can see now that a spirituality that is solely light oriented only ever deals with surface things. It lacks the depth and grounding to nourish and promote balanced growth. Now I am more willing to face my shadow side and attempt to deal with the shadows, integrate them into my life and so benefit from the insights and personal growths that result. I am also less afraid of the dark, of inner silence and of death. The way of the unconscious mind or 'right-brain' is the way of darkness.

In my short journey so far, I have come

across many traditions, religions, philosophies, cultures, schools of science and spirituality. Glimmers of wisdom are to be found in all of them. From the ageless realms of prehistory a remarkable teaching has existed which is universal in its application. Streams of this 'wisdom of the ages' are discernible in every culture and religion. Studying and practising these teachings reawakens within my heart an intuitive knowledge that helps solve my personal problems and leads me to the ultimate Source of that wisdom — the Divine Home for which I am heading: Blessed be!

In the realm of spiritual growth, there are no free lunches. I have found that sitting back and waiting for things to happen is a sure recipe for frustration and disappointment. 'As above, so below' runs a well-known Wiccan saying. Where spiritual development is concerned, as with physical fitness, I need consistency and discipline in the practice of what might be called 'spiritual exercises'. Whenever I neglect the means of nurturing and sustaining my spirituality, my motivation and zest for life begins to dry up. So what are these spiritual exercises?

You describe some very helpful ones in your books, Dawn. For a living I drive buses for the local city council, and each morning before leaving the depot I White Light my bus for protection and so that all who travel with me are bathed in peace and love. Visualisation and meditation provide opportunities to receive energy and inspiration from other realms as well as providing a relaxed time in which to balance and ground myself. But I have found that consistency and learning to be still and listen are the keys to success. For fifteen years as a Christian Brother I meditated daily; but they were mentally noisy affairs, as I was always making prayers of praise, thanksgiving or petition. I am sure God must have been left feeling quite ear-bashed. I did not understand at the time that meditation is more useful for receiving divine light, love, wisdom and guidance, then marvellous things can happen.

Another means of stimulating spiritual growth is by reading worthwhile books. Reading stimulates me to think about life, to clarify my ideas, receive fresh insights and develop new beliefs and outlooks. Being open to a wide range of views has been an excellent stimulant to my own thinking. Together with reading, another way to benefit from the wisdom and experience of other voyagers is to allow myself to be questioned and challenged. No one person has the monopoly on truth and wisdom. I hate conflict and prefer to avoid it or hold my silence in an attempt to maintain my Mr Nice Guy image. Living with Joy, however, has helped me realise that being vulnerable, allowing challenge, confronting conflicting situations and sharing my own thoughts and feelings can actually help me to grow as a person, and others to know who I really am.

Joining with others in ritual celebrations and sharing have also been important to me. Life is my most valuable and only true possession. Therefore it is worth celebrating at every opportunity — and there are plenty of those: special occasions, seasonal high points, relationships, births, deaths, gains, losses, arrivals, *departures, the list is endless. Any reason or any excuse is valid when it comes to celebrating life. In our modern, hyperactive civilisation, the art of ritual and celebration are seriously undervalued.*

During my earthly existence I am immersed in the physical. The quality of my physical health and vitality is directly related to vitality in the spiritual dimension. Therefore I believe the maintenance of good health and plenty of exercise are invaluable aids to the spiritual life as well. My body is indeed a temple; and a beautifully sensuous, sexual and pleasurable one at that. A balanced and vital energy flow is enhanced immensely by looking after myself.

On occasions I have taken part in therapeutic processes such as massage, counselling and psychodrama. These guided journeys of self-exploration have been invaluable means of spiritual growth because they provided insights about myself and revealed emotional blocks to personal growth. I have been helped to deal with personal issues in a creating and liberating way and this, I believe, has accelerated my personal evolution.

Taking time to develop my creative side through music, creative dance, poetry and the like has also been uplifting. Music in particular has often lifted my spirit and motivated me to pursue worthwhile paths.

Talking of paths, tramping and climbing have been great spiritual exercises for me. When I am out in the bush or other natural surroundings, I experience a certain rejuvenation and feel more centred; more connected with the natural world. From time to time I write poetry. Often the creative urge comes upon me after being in the wild; away from the usual bustle and stress of city life. This seems to be true for relationships as well as for individual physical and spiritual well-being. Joy and I have made a conscious effort to go on at least one honeymoon a year during which we seek out places of natural beauty and tranquillity to be together. I believe this has served our relationship well.

One very interesting spiritual exercise I have practised over the last twenty years is the keeping of a personal journal. In this journal I write about my feelings, dreams, plans, aspirations, thoughts and experiences. It is not kept on a daily basis, but just as I feel the urge. This happens when I get stirred up about something or have some meaningful experience. Writing is a marvellous release for strong feelings such as anger, sadness, love, excitement, outrage and the like. In some way this document plots my spiritual journey and my beliefs over the years. It is a very private document, but parts of it I share with close friends when appropriate. Joy also keeps a journal, and part of our New Year's Eve ritual is to swap journals and read about each other's year. Sometimes surprises lie hidden in the pages, waiting to jump out on me as I read about the things that have touched the life of the woman who to me is partner, friend, lover and guide. Keeping a journal is an exercise I can recommend to anyone, especially if one likes writing. Often, writing in my journal is a way of bringing into focus things that I have been feeling or half-baked ideas that need knocking into shape.

The spiritual quest will always go on for me. Your books, Dawn, have been a great source of inspiration and have motivated me to use the spiritual exercises described above with more consistency and discipline. Your common sense and eclectic approach have helped me immensely. I am now even clearer about the qualities of authentic spirituality which I would list as: positive, open-minded, eclectic, post-patriarchal, pro-feminist, nonviolent, liberating, humble, pagan, universal, cosmic and fun.

Positive because a healthy spiritual outlook is always optimistic, believing the best is possible.

Open-minded because a closed mind is a closed heart, dogma is the death of an idea. Wisdom comes to me from every experience in life.

Eclectic because no one has the monopoly on wisdom. A truly balanced outlook needs the insights of every tradition. All streams of wisdom ultimately have the same source.

Post-patriarchal because no longer can I subscribe to a religious tradition that is hierarchical, dogmatic, sexist, dualistic and divorced from nature.

Pro-feminist because to be made in the image and likeness of the Divine is to be a co-creator, continually giving birth to a new creation. Therefore my spirituality is necessarily matrifocal, recognising my mother function, nurturing and caring for all beings, recognising and holding sacred the connectedness of all life.

Nonviolent because if all life is sacred I need

to avoid doing harm to myself, to others or to the environment in which I live. 'If it harms none, do what you will.'

Liberating because to seek truth, my own truth, is to be set free.

Humble because I am of the world, not just in the world. In my physical dimension I am from the humus and am called to be a fertile ground for the sprouting forth of Divine Life.

Pagan because I desire to be a 'country dweller', learning to walk with reverence on the Earth Mother as well as being opposed to those cultural, economic, social, consumer and political forces so evident in large urban centres and so destructive to personal well-being.

Universal because a truly useful spirituality is not sectarian or confined to any single tradition, culture or religion. As the saying goes in Wicca: 'All the Gods are as one God'.

Cosmic because spirituality is a way of being without boundaries; ever-expansive and connected to every other part of creation. The word 'cosmic' derives from a Greek word meaning 'order'. A cosmic spirituality concerns itself with right order, balance and justice because every individual out of balance throws the whole of the cosmos out of balance. Nothing and nobody is isolated from or unaffected by lack of balance in the world. The improvement of life and personkind on our planet must start with individual efforts, as the whole depends on the atoms composing it.

Fun because life is a joke and seeing the funny side opens me to love, laughter and the infinite blessings of well-being.

Your books, Dawn, have affirmed some of

*these beliefs and helped me realise that every
other person is also a unique and precious
individual. Behind each pair of eyes and each
ego lies a spark of Divine Life that deserves
acknowledgement and respect as it, too, travels
the path it has chosen. I believe there are no
wrong paths: life is but a series of cycles of
learning with experience as the teacher. So
where to from here? What are my ideals and
hopes for myself and for the world?*

*Well, I believe I am a person of unlimited
potential; that my reality is of my own making
and that I am limited only by my own beliefs.
So the future holds an infinite number of
options for me. However, for some time now I
have been developing a particular vision
towards which I am slowly moving. Before too
long I would like to be living away from Otautahi (otherwise known as Christchurch) and
develop a truly pagan existence. The root word
from which 'pagan' derives literally means
'country dweller'. But in its deeper sense it also
implies one who has learnt to walk with reverence on the Earth Mother and lives in harmony
with natural and cosmic forces. A truly pagan
spirituality, though quite possible, is more
difficult to sustain in a city setting. So I'm
working towards living in a less stressful location, surrounded by trees, birds and tumbling
waters. To this end, Joy and I have secured title
to three and a half hectares of land just over an
hour away from Otautahi. I hesitate to say we
own the land because one cannot really own
land. As the great Maori prophet Te Whiti
would say, land is the mantle of the Earth
Mother and not to be carved up into little bits
of real estate.*

On this land of which we are now the legal guardians, I plan to live in creative simplicity, building a dwelling that is environmentally sound, maximises the use of nature and minimises waste of space and materials. A small orchard and garden are envisaged to meet as many of our nutritional and medicinal needs as possible. Eventually, there may be one or two other households of like-minded people. One-third of the land has already reverted to native bush and I plan to return the rest of the property to native trees, especially those which are indigenous to the area. As the project progresses, walkways, groves and picnic areas will be developed throughout the bush and along the two streams that tumble through the property.

My hope is that this place will become a Wiccan centre of pagan spirituality where people can come and learn the principles of a simple, healthy, holistic, connected and economic way of living. My vision pictures this centre as a healing and meditation centre where those who are stressed out, off centre or ill can retreat for a while to reconnect with themselves, experience the healing energies of nature or receive a treatment of some sort. That could be a massage, counselling, a spiritual reading, a herbal treatment, taking part in the ritual celebration of a nature festival in an outdoor setting, or just taking time out in a tranquil place. In this way I hope to adapt my outward life to fit more closely with my inner goals and beliefs. My hope is also to be able to share that life with those who are interested in or attracted to the project. I believe that mutual understanding leads towards mutual co-operation and that mutual co-operation leads to peace; the only way of survival for personkind. I do not seek to isolate myself, but believe that improving the lot of personkind on this planet begins with individual efforts. Every action has its consequences. What I do with the rest of this earthly incarnation will affect those around me, the planet as a whole and reverberate around the entire cosmos. Doing something which I believe to be worthwhile will facilitate my spiritual evolution. I know there will be plenty of lessons to learn along the way — but that is what life's about.

What of the world at large? I believe humanity can transform the tide of destructive forces that threaten to engulf us by recognising and developing its spiritual dimension and recovering the concept of the Motherhood of God. We live here on this jewel of our solar system where the Earth Mother in her bounty provides sufficient for us all. It was not intended that personkind become locked into materialistic, grasping and exploitative patterns of living where wealth, power and decision-making become the prerogative of a few.

At this point, Dawn, I must let you in on a private joke of mine. You will have noticed that this epistle is written under the letterhead of the 'Peoples Liberation Movement'. Does that sound like some armed subversive revolutionary group devoted to the overthrow of the establishment? Well it's not. The Peoples Liberation Movement is actually a figment of my imagination. Yet it also has some basis in reality. You see, I have no faith in revolutions. By definition a revolution is the overthrow or

292

repudiation of a regime or political system by the governed. In Marxist theory a revolution would be the inevitable, violent transition from one system of production in society to the next. But a revolution is also by definition a complete turn in a circle around a point: and that is the point. A revolution always returns to the same point. History bears witness to many revolutions and most of them seem to go full circle to produce yet another tyranny. The industrial revolution led to the tyranny of capitalism. The Russian revolution led to the tyranny of viciously totalitarian regimes, and so on. Our society needs not a revolution, but a quantum leap in awareness; a movement so forceful that people are liberated from the bondage of outmoded and destructive patterns of living. Therefore, in my enthusiasm and glee, I created the Peoples Liberation Movement, which is the figment of an optimistic mind, but also has a concrete reality where people are striving to use their creative energy to transform themselves, society and the planet; a 'new Heaven and a new Earth' no less. The letterhead creates interest for some people and paranoia in others. About ten years ago I put together a short tract to celebrate the birth of this worldwide movement. I would like to share it with you, Dawn.

GLIMMERS OF HOPE

I am Te Ruru. Afraid of the war-loving men of this world, I often retire to the darkest corner of my forest home; for I see many destructive forces at work in Earth Village.

These destructive forces have produced a disease of immense proportions. This global disease is marked by the concentration of wealth, power and decision-making into fewer and fewer hands, together with the unprecedented growth of militarism. The advanced state of this disease is made obvious by the intolerable suffering and inequalities that burden so many millions, by the widespread unrest in the world and by the extent of personal, mental and physical illness among people everywhere.

It is quite apparent that the great anguish and severe inequalities that exist point to basic social weaknesses — like centralised power, white-male-capitalist decision-making and a permanent war economy. Yet, from my dark forest perch, I also see a new day dawning. The very tension and unrest at work, in the world today is cause for hope. The powers of destruction have unwittingly generated within Earth Village an energy and groundswell that is beyond their control.

The long bondage of sexual, religious, cultural, racial and economic oppression — culminating in blind commitment to a system of technological progress based on domination and exploitation — has created a climate of fear together with intolerable living conditions for the majority of people in Earth Village. Friction so generated has unleashed a transitional movement rooted in the deepest aspirations of ordinary people — a movement for people's liberation.

This Peoples Liberation Movement seeks a greener and more peaceful Earth: a new social order based on equality, justice and love. It cuts across sexual, class, age, political, religious, racial, cultural and national boundaries. It is an ever-swelling torrent, fed by a thousand streams of discontent and frustration.

Once separated by differences of culture, cult and economic development, more and more people are emerging to stand on common ground. They realise that there must soon come a time when people will stand somewhere and not be moved.

Those who join the movement for people's liberation contribute to a vast and ever-expanding pool of personal energies so powerful that it will, given the right conditions, radically change society, which at present is dominated by forces of greed, power, individualism, materialism, status, consumerism, competition and exploitation of the weak.

Many characteristics of the Peoples Liberation Movement make it radically different from the dominant forces that control people's lives and environment today. The movement recognises the spiritual dimension of personhood and seeks to allow it full expression by unlocking the individual creativity that is in each of us; it seeks as well to make politically acceptable consideration of such values as diversity and creativity through a love of beauty, justice, imagination, involvement and a responsible approach to our relationship with nature and to one another.

All who join this movement seek a modest lifestyle which is marked by a great concern for environmental protection. Realising that people and environment are integral with each other and coexistent with the universe, people *in the movement for liberation grow through continuous mutual interaction with their environment.*

This movement recognises people's boundless potential for helping and healing themselves and one another. Every person is an indispensable expert on her or his needs. That is why the movement derives its momentum from the power of human creativity — a constant stream of energy emanating from many minds and hearts.

People for liberation instinctively distrust the present power and decision-making structures in society. In their effort to decentralise power and demilitarise Earth Village, they indulge in both nonviolent direct action and in a variety of awareness-raising activities. They seek to accelerate the flow of ideas, information and resources all around the world. Through co-ordinated and diversified action, groups of individuals will prove that people have the power to change the course of human events.

Those who toil for justice, fight racism, resist sexism, dismantle imperialism, foster civil liberties, oppose a nuclear society, resist war, protect the environment, shun intolerance and promote life in its fullness, all belong to the movement for liberation.

That is why the Peoples Liberation Movement is devoid of hierarchical structures, having no gurus, leaders or opinion makers to force their will on others. It has been said that whatever finally happens in the evolution of Earth Village will be settled by political forces. I say that the most potent political force is the power of people. Who would not be part of such a movement?

TU TANGATA!
PEOPLE, MAKE YOUR STAND!

*Much of what I have said in this letter is critical
of institutional religion; Christianity and
Catholicism in particular. I believe the criticisms are well founded. The institutional
church's sin of neglect and silent collusion
during the past fifteen centuries in which
human creativity has been stifled and allowed
to run amok; murdering, raping, pillaging,
spoiling, impoverishing, oppressing and
manufacturing horrific weapons of genocidal
proportion, is a matter of history. However, it
must be said that from the earliest times there
has always existed within the bounds of Christendom a 'prophetic church' — individuals
and communities that have consistently
worked for social justice and actively opposed
the oppressive power-centred structures of
both organised religion and chauvinistic
governments.*

*In highlighting the weaknesses of the
church, I also do not deny the benefits that have
occurred for me during my years within the
walls of Catholicism. All experiences in life
have their lessons. No longer do I feel bitterness
about the stunting effect of living within such
a system. I did go through a rage stage; a
necessary part of the grieving and separation
process. Now I can see institutional religion
for what it is, and that the experience of its
effect on me was merely part of my personal
evolution. Having grown out of it, and moved
on to better things, I can also look back and see
how I have benefited from that period in my
life. I have received a good general education. I*

*have developed a love of words and an aware-
ness of the richness of the language I speak. I
have been touched by the kindness of many
good people and have been able to touch the
lives of others myself. A certain discipline and
methodical approach to life have remained
with me. Skills in public speaking and communication have come my way. A love and
appreciation of good music were also fostered
during my years as a young Christian Brother.
Two or three friendships have survived those
years. Ironically enough, my experience in the
Catholic Church and close association and
involvement in liturgical practices have given
me a grounding in many of the elements of
ritual; something that I have been able to utilise and build on as I come to develop a Wiccan
spirituality. Many of the elements that have
been adopted in Christian rituals existed for
millennia in pagan religions. My adoption of a
pagan spirituality has revitalised many of the
symbols and practices that seemed empty and
repetitive within the Catholic liturgy. Perhaps
deep within me, pagan origins from former
lives have been stirred up but not allowed to
manifest themselves freely until I broke the
onerous yoke of Catholicism.*

*My time of religious formation in the con-
gregation of Christian Brothers and in the
seminary developed within me a thirst for reading and poetry. Now I love writing poems, and
books are a passion of mine. During that time I
was exposed to the major systems of Western
thought. In particular, scriptural studies gave
me access to scholarly, modern and well-
researched information on the Bible. This*

offered me an understanding of the Bible as a complex and fascinating document with identifiable sources and many literary forms. Each book of the Bible has its own literary genre and authorship which was influenced by the social, political, economic and religious environment in which it was written. This information enabled me to avoid the pitfalls of literal interpretation of the Bible while at the same time benefiting from the inspiration and wisdom it contains. I also became aware of other source documents.

There are a host of writings, many just as interesting and inspirational as those that finally made it into the Bible. For example, the Essene Gospel of Peace is contemporary with many New Testament documents. The Essenes developed a major stream of spirituality within the Hebrew tradition and had a major influence in the centuries immediately before and after the earthly incarnation of the character known as Jesus Christ. In fact many teachings in the Essene Gospel of Peace come from the mouth of an Essene master known as Jesus. In contemporary historical documents written by characters such as the Roman naturalist Pliny, Philo the Alexandrian philosopher, the Jewish historian and soldier Josephus, Solanius and others, there are encounters with both Jesus and Essene communities. The Essenes themselves were the most down-to-earth mystics in history. Among the Essenes were healers, teachers, gardeners, arboriculturists, builders, herbalists and prophets. Some who followed the Essene way lived in a community lifestyle away from the cities, as in the Maroetis in

Egypt, where they were known as therapeutae or healers. They were vegetarians and committed to nonviolence, refusing to carry weapons or be involved in their production. They had no servants and were said to have been the first to condemn slavery in both theory and practice.

There were no rich and no poor among the Essenes, as they believed both conditions were deviations from the natural law. They established their own economic system based on the belief that all food and material needs could be supplied without struggle, through the knowledge and use of natural and cosmic forces. They spent much of their time in the study of ancient writings and special branches of knowledge such as education, healing and astronomy. Their simple regular life enabled them to live 120 years or more. In all their activities they strove to express creative love. Essene communities sent out itinerant healers, teachers and prophets, among whom are said to have been Elijah, John the Baptist, John the Beloved and the great Essene master, Jesus. Some of the Aramaic text of the Essene Gospel of Peace was actually found obscured and neglected in the Vatican archives by Edmond Bordeaux Szekely, co-founder of the International Biogenic Society, which is devoted to spreading and applying of Essene principles of living to modern day life. Well, despite being a major contemporary spiritual movement, all mention of the Essenes has been edited out of the New Testament documents, although traces of their particular brand of spirituality remain. It helped me to put Christianity in perspective when I realised that the documents of the New Testament were constructed by their authors to fit in with the dominant religious and political forces operating at the time of writing, and to affirm the beliefs of the Christian community. To support a particular tradition, events were often fabricated that bore no resemblance to chronological facts as we understand them. While this is a perfectly valid literary device, it remains just that — a device.

I have digressed here to mention the Essene way because it has had quite an influence on my own spirituality. Knowledge of and alignment with the forces of nature was an integral part of the Essenes' biogenic way of life. In the New Testament, for example, only the Heavenly Father is mentioned. The Essene writings give equal weight to the Earthly Mother and the Heavenly Father.

So much for my ramblings. This letter does seem to have dragged on, Dawn. I did not set out to write at such length, but your books have really stimulated me to think about my own life and beliefs. Writing has helped me focus on my journey and where I am heading. I will not keep you any longer, Dawn. In my journey from dogmatic Catholic to practising pagan, I believe I am developing a worthwhile spirituality, one which for me is liberating and cosmic in its dimension.

This letter is but a response to your three books which you have so generously published and which, I am sure, have touched many people among your reading audience. To avoid writing a whole book myself, I leave you with this sketchy account of some of my own *journey and beliefs. As I sign off, it is the eve of the winter solstice when the Sun King will be born again and daylight will once more begin to grow longer as we head for that great bursting forth of life and colour in spring. I wish you the fullness of life, sending this letter off on the cosmic tides of love with that ancient Essene greeting:*

PEACE BE WITH YOU!

Te Ruru
Winter solstice 1990

CHAPTER TWELVE

Harmony and Balance — you and your environment

Concern for the global environment is very much a New Age issue. It interests me, not only because of the obvious need to protect the planet upon which we depend for our physical survival and well-being, but also because of what it reveals about our evolution in terms of spiritual consciousness.

Spiritual development depends on the establishment of balance between the physical and the spiritual, for these aspects of our being are not separate but interlinked. Our lives are an expression of our minds; what we do and say at the physical level is the expression of what we think and understand. 'Right-brain' consciousness has been coming to the fore in recent years, bringing with it a more holistic way of looking at life, giving credence to intuition as well as intellect, being aware of relationships and patterns rather than separate forms existing in isolation from each other, and so on. We are learning to see more about the ways in which all forms of life are interlinked and interdependent, and to understand the effects we have on the other lives around us.

It is inevitable that these changes in our ways of thinking will be reflected in the way we relate to life in our world, and the issues that assume the greatest importance in our minds. It is also natural that, as human spirits develop a greater awareness of the interrelationships connecting our lives to all others, our attention at the physical level becomes more focused on the way we are relating to our fellow spirits and to the planet itself, along with the other forms of life that draw their sustenance from it.

Another characteristic of New Age thinking is a growing respect for the sanctity of all life; the awareness that everything has its place in the overall scheme of things, and performs some vital function (although to be honest, I have yet to discover where mosquitoes fit in, or what beneficial function they can possibly perform!). This, too, is reflected in our increasing concern for the preservation of life in all its various forms on the planet we call Home.

There is also a resurgence of awareness with regard to the feminine aspects of the godhead, or universal life-force, and its relevance to the balance of life energies by which we are sustained, and in which we have our being. It is intriguing to note that this awareness of the feminine aspects and qualities of life has been rising in concert with the concern for preserving our earthly habitat. It seems hardly coincidental that there has always been a tendency for us to refer to the planet as *Mother* Earth, or that the period of time during which human society has inflicted the most damage on our physical environment has been characterised, socially, politically and religiously by male domination. The revival of belief systems in which the Goddess is afforded equal status with the God in the form of structures collectively known as Earth Religions can also be seen to be closely connected with concern for, and alignment with, a greater harmony with nature.

From an observer's point of view, it is not difficult to see how the growing concern for the care of our environment reflects the progressions being made in terms of New Age thought. At the practical level, however, there is a need for more than thought and, like many other people, I have had cause to examine my own level of input. I have steadily been introducing changes in my lifestyle, such as buying environmentally friendly household products in preference to the destructive 'conventional' alternatives, recycling wherever possible, growing vegetables organically for the kitchen and so on, but I have often been perplexed by the thought that maybe I'm not doing enough. The letters I receive from readers indicate that many other people share these feelings: we all want to do our part to help preserve the environment, and we do what we can to the best of our ability, but the problem seems so enormous. Are our efforts merely an ineffectual drop in the proverbial ocean?

When I was in the process of preparing the material for this book, I kept feeling strong inner promptings to write about environmental concerns. I recognised these urges as coming from the spirit friends who work with me (to whom I often refer, somewhat facetiously, as the 'Upstairs Management') and I realise that the environment is an issue of some compelling importance. At the same time, I was dubious about writing on a subject in which I don't have any specialised knowledge, and I couldn't see how I could possibly write anything that hasn't already been written and said countless times by people whose knowledge on the subject is far greater than mine. In meditation, when I asked for guidance, I kept receiving the words 'points of view' which, quite frankly, didn't seem to offer a great deal of illumination at the time. Knowing that the Upstairs Management has ways of getting things done, however, I accepted that the appropriate information would be drawn to my attention when the time came, and that the best thing for me to do was stop struggling with the issue and let the universe take care of the details. A short time later, I received a letter that helped to set the ball in motion.

Dear Dawn,

I am at present residing on the property of the King family. This family was poisoned by pesticides in Queensland some years ago and found the safest refuge for them to recover physically, mentally and, therefore, spiritually, here on Kangaroo Island.

The King family has been featured by the media at various intervals of their stay here. Their aim is to have their problems recognised so that they can in turn help others and influence government bodies.

They are succeeding, and Mrs King — Marilyn — has greatly developed her spirituality and consequently her psychic ability.

I came to stay with the King family because I also fell victim to twentieth-century poisons. I realised Marilyn, Howard and children, Sasheene and Casey, with their positive attitudes due to their spiritual growth, could greatly help me and my family. We also share the same desire, i.e. to set in motion a refuge for 'victims of the twentieth century'. Particularly those labelled as ME sufferers, and parents with small children suffering hyperactivity, etc.

We feel that Kangaroo Island, not far off

Adelaide, with its predominance of SE and SW sea breezes and cleaner seas, is the physical area for such a refuge.

The water, though hard, appears of good quality. Quality, chemically uncontaminated produce is becoming more available, plus what is grown here on the property.

The food, air and water needs can therefore be dealt with and so enable those affected to free their souls to their true spirituality, which is theirs by Divine Right.

I feel that you and yours have important roles in the establishment and success of this refuge. Whether it will be as teachers, guides, therapists, on a physical level or a purely spiritual level, will become clearer in time.

As a nurse, a mother, a victim and a reader of your experiences, and your spiritual and psychic achievements, I know you and yours have much to offer. I thank God for the wonderful skills of communication He has manifest in you through David that have enabled me to attain an even closer relationship with Him, and the growing strength to do God's will.

Whether your response is in a physical form or a spiritual form, I know it will be there.

Most sincerely
Anne

It is not uncommon for me to receive letters from people who feel or believe that in some way I am meant to have some sort of personal involvement with them, or with some project of theirs, but it is not possible in all cases. The Upstairs Management have ways of making sure that I sit up and take notice, however, when it is intended that I should do so: goosebumps that start on my arms and then travel down my back, along with a sensation that I can only describe as the psychic equivalent of white strobe lights flashing in my mind. Both of these sensations happened while I was reading Anne's letter so, although I was still unclear as to just how I am supposed to be of help, I responded and asked if Marilyn would write to me, telling me more about her family's history.

I have a friend who also suffers from the twentieth-century allergy syndrome as a result of being exposed to toxic fumes in his place of work for many years, and while I feel a great deal of sympathy for anyone who suffers from this complaint, the idea that I could do anything to help such people had not occurred to me. After receiving Anne's letter, I went back to the Upstairs Management in meditation, asking just what it is that I should do to be of help. Into my mind, in David's distinctive pattern of resonance, came the answer, 'You are a writer. Your purpose is to write.'

'Just write?' I queried. 'Is that all?'

'My daughter, what else do you do?' He had me there!

'But *what* will I write?' I persisted.

'Points of view,' came the enigmatic reply. Economical with words, my spirit friends!

After reading the letter that subsequently came from Marilyn King, I felt that the best thing I could do was to present her family's case history in her own words, as she described it to me. I also asked her to write a letter, telling me what she would like to say to the people who will read this book. Back came her reply, as follows:

Dear Dawn

Thank you for the opportunity to tell your readers about our project.

As the result of herbicide poisoning, we developed chemical sensitivity and had to move to Kangaroo Island from Queensland. The island was the only place where we could find land away from farms and near the sea. We knew that we need clear, safe air.

In the following years, we realised that we couldn't be near gas, cigarettes, perfumes, clothes washed in soap powders — in fact, anything that is made using manmade chemicals.

We suffered intense headaches, nose bleeds, ear and throat infections, rashes, bleeding from the bowel, continuous exhaustion, chest pains, vomiting, and lack of bladder and bowel control, to name a few symptoms. After many trials and errors, we were able to control the illness and, using only natural medications and oxygen, we can go shopping and dip into society whenever we want to.

We now live in a house made only of natural timbers — no chipboard, laminates, carpets, paints, etc. We eat only chemical-free foods (organic or biodynamic) and wear only cotton or wool. We also wear only canvas or leather footwear; however, because of the chemicals used to manufacture leather and materials, we still have to treat them by washing in bicarb. soda and airing them in the sun for weeks.

Over the years, we've learned how to do reflexology, massage and acupressure. All of these help to stimulate the lymph glands and so remove the lumps. They also help relieve headaches and lessen the reactions. With the help of relaxation tapes and other self-healing aids, we are now in far better health than when we came here. Over the years, we've received numerous phone calls and letters from people who also have this crazy illness — all asking for help.

Then we received letters and phone calls from folk begging us to let them live on our land for a while, so we said, 'Sure, bring a caravan'. One lady was advised by her doctor to contact us — she'd been given two weeks to live. She arrived on a chartered plane, skin and bone, and yellow as mustard. I picked her up at the airport and, for a fleeting minute, I was scared she'd die, so I prayed for help. Eighteen months later, she's alive.

As more and more folk called needing help, we realised we needed to establish a centre, and so the 'Wilwindri' Allergy Rehabilitation Centre is in its infancy. At present we have three caravans in use, and the council has threatened to evict the people we are helping. But we are doing as we are guided and, so far, we haven't been prosecuted.

We are having plans drawn up for cottages, a community kitchen and recreational building, and a chapel. Also a counselling room. The local doctors visit the 'tenants', doing blood tests, etc. We are grateful for this, because these people are often too ill to even go in a car without having a severe reaction.

We put people on to chemical-free foods, natural medications (they see a practitioner), do reflexology, massage, etc. and have weekly group workshops, as well as private counselling. We teach people how to control the *illness and stop it from controlling them. Positivity is the keyword. This illness has strengthened our faith and so we are able to love and help others. We are not religious and have helped people of different faiths, as well as non-believers.*

We are registering as a charity so that we can ask for financial help to build the accommodation cottages, etc. For years we've done it on a pension — buying an amenities caravan and other much-needed items. Beasley donated a solar hot water system; we are so grateful to them. No longer do the folk have to boil kettles and bath in little tubs!

As this world becomes more and more polluted, this illness becomes more and more common and severe, and so more folk need our help.

I ask your readers to go to their kitchen cupboards. Look at all the bug sprays, dish detergents, cleaners, polishes, air fresheners, etc. Look in your bathroom; scented soaps, hair sprays, after-shave lotions, deodorants, perfumes, make-up. Now the laundry; soap powders, fabric softeners, spray starch, stain removers. A good guess would say all are manmade chemicals. Read the labels. Then think.

Anything you take out of its wrapping or can goes into your immediate environment, where it can affect you and your family's health. Then it goes into the greater environment, where it affects the planet's health!

There are so many 'safe' products that Grandma used: vinegar and salt or bicarb. soda to clean everything, and pure beeswax and olive oil makes a great polish.

Now I'll ask your readers to go to the medicine

311

chest. Do they have antibiotics, aspirins, etc.? Do they need to regularly take medications? If so, maybe they are chemically sensitive without knowing it. Stop using toothpaste (salt and water or bicarb. works great). Take a break from all the cleaners, box them up and pop them in the garage. Change to organic foods and cotton clothing and bedding — and see if it helps. Even if you aren't noticeably being affected, everything you use is affecting the environment and so creating a chemical time-bomb.

Some folk say, 'What difference can one person make?' A great difference. YOU can then teach others. Teach them how to pull out the weeds in their garden instead of spraying herbicide; how to use garlic sprays and other natural methods of pest control. Teach your local council about the effects of chemical sprays; how to use eucalyptus oil on cotton wool instead of air fresheners in toilets — or an open packet of bicarb. soda. Teach your local school to use safer products (water-based felt pens, natural cleaners, etc.) Teach your family and friends to use safer products. Basically, teach folk how to love and protect each other, and the environment.

By doing so, you will help to protect present and future generations from this and other illnesses. God gave us a beautiful world — we owe it to Him to take care of it and to take care of each other.

If anyone wishes to contact us, to find out more about the centre, to offer help or to ask for it, we'd love to hear from them. A gentle reminder to send a stamped, self-addressed

envelope and notepaper (or extra stamps). Our
postage bill is astronomical.

May God's love be with you and all your
readers.

Love and laughter
Marilyn

PS Remember that when people stop buying
products, companies stop making them!

The story of Marilyn's family and how they developed the disease is quite horrific. Here is an
extract from the case history, in Marilyn's words.

When our son, Casey, was four months old, we
moved on to our block of land at Cedar Creek
(in south-east Queensland). I was pregnant
again and thrilled about it. After we'd been on
our land a couple of days, Casey ran a fever and
had diarrhoea; so did Howard and I. Then we
all came out in a red, itchy rash. Before becom-
ing ill, we had carried Casey outside to watch a
helicopter 'watering the trees' on the creek bed
at the bottom of the hill. Later we found out it
was herbicide. Within a week, I started 'spot-
ting', and the pregnancy was touch and go. We
were all ill with what the local doctor called
'the summer wog'. Then I miscarried.

A couple of months later, I was joyous to
find I was pregnant again. I was ordered to take
it easy, so I did. However, with this pregnancy,
I wasn't 'blooming' as I had with Casey. I was
ill often and suffered a threatened miscarriage.
I gave birth to a daughter prematurely, after an

emergency Caesarean. Sasheene was put under the ultra-violet light because she was slightly yellow.

Then followed years of illness for Casey and Sasheene — ear and throat problems, rashes, fevers, etc. Poor little Casey had been having infections ever since we moved to the land. Once Sasheene kept being ill, Howard's mother told us it was something in the air, because she got headaches and a 'tummy bug' when she came to visit. 'Sell up,' she advised us, but we didn't.

By this time, Casey was diagnosed as hyperactive, and he responded a little to the Feingold diet. Then a lady visited and said she'd seen a spray contractor dump some poison drums out near the local swimming hole, by the primary school. She didn't tell the police because she was afraid to be involved. I went down and the drums were still there, so I called various people in the law and government offices, to be told, 'Not our jurisdiction'. Eventually I called the local paper. They ran the story with photos, and the media then took up the story. THEN a local health inspector phoned me and told me to pick up the drums because he wanted to prosecute the spray operator.

I went down, leaving the children in their car seats. I picked up the drums and checked the identification number as instructed. Something splashed on my legs and everything went bright white — I had trouble breathing. I felt very ill, so left the drums and drove home. I then carried the children inside and don't remember much else for two weeks.

Apparently I called a friend who went down

in his truck and collected the drums. He put them at the back of our property, then came in to see me. He told Howard when he came home that our house stank of chemicals from my clothes and that both children had it on them. He helped me shower and then helped bath the kids. He said I was hallucinating and all three of us were vomiting and crying. Surprise, surprise, in a few hours, the rash returned!

During the next few days, I handed over the drums to the health inspector, who wrapped them in brown paper and put a wax seal on them. I also did interviews and saw the doctor for tests etc., but I remember very little. The doctor told us that now he knew what was causing our 'summer wog' — herbicide poisoning.

Over the next few months, we were inundated with calls from all over the valley, from folk who were all ill from roadside and aerial spraying. Horrific stories of women losing their babies because the placenta broke up (which was what happened to me), also stories of liver troubles and babies being born deformed. During this time, I found that foods I had eaten all my life were now making me ill; breakfast cereals, margarine and sugar, to name a few.

Our tank water made us itch and feel ill, so we had it tested. The result — '5000 times the safety level of 245T and extensive amounts of 24D'.

'Don't use the water,' warned the analyst. This water was rainwater, collected off our roof over a three-year period. We and many others tried to stop the spraying, to no avail.

Finally, we left. The children and I were so very ill and Howard was also developing problems, diagnosed as chemically induced asthma. I was bleeding from the bowel, coughing up blood, and nose bleeds, rashes and all sorts of crazy symptoms. We travelled around, trying to find a safe place to live, and ended up on Kangaroo Island.

I could not help feeling deeply disturbed by Marilyn's story, and I began to wonder if perhaps she, her family and the other people she mentions as suffering from this disease, might not be a harbinger of things to come unless the conditions in our world are dramatically altered. A lot of people remain relatively unmoved by stories about native animals having their habitats destroyed, and deformed, cancerous fish being found in our oceans, but when they hear of the effects of pollution on human beings, there may be cause to wonder 'Can it happen to me?' and Marilyn's story shows that it certainly can. How easy it is for us to innocently expose ourselves to deadly poisons without even knowing they are there. I am reminded of a time when Roland and I were living on a two-hectare block of land, also in south-east Queensland, along with our friends Beverley and Ken, and their son Luke, who was only a toddler at the time. Beverley was delighted to discover that she was expecting another baby, but a few weeks after we received the joyful news, the local council sprayed our area with the herbicide 24D to eradicate a weed problem. Within a few weeks, Beverley miscarried.

How often, I wonder, are we exposed to such dangers and assured by 'the authorities' that the chemicals being used nearby are 'within safe limits'

316

or not dangerous to human beings... and how often are we simply not told that such things are being used? As Marilyn points out, many of us could be suffering from low-level chemical reactions and feeling slightly under par a lot of the time as a result of using common household products. The more I thought about these things, the more overwhelmed I became. Just where does an ordinary person like me start when faced with problems of this magnitude? What can I do? What can I say, and who should I be talking to? Moreover, what should I be *doing*?

Inspiration sometimes strikes at the most unexpected times. Not long after I received Marilyn's letter and case history, in a discussion about something entirely unrelated, a friend remarked on how often we search far and wide for answers when the most obvious ones are right under our noses. No doubt my reaction seemed a little disproportionate to the remark, but it had triggered a brainwave.

I live in Tasmania, a state that made headlines after the 1989 elections when five Green Independents led by Dr Bob Brown gained the balance of power in parliament. Dr Brown first hit the headlines when he led a successful campaign to stop the Hydro-Electric Commission in Tasmania from proceeding with a project that would have caused the flooding of the Franklin River in this state's rugged wilderness area. I was living in another state at the time, and knew very little about the confrontation, except for televised news reports, and at the time the total of my involvement was a degree of annoyance whenever someone, hearing that I was born and raised in Tasmania, insisted on hearing what I thought about the damming of the river. Since I hadn't lived in this state for almost twenty years and was quite out of touch with local events, I really didn't feel in any position to make an informed comment, but I can see the need for action on environmental issues and I admire any person who has the courage to stand up in defence of what they believe to be right. As far as Dr Brown is concerned, however, any admiring on my part had been done from a distance: it had simply not occurred to me that it might be possible for me to speak with him personally.

Nothing ventured, nothing gained! I rang Parliament House and spoke with Dr Brown's secretary, explaining that I was writing a book about New Age issues and that I would like an opportunity to speak with Dr Brown if it were possible. At first his secretary was polite, but understandably noncommittal. Then she asked my name and, when I told her, she answered with a laugh: 'I can't answer for Dr Brown, and he's interstate at the moment, but I'm sure he'll be happy to speak with you, Dawn. I've read your books!'

A few days later, she called to tell me that Dr Brown was quite happy to talk with me, and to make an appointment for me to see him. I was quite nervous when Craig and I arrived at Parliament House on the big day, partly because I am not a journalist and have not had any experience with conducting interviews. In interview situations, I am usually on the 'receiving' end! I was also nervous about speaking with Dr Brown, who has won international awards for his work on environmental issues. I felt quite small and a little lost as I waited in the lobby after the guard at the desk had called Dr Brown's office to let him know we had arrived, but I was put at ease as soon as he came to meet us. On television he often appears stern, almost to the point of implacability, but in person he radiates a quiet warmth and gentle good humour, without any of the calculated charisma that we tend to expect from politicians.

After he had located an empty room in which we could talk, I explained that I didn't have a clue how to conduct an interview, and asked if we could simply talk about his philosophy on life and his views on the issues for which he campaigns so strongly. Could he tell me something about his personal background, and what had led him to become involved in the Franklin Dam issue? 'Sure,' he agreed, so I switched on my tape recorder and we began.

'I grew up in country New South Wales,' he said. 'My mother had come from the land, on a small dairy farm near Glen Innes, and my father was a policeman. I was born at Oberon, near Bathurst. We travelled around, and I started at a little school at Trunkey Creek, where there were about twenty-four kids. It was a mining town. My father was the local policeman in these places and the bush was just through the back fence and I found that there was something really special about the bush itself. I was always intrigued by it. When later I went to bigger towns, I used to go back to Glen Innes, to relatives, and spend time in the bush there, on holidays.

'Then I went to Blacktown High School, then to Sydney University, and did medicine there for six years. I didn't like it. I didn't like the university. I did like medicine, only when I got to the stage where I was actually meeting with people who were ill and talking with them, and so on. I remember the very first person I met was a man from central western New South Wales, from right out in the bush, who had a stomach cancer. He sat there in Prince Alfred Hospital, he'd hardly ever been to the city, he had involvement of the lymph nodes and that meant incurable, and they were still there doing tests. It just seemed to me that he should be helped on with his dressing gown and

319

taken down to Central Station, put on the train back home and allowed to enjoy himself, instead of being in that foreign, highly technical environment, where it was very similar to being in a laboratory.

'I was ten years in general practice. I came to Tasmania in 1972 to look for the Tasmanian Tiger, which I didn't think existed (and I think unfortunately it *is* gone) and to have a glimpse of Lake Pedder. I just flew over it before it was flooded, but I found the whole place beautiful. I was then asked to go on a trip along the Franklin River, and walks in the south-west, and to me it was a case of . . . the majority of the people who go to general practitioners are there because of the modern rat-race. They've got allergies, blood pressure, stomach ulcers, asthma and migraine . . . things called multi-factorial, but nevertheless things that happen much less when you go back to people who are still living in the natural environment rather than a built environment. It seemed to me crazy that we should be knocking down more of the wilderness, which is a storehouse for rest, and relaxation, and inspiration . . . to put up more tranquilliser factories.

'In a way, I've never stopped doctoring. I still find being involved in this is really preventative medicine, and that's what you're talking about, Dawn, because it's saying we shouldn't wait until we find ourselves in a ward somewhere with all sorts of machinery being attached. That may be necessary in some cases, but by and large, we will have a far better run through life just by thinking about our connection with the planet and about how to make sure our environment is tipped towards the natural side of things.'

'You've reminded me of something that happened when I was nursing,' I remarked. 'We had a child there, a little boy of about seven, who suffered from lymphosarcoma and gamma globulin anaemia. Everyone knew he was dying, yet they kept giving him transfusions to keep him going for a little longer, even though it was agony for him even to be touched gently. When he went into his final coma, I was assigned to stay with him and keep taking his vital signs and so on, and it wasn't long before I found myself praying for him to die, to be released from all that . . . it might sound hard-hearted to some people . . . '

'It doesn't to me,' he answered. 'Death is coming to all of us. It comes to some young and it comes to some old, and we're neurotic about death. We're a society that's neurotic about it, but it's an inevitable part . . . it's one of those things we all have in common. Elisabeth Kubler-Ross, in the 1960s, really broke through that and I suppose it's somewhat significant that it was a woman who did it. It's starting to break down now; people talk about death much more readily. Hence my tiny little move with the Death with Dignity legislation, which is simply to allow an adult the right to say, 'I don't want to be kept hooked up to a machine, I want to die naturally'. And what a thing, that we have to be looking at *legislation* so that people can die naturally and not be hooked up to machines!'

'I think people focus too much on just staying alive,' I suggested. 'Maintaining what they've got and not looking, for instance, at . . . reincarnation is obviously a very New Age thing and not everybody accepts it, but if the man who owns the chemical factory were to realise that he will have to come back again and inhabit the world he's creating, there might be more incentive for people to stop polluting.'

Dr Brown nodded. 'I don't know where life goes

to,' he said. 'And I don't know where life comes from. I know we have this magnificent life force, of which we're a part, because here we are, which proves that we were in the design books of the universe. Each of us is inherently different and special, and unique. Whatever else happens, I'm very strongly motivated in what I do by knowing that people just like us will be around five hundred or five thousand years from now. Not clones, but made up of all the various bits and pieces in all of us, because we have an enormous environmental, genetic and cultural heritage, which is all inter-mingled in each of us, and it keeps moving itself along. There are five billion of us on the planet at the moment and there are going to be more. Then, I suspect that this is where common sense will start bringing our population back to one which can live in harmony with the planet instead of at the expense of continued deterioration of the planet, and the increasing of the "garbage bin" effect.'

'A lot of New Age people don't really know what comes after this life, either,' I agreed. 'But it's not so much life after death that I'm looking at right now, because that's going to happen regardless. It's the quality of what we're doing here, and the fact that we can't do a thing without affecting some other form of life, human or non-human. I really don't see any difference. You mentioned going into the bush as a child: I used to do the same thing when I was growing up on King Island, talking to the tree-people and the pixies and so forth. I thought all the other kids did it, too, because it seemed such a natural thing to do. I think that kind of background gives you more of an appreciation of what we get from nature.'

'You're very right, too, about our fellow crea-tures and life-forms and the rest of the planet being interdependent,' replied Dr Brown. 'There is no dividing line between what is the form of the planet, and life and intelligence, all of which are expressed in human beings. And as we do unto ourselves, we certainly do unto everything else, to future generations and in a way, I believe, to the past, too, because people in the past, and life on this planet in the past, aspired always towards a future. Have you read Chief Seattle's statement?'

'I read it once, some time ago,' I answered. 'I don't remember a lot of it, but he was pointing out that we can't sell the land, because we belong to the Earth, not the other way around.'

'That's the one,' smiled Dr Brown. 'Well, in 1854, he expressed this idea and said we are not the web of life, we're a strand in the web and, as we do unto ourselves, we affect the rest of the world; and also the Earth doesn't belong to us, we are just a part of it and we belong to it. Unfortunately, in the big cities nowadays, where everything is basically concrete and straight lines, people are getting cut off from that bond with nature, but it's still there in everybody. You see pictures of nature on walls, not pictures of bulldozers, and it's particularly restful for people. The bond with nature is, I think, best expressed by saying, for example, that if you told somebody, "This is the last time you can have a flower in your whole existence. Here's a rose that has a few tattered petals; and in my the other hand I have a plastic rose that is perfect, scented, beautifully coloured and it will last forever. Which will you have?", give people time to think about it and they'll take the real rose. You can't explain why you'd reject the artificial and take the real, but people's whole feeling is towards that. The plastic one is ornamentation, the real one is part of us. It's an easy way of expressing to people that thing which is beyond being put down into words. You could write books about it that nearly get there, but in that flower... the handmade one might be perfect according to the cultural way we look at things; its form, its colour, its scent and so on. The other, being natural, will always have imperfections, but it's the one we go for. I think you'll notice another thing: we're all imperfect and we're in a society which tries to teach us, through television and so on, that we've got to be perfect, and we've got to be beautiful...'

'And strong!' added Craig, who had hitherto been sitting quietly to one side, absorbed in the conversation.

'Yeah!' agreed Dr Brown emphatically. 'Yeah, and you've got to be like those people you read about in magazines!'

I was thoroughly enjoying myself, all traces of nervousness forgotten. Dr Brown was so easy to talk to, and so relaxing to talk to, the 'interview' had fallen naturally into an easy, spontaneous discussion.

'The people I'm communicating with and hearing from are all looking for something they can do as individuals,' I said. 'They are tuned in to a kinship with all life. They might work at a checkout in some inner-city supermarket, but they are still concerned, and they aren't sure what they can do in that sort of situation. Living where we do, we're fortunate, in that we can drive for ten minutes and we're in the bush, but in inner-city suburbs, there are kids who think milk comes from cartons at the supermarket. A lot of people in those places need to know there is something they can do. They also feel very helpless. They look at the whole 'looking after nature' thing, they realise how important it is, but they don't feel confident that they can do anything worthwhile about it. I wonder if you would direct some remarks to people in those situations, who are looking for something they can do but feel overwhelmed by the enormity of it. Okay, we can all buy string bags instead of accepting plastic ones, we can buy environmentally friendly household products instead of the chemicals and things like that, but if you were to talk to these people, what would you say to them?'

'A number of different things,' answered Dr Brown. 'First of all, I'd say hop into the car on the next fine weekend and head off into the bush, and for good or bad, get a little bit of the feeling of the planet, as all our ancestors did over thousands and millions of generations. That's what we were made for, that's where the curl of our ears comes from, and the nails on our toes. The other thing is, I think at the local level, to say where has this (substance) come from, and where is it going to? None of us should panic because we're having a bad impact on the environment, just by degrees keep comfortably moving in a direction that is helping the world. If it takes you a month in your household to get used to turning off the lights as you leave a room, just keep at it. Turning off your porch light stops over a kilogram of carbon dioxide going into the atmosphere: that's from the coal burnt at a power station to keep that light going. The same if you walk down to the store instead of taking the car, and if you recycle a lemonade or beer bottle instead of putting it into the waste bin. You can help the whole planet. You've helped the forests, you've helped the animals grazing on the plains in Africa by doing that. I think it's just so important to remember that all of us are part of the planet and, as you say, what we do in our own little environment we're doing to the whole world. We've got to think when we're doing that, we're helping the whole planet and it's like ripples in a pond. A little stone will make a whole pond move.

A frog, jumping from one leaf to another, will make a whole pond move. It's very important that we recognise that not only are we affected by the people we run into, but we affect them as well. We affect everything around us, and forever. The whole pattern of the planet is changed by each one of us being here. And finally, tell those people to be nice to themselves . . . be very kind to themselves.'

I smiled. 'People *are* very hard on themselves, aren't they?'

'Yes, they are. If you're being nice to yourself, you're being nice to everybody else. I think a lot of the most sensitive people are very self-conscious and shy, and feel "What can I do?" They're self-critical.'

'In a nutshell, you seem to be telling people not to think that what they're doing isn't much, but rather, "A whole lot of people like me, just doing this much, can make a big difference". So it's something important that each person is doing, and they needn't think of it as small.'

'Yes,' Dr Brown replied. 'I have rarely been out of this country but I've been twice to the other side of the world, to North America and Europe this year, and *everybody* is thinking the same way. We're all hooked into a whole mind change. It's part of the whole human organism thinking, "Well, we're intelligent about this". Information is coming back through modern mass communications in our own living rooms at night. We see what's happening to the world on nature shows and the news. This is the whole greening in the thinking of people everywhere, and so, yes, we're part of the biggest catastrophe that's ever occurred — the destruction that's going on at the moment — but also one of the most exciting periods. People in the future will never be able to come back and undo what we're doing now, or be part of this change. So we've got to stop just being gloomy about it. Recognise that it is a fantasically exciting time to be alive, and I think as long as each of us can say, "I'm handling the environment better than I was this time last year" . . . if we keep doing that for the rest of our lives, we'll all have moved with this tide.'

'That's a very New Age outlook!' I laughed. 'Everything you are saying tends to be the motivation for people who are inclined towards New Age thinking. We see this as a really exciting time to be living. We are seeing the transition into the forecast Age of Enlightenment, but we are also seeing that many things are here *in potential* and if we don't do anything about it, the opportunities are going to pass by. We're looking at approaching things in a more practical, down-to-earth, physical way, not just sitting and waiting for an entity from another dimension to arrive and deliver a lecture. The spiritual communication is an important part of it, but it's what we *do* with the knowledge we're given that has relevance to the here and now . . . and the future.'

'It's one of the hazards of the great old religions, which don't hold the sway now that they did,' mused Dr Brown. 'There was this feeling that it was okay, we'll be all right when the world goes to destruction, we're going to be selectively saved out of that. I think people feel let down by that now, because they don't want to rely on it, and nor should they. With the reasons beyond our ken, we are the universe, thinking about itself, and able to change itself. To say, "Well, I'm not responsible", is to duck out on the most exciting part of being alive. The onus *is* on us, the Earth *is* in tremendous . . . a period of tremendous destruction. We know the cause; it's us. We know the cure; it's us. You can either be gloomy about it, and pessimistic, or you can be active about it, and optimistic, and that's when life starts getting to be thrilling.

'Scientists have gone right through... they've spent two centuries trying to prove you can get down to an ultimate thing and therefore explain everything. Now they recognise that it's all chaos, and what they really mean is that they're a bit desperate in giving it a name. But as you say, everything is interdependent and infinitely complex, and we shouldn't forget that either. We should just enjoy anything we're looking at, at any given time, and recognise that it *is* all linked up and because it's all linked up, we affect it.

'There's another thing, that's for people who feel desperate. You know the old saying that today is the first day of the rest of your life? I think it's very important for people not to feel that they're too young or too old or they're not well educated enough, or all of these myths that we have, that in some way other people are better than us. I find it's really instructive when people say to me, "You're so confident"... and I'm not.'

'People aren't really conditioned to be self-confident,' I remarked. 'We are raised with the idea that the real power is outside us, but really it's within us all. It's from within that we make the important changes. We all have more capabilities than we realise, and we need to recognise this and use it. It means people tuning more in to themselves and less in to institutions. Instead of saying, "The government should do something about this" or "People should do something about that", it's saying, "I can do something here", and looking for what we can do as individuals, understanding that the world is composed of individuals.'

'Yes,' agreed Dr Brown. 'And all of the big changes that have happened in this world, the people who have got involved in them were out of step with their times.'

'Well, you didn't start out with an ambition to enter Tasmanian politics, did you?' I laughed.

'Oh no. And people got tarred and feathered trying to abolish slavery; and women . . . the House of Lords held a debate about giving women the vote! I mean, how can you have a proper debate about that, without women having a say in it?'

'Well,' I responded, only half in jest, 'with the experience we gain in organising households, managing budgets and bringing up children, I think we need to have women in charge of running governments.'

'Exactly,' smiled Dr Brown. 'It is something we need very much more, in politics and in public life. This is a generality and they're always bad, but there are fewer women in positions of power because the two things don't readily sit together. I think it's going to be very relaxing for men when they stop wanting to *have* power and start tuning in to the fact that we live very brief periods of time, we don't have all the answers, but we can make things go a lot better.'

'Let's find out a few things from women?' asked Craig.

'Yeah,' replied Dr Brown. 'And let's relax about it and stop trying to run things, instead of working with women and working through them, and see how we can include them in the future.'

After that conversation, I felt glad that I have no professional skills as an interviewer: if I had, I might have led the discussion through a list of questions that I had formulated in advance, making it necessary for Dr Brown to answer in a 'professional' way. Allowing the flow of conversation to follow a spontaneous course permitted us to be ourselves, and I learned much more than might have been possible in a more formal interview. It would not, for instance, have occurred to me to ask Dr Brown for his opinion about the role of women in society or the right to die with dignity, and I would have missed out on those enlightening insights. I would also have missed the opportunity to talk with the man as a person had I cast us in preconceived roles as interviewer and politician.

Dr Brown spoke in a straightforward, down-to-earth manner, with no overtones of artifice. Watching him on television since then, I see that what I once perceived as a rather stern demeanour is more an uncompromising 'What you see is what you get'. He is polite and he does not give way to impassioned displays of emotion, but he cares a great deal about the quality of life for all, and he tells it as he sees it.

In Tasmania, there is sharp division among the people, in their opinions about Dr Brown. There are many whose livelihoods depend on the industries that he has sought, often successfully, to curb. Among these people, many come from families whose members have been miners or logging workers for generations, and they see him as a threat, not only to their means of livelihood, but to their way of life. On the other hand, there are those like the young woman who recently wrote in a letter to the local newspaper that she would rather be blamed for the loss of jobs in the short term than be responsible for contributing to the long-term destruction of our planet. There are extremists on both sides of the issue, of course, but Dr Brown did not strike me as being one of them.

I come from a family of miners, and I have been enthralled by discussions with some of these men, whose affinity with the earth is deeper than the deepest mineshaft and whose philosophy on life is as profound as it is earthy. I know one old-timer whose home is a ramshackle old shed in the mountains, cluttered with an amazing variety of tools, bits and pieces of dismembered machinery, ore samples... and books. Treasured encyclopedias, old and well used, but still in an excellent state of repair. He spends most of his time away with his dog in the bush, prospecting (he refers to it as 'tin-scratching').

Many years ago, he discovered a rich lode of tin. He said very little about it, simply registered his claim to the mining rights and went on tin-scratching elsewhere. Years later, his lode was discovered by a large mining company, who then had to negotiate with him for the mineral rights. Out of the proceeds, he bought himself a brand new E-Type Jaguar, which he wrote off within a few days when he rolled it on the way home after a few convivial drinks with some friends. He just shrugged his shoulders and carried on with his tin-scratching. He doesn't want all the bothersome business of mining huge lodes of ore, he just likes being off in the bush with his dog. His survival skills and feats of endurance in the bush are legendary, and his advice is sought by scores of young miners with admiration glowing in their eyes. Left to his own devices, this oldtimer would mine nothing more than what he needs to support his few requirements. It is big, multinational mining corporations who rip out the ore in millions of tonnes every day. Perhaps from an old prospector's point of view, it is inevitable that the mining companies will find those lodes of ore one day and, when they do, he can't stop them from greedily raping the earth, so he might as well let them pay him for the privilege. If the policies of mining companies were decided by men like him instead of by company executives who work with profit sheets, how might the picture be altered? To stretch the possibilities further, what would the picture be if people like Dr Brown had people like the old tin-scratcher to deal with, instead of executives and power brokers?

It does not surprise me to find antipathy towards Dr Brown among people who depend on the industries that have been slowed down in recent times, but I did not expect to find it among other environmentalists. I was therefore quite taken aback when, not long after I had done the interview with Dr Brown, one of my friends declared, 'Bob Brown makes me furious!'

When my friend Tom explained the reasons why he feels frustrated with Dr Brown, I heard yet another point of view; equal in value but with a different focus. I asked him to write his thoughts down for me and he did.

When our settlers first came to Tasmania, they found a land which was sparsely populated by small groups of Aboriginals who moved around the state, living from the land, following game and naturally occurring food cycles. These Aboriginals tended to live comfortably, as there was ample game even in the winter months. They used only a tiny fraction of the available native foods. On occasions fires, caused by lightning or which were lit accidentally or purposely by the Aboriginals, destroyed large tracts of land without causing any major upsets to the ecology. Time and nature soon restored the flora and fauna lost.

The settlers used the land in more orderly fashion and they found that they needed to clear large areas, often removing the trees in the richer, more densely growing areas to create their farms and grow the crops they needed to survive. These settlers worked under terrible hardships, working long hours for little reward, and often whole families were destroyed by untreated disease. Women died in childbirth and men were killed by falling trees, children drowned or were burned to death. Still the families toiled on and eventually, after generations of work, they succeeded in wresting a good living from the earth in the most natural way known to man, by cultivating those plants and trees that could best provide for their needs.

As a young teenager, I worked on a farm which was mostly bush. I helped plant crops on the few acres of paddocks and cut firewood from the bushland. We did not have power or telephone and, while we lived comfortably, we did not have the benefit of television or easy access to shops or entertainment. In that way, I feel that I lived just a little bit closer to the kind of life that many of our settlers endured.

On that farm, we needed to use our natural resources to live. We pumped water from a river, both for personal use and to water the orchard and garden that stood beside the house.

We had to empty the toilet pan and bury it deep in a patch of the garden that was used later to grow vegetables.

Wood from the bush provided us with heat, hot water and fuel for cooking. It provided timber for the hay sheds and shelter for the stock and, when things got tough, we sold timber for telegraph and power poles.

We didn't waste much. The heads of the trees felled were dragged to the flats and cut up for firewood which could be sold or used on the farm. the larger log butts were kept long enough to split for fence posts, and the leaves rotted back into the ground to provide soil cover and humus for other growing things.

One boundary line was a river which flooded a number of times each winter, and I used to watch huge logs float down the river, to end up at sea or sometimes on paddocks lower down, where the water spread out a little. The carnage to the environment by natural means was tremendous. I saw kilometres of river banks seriously eroded, trees shredded, and the river bed scoured three or four times a year. That lasted until the Hydro-Electric Commission built a dam which not only provided electricity for industry and comfort, but controlled the water supply and allowed nature to rebuild along the river banks.

I believe this taught me that there was room for conservation and for development, particularly where man could obtain a balance by providing for our own creature comforts and by reducing the incredible damage that nature could inflict on the environment. There are those who would argue that man created the imbalance in the first instance, but when I see what nature can do, the somewhat puny efforts of man seem to be rather insignificant.

I am reminded of the self-destruction of the sun, which will continue on until all the things we now argue about and seek to preserve will be destroyed by the system that once created us.

As I grew to adulthood and finally found the work I have actively pursued for a number of years, I sometimes found myself in conflict with conservationists who seemed to fall roughly into several categories.

There were those who were mildly conservationist, who grew their own vegetables and planted trees in their gardens, and grew a little concerned over some of the more emotional issues thrown up factually or embellished by the media. These were the average citizens who had no focus for their concerns and preferred to sit back and let the world go by. They are comfortable in their three-bedroom homes, which collectively were provided through the destruction of countless hectares of forest trees.

They buy every possible gadget, usually powered by electricity, which is provided by the dams they might have protested against at one time or another (usually quietly, because they didn't want to get involved). They cook their food, dry their hair, watch their television and listen to their radio, and use a very wide range of equipment and goods.

Usually they sit in a room warmed either by electricity or by a good wood fire which burns six or seven tonnes of wood each winter, and when they go to work, they drive in a car made from metal obtained from an environmentally undesirable mine and smelted at a similarly undesirable smelter, and which uses the rapidly reducing fossil fuels. They eat vegetables which are sprayed with insecticides, eggs laid by battery hens and meat from animals bred by man for slaughter. If you told them they would have to give up all that and eat nothing but organically grown vegetables, they would be in revolt immediately.

Some of them work in the timber industry, or sell furniture, or build houses.

The next category are the moderates. They still enjoy all the creature comforts but tend to become involved in the wider issues and write letters of protest and sign petitions, and march in rallies or such things. They, too, are not likely to give up their comforts but they are a bit more uneasy and vocal about the environment.

There are the true environmentalists who see a need for a balance between nature and the needs of man. The people who are mature and totally concerned with the environment and the future and who will do all they can to work towards a compromise so that man can live in and work with the environment. These are the people I can relate to.

Then there are the radicals. The foaming-at-the-mouth, raging, banner-waving, drum-thumping radicals who see everything as an insult to the environment (most of them still live in houses and enjoy the comforts, etc.). Some of them have switched off the power and cook over and warm themselves with an open fire, burning wood, of course, and trying to kid themselves that their life is the healthiest and best of all.

I once had cause to work near a remote river in the south-west, and saw where the river rafters, many of whom screamed loud and long to protect the environment and attended all the right rallies and all that garbage, had hacked their way around a portage so they could raft down the river with a little more comfort. The trouble was, they had hacked their way through a stand of Huon pines, killing many hundreds, if not thousands of small trees and cutting a great slash in the undergrowth along the river edge in pursuit of their favoured

336

hobby, which was the 'flavour of the day' at that time.

How easy it would have been to have taken those small trees of this precious wood and replanted them in an area where none existed. What was wrong with planting them, with other native trees, along the edge of the man-made lakes these people hated so much, so that in time to come they would expand the number of stands and give nature a helping hand?

I saw conservationists refuse to listen to a request that something be done to save the trees or have them replaced as they were felled. This was years before the forest debates became topical, and I was told the conservationists were too busy with the dams issues to worry about the trees. They could have done so much to help but didn't want to, because it didn't suit them at the time.

What I would have expected was that the 'Greens' would have set up and agitated for a proper management programme which would have allowed trees to be used, but which demanded their replacement with a similar species rather than the pines that were popular years ago. I would have supported that and worked with them, as would many others, but I am now very anti-Green while still remaining a conservationist.

I own a large block of land which is heavily timbered and I want to take the more mature trees out and mill them for my own use before they get too old to be practical. I also want to clear a two-hectare block to build a small house on, so that my children and their children can enjoy the benefits of nature for a few weeks

each year. The clearing must be done as a fire
break for the house, and the area would be
grassed down for stock or horses.

I am now afraid that the radicals will soon
influence parliament to the degree that I will
not be able to clear the two-hectare block or fell
the trees to build my little house. This will
imprison my children and grandchildren in a
city and they will never know the benefits of
natural living in a forest area, where they can
yell and scream to their hearts' content, get wet
in long grass, ride a horse, sit in front of a wood
fire in the open, see native animals feeding at
night or enjoy the sight and sound of the bush.

I think Bob Brown has a lot to answer for.

Tom

Points of view indeed! It is fortunate that I have
not been asked to take any sides in this issue,
because there are so many perspectives from which
the same subject can be viewed, and each point of
view shows different areas that need to be taken
into consideration. In a discussion with Tom after
reading his written material, I pointed out that I
cannot see Dr Brown as a radical, having spoken
with him as I did. Doubtless, there are radicals
within the environmental movement, but Dr
Brown's message, as he explained it to me, did not
carry those overtones. I can't claim any intimate,
first-hand knowledge on the subject, but to me it
seems that Dr Brown is not trying to stop all
resource-based development period, but rather
that he is saying, 'Stop and *think*... find better
ways of doing this'.

Most people today are prepared to acknowledge
the need to utilise natural resources more wisely,

but I can't help wondering how many ordinary citizens would have become aware of this need had it not been for the people who are prepared to campaign and make waves in order to draw attention to the issue. Sometimes, I think there is a need for drastic measures, to shock us out of our inertia and make us take a closer look at what is happening in our world. Back in the 1960s, there was a lot of radical, banner-waving, drum-thumping marching in rallies for the Women's Liberation Movement. As a woman, I couldn't see what all the fuss was about at the time, but I had never really taken an in-depth look at the position of women in our society and, in retrospect, I can see that the Women's Lib Movement had a number of valid points to make, and out of those radical demonstrations have come a lot of improvements for women in our culture. As further progress is made in this area of social concern, the rallies and protest marches have become somewhat obsolete, but I wonder how much progress would have been made if that drastic action had not been taken initially.

Concern for the environment is still in the early stages, but already we are noticing changes on supermarket shelves and in the way people are learning to consider the environmental impact of our living habits. We can't achieve everything overnight, but we are making progress. I think it is possible to become too panic-stricken about the subject and I don't think extremes of any kind promote clear thought or appropriate action. Tom makes a very telling point about the conservationists a number of years ago, who were so engrossed in the dams issue that they couldn't see what was happening to the trees. That kind of tunnel vision doesn't lend itself readily to positive outcomes.

The issue of environmental concern is enormous

339

in its proportions and it is easy to be overwhelmed, but Dr Brown's advice to just keep steadily working on improvements, doing what we can in our own lives from day to day, is both realistic and reassuring. Instead of thinking, 'I'm only one person, my puny efforts aren't going to make much difference', we need to remember that the biggest changes are often brought about by a lot of little people, each doing what they can within their own spheres of activity. Maybe one person switching to environmentally friendly household products won't make a big difference to the pollution problem in our rivers and oceans, but a whole lot of people doing the same thing can change the picture quite significantly. As Marilyn points out, when people stop buying the harmful products, manufacturers will have to stop making them.

It is not for me to say whether other people should support environmental causes, or any other causes for that matter. What we need to consider, however, is whether our activities are in accord with our beliefs and ideals. For instance, if a person tells me that she is concerned about the environment, and I see her pouring a phosphate-based detergent into her washing machine, heating convenience foods in a microwave oven, spraying bugs with aerosol chemicals and driving her car to the corner shop, I might find it difficult to take her very seriously. I wouldn't expect that she should march in rallies or return to living in the Stone Age, but making small changes around the home can make a big difference to the planet.

While I believe implicitly in the value of things like meditation and spiritual communication, we also have bodies in which we inhabit a physical world. I believe in the value of planetary healing meditations as a necessary aid to the recovery of the

340

Earth, but it doesn't stop there. What we think is important, and so are the words we say, but they are no more important than the things we do. Without action, thoughts and words are largely ineffectual. Let us be wary of becoming 'armchair idealists' and look for positive ways in which to practise what we preach.

CHAPTER THIRTEEN

Channelling

Whenever a New Age phenomenon receives extensive publicity through the entertainment media, the event is inevitably reflected in the letters I receive from readers. Since a recent visit to this country by a woman who functions as the 'channel' for a personality known as Mafu, people have been writing to ask my opinion of the channelling phenomenon in general and Mafu in particular. On the whole, the readers' questions have been centred around whether or not I believe that particular entity to be genuine. At the outset, I must point out that it is not for me to set myself up in judgement on others. I do not know all there is to know about Life, the Universe and Everything, nor do I have the right to pass judgement upon anyone else, irrespective of my own personal opinions. It benefits no one to rely on external sources for decisions on what should or should not be accepted as personal truth; that kind of guidance should always come from within. I will write of my observations, based on what I have seen of the channelling phenomenon and what I have personally experienced, but while my words may be given due consideration, you must always make your own decisions with regard to what you will or will not believe.

Public reaction to the emergence of the channelling phenomenon has been mixed, even among active members of the New Age community. Judgement on any issue is by nature subjective, but as a writer/researcher, my purpose is best served by maintaining a degree of detachment and being as objective as humanly possible.

For anyone who may be unfamiliar with the term, a 'channel' is a person who enters an altered state of consciousness, during which it is claimed that the body is used as a vehicle for communication by a being from a higher level of spiritual enlightenment. The purpose of these communications, it is said, is to assist in the upliftment of the human race, to usher in the long-awaited Golden Age of Enlightenment. Until quite recently, I believed that the words 'medium' and 'channel' could be used interchangeably, and my dictionary appears to support that idea; however, according to the woman who channels for Mafu, this is incorrect. In a television interview she explained that channelling differs from trance mediumship because with channelling the consciousness of the channel actually leaves the body while the 'Exalted One' is speaking, so that when the visiting entity departs, the host personality has no recollection of anything that took place during the exchange of consciousness. I find this claim somewhat puzzling: from what I have observed, there do appear to be some differences between channelling and trance mediumship, but the absence of conscious awareness during the process is not one of them. Listening to what that lady had to say, it seemed to me that she is unaware of the distinction between conscious and deep trance mediumship.

There are levels of trance, just as there are levels of consciousness. In medicine, for example, the level of consciousness in an apparently comatose

343

patient can be determined by the presence or absence of physical responses to stimuli such as sound, touch and pain. A 'conscious medium' may experience nothing more profound than a slight change of mood and can be fully aware of everything that takes place during a trance communication. A deep trance medium, on the other hand, will enter a state closely resembling deep sleep and awaken from the trance with no awareness of anything that took place while he/she was 'out'. Between those two states, there are levels of trance in which the medium's consciousness leaves the body yet he/she remains fully aware of the proceedings while the visiting entity is in control of the body. Some mediums have reported observing the proceedings from a point somewhere near the ceiling, others are unaware during the trance, but experience a mental 'replay' of everything that happened during the trance *after* they awaken. Listening to the experience of channelling as described by the visiting celebrity, I heard nothing that could not as easily be applied to the process of deep trance mediumship.

Medically, a person may be incapable of registering any reaction to sounds, physical touches or even pain, yet still be mentally awake and alert. As a student nurse, I was taught never to assume that 'unconscious' patients are not aware of anything that takes place in their vicinity. There have been well-documented cases in which people have regained consciousness and faithfully repeated every conversation carried out within their hearing during the period of unconsciousness, often to the acute discomfiture of anyone who has spoken indiscreetly in their presence. In books such as Dr Raymond Moody's *Life After Life* the author relates numerous cases in which people who have been clinically dead for a period of time have recalled observing the activity taking place around their apparently lifeless bodies and hearing every word spoken by those present at the time. All of these examples would seem to indicate that loss of conscious awareness and/or out-of-body experiences are by no means limited to the phenomenon of channelling. Consciousness is a remarkably flexible state of being. In addition to the states of consciousness already mentioned, mediums who undergo profound shifts in awareness may also experience being in some other place, as in being drawn into a light or visiting a hall of learning. All of these states are valid and none is inherently better or more reliable than any other... or less vulnerable to misuse. The method by which a medium or channel may be activated is not always relevant, but the quality of information received through that agency, and its effect on those who are touched by it, are of vital significance to us all.

Between channelling and deep trance mediumship, one major difference I have observed is that channelling seems to be unaffected by the highly charged electromagnetic fields generated around television equipment, and seems to have no appreciable effect on the function of that equipment. This may be due to some supreme level of control on the part of the visiting entity, but it is not common in my experience with deep trance mediums, even though some have been the vehicles for entities equally advanced, or in some cases perhaps even more so than the luminaries who communicate through celebrated 'channels'.

It is *possible* to film a deep trance medium in action, but from my observations so far, the more highly advanced a communicating entity may be, the more interference is generated in the presence of electrical activity, whether naturally occurring or artificially produced. Although some deep trance mediums ask to have electric lights turned off while they are working, communication between the spheres seems relatively unaffected by such low levels of activity. I have seen communication with entities from spheres of great illumination taking place in brightly lit rooms, sometimes even with tape recorders running, so it is evident that there is some kind of cut-off point at which electrical activity becomes a hindrance. I have known instances when it has been requested that all nonessential electrical appliances be turned off, and occasions when planned sittings have been aborted because of thunderstorm activity in the area.

In the fifteen years that Roland and I were together, only two brief visits from the spirit teacher David were ever recorded on film (or, more correctly, videotape) and on one of those occasions the effect of electrical interference from television equipment was vividly demonstrated. There were two video cameras and a couple of microphones in operation, recording a meditation circle during which Roland entered a trance state. After identifying himself, David began to speak about the purpose of meditation. He seemed hardly to have introduced his topic when the communication came to an abrupt halt. Roland's head drooped forward and silence reigned for a few moments, then just as suddenly his body was again activated, this time by David-Michael, an entity who exists at a lower level than David himself, and who frequently assisted in our trance work.

'I'd be thinkin' he's gone, me darlin',' he told me, in his distinctive Irish brogue.

'Was it because of the electrical equipment?' I enquired.

'Aye, that it was,' he agreed cheerfully, then he was gone.

If all this is beginning to sound like gobblede-gook, please bear with me. If there had been nothing more remarkable than an abruptly cur-tailed address purporting to come from a Higher Intelligence, spoken through the lips of an appar-ently sleeping medium, the incident would have rated no further comment, but an intriguing devel-opment connected with this incident was related to me on the following day by several members of the film crew. When they told me that 'something spooky' had them quite bewildered, my interest was piqued, because I knew that they had not had a personal belief in matters supernatural previously. In a conversation on the previous day, they had told me that although they did not question my sincerity or that of my colleagues, they had yet to witness anything really convincing. Now they seemed considerably less sceptical and even a little shaken.

As a preface to their tale, they told me about a malfunction known as a technical dropout, which happens when a segment of videotape fails to take up the picture being filmed. The result, they explained, is a momentary 'blank' on the televi-sion screen when the film is run. To give some idea of how often these dropouts occur, they told me that a full-time television news cameraman work-ing with videotape might encounter a dropout maybe once a year.

After filming the meditation sitting during which David had visited, they had as usual returned to the studio and played back the film footage as a preliminary to editing. When it came to the segment involving the trance, they were amazed to see that at the moment I spoke the words 'electrical equipment' there was a simultaneous technical dropout in *both* independent video cameras. The film crew members assured me that the odds against a simultaneous double dropout are too ridiculous to be imagined.

'Lady, this kind of thing just doesn't *happen*!' said one of them.

I surveyed him with just a hint of mischief in my smile. 'Correction,' I grinned, 'maybe it hasn't happened to you before, but it has obviously happened now!'

For the benefit of those readers who may not have personally witnessed deep trance communication, superficially it seems to have a number of things in common with the channelling process as demonstrated on television and commercially released videotapes. Deep trance mediums and channels (for the sake of simplicity I'll refer to both as 'instruments') both enter a state resembling sleep, after which their bodies are apparently animated by a personality from beyond the realm of physical substance. During the transition phase, when the instrument's personality withdraws and the incoming entity is taking over control of the body functions, the eyes are usually closed, there can be noticeable alterations in the breathing pattern and sometimes facial grimaces. There may also be certain characteristic muscular movements, such as a rhythmic pulsing of an arm, nodding of the head, even occasional jerky spasms. At other times, the transition from one level of consciousness to another can be so smooth that it takes place before anyone present notices a difference, at least in the case of mediumship. In channelling, however, the breathing pattern seems to undergo pronounced alterations at the onset of every trance, regardless of circumstances.

In deep trance, a medium's body can be activated to move, walk around or even dance if required, but in general the body is kept at rest to conserve energy. It has been explained to me that a medium's energy field is altered during the trance process, therefore precautions must be taken to avoid undue strain on the body's resources. It requires the expenditure of a considerable amount of energy just to hold the trance steady so that the visiting entity can verbalise, and some of that energy is drawn from the medium's physical reserves even though the body may be at rest. To make the body stand and move around considerably multiplies the drain on energy. Of the trance sittings I have attended, those in which there is physical mobility are shorter in duration than when the medium's body remains at rest. This would seem to indicate definite limits on the amount of energy that can safely be expended at any given time. The operation of electrical items such as video and sound equipment during trances also seems to demand the exertion of a greater amount of energy to hold the trance stable, although it has been noticed that the effort required is not as great when the incoming entity is from a level close to our own. It would seem that the more highly advanced the visiting entity, the less movement is exerted and the more interference is caused by the operation of electrical appliances.

Given that both channels and deep trance mediums are said to enter altered states of consciousness to provide the vehicles through which Higher Intelligences may communicate, I would have expected similar precautions to apply in either case, but apparently I have been mistaken.

I have witnessed numerous deep trance communications, but all the sessions of channelling that I have seen have been on video and television, where the proximity of all the associated electronic equipment seems to have no appreciable effect on the proceedings. Since an entity communicating through a channel will often animate the host body to rise and stride around while speaking and to use energetic gesticulation, I expected at first that such episodes would be quite brief by comparison with the more sedentary deep trance mediumship, but the channelling entities seem able to maintain the flow irrespective of television equipment, large audiences and bright lights for extended periods of time. People who function as channels appear to be capable of producing high-performance trance states frequently, at will, and under conditions that could deter the worthiest of trance mediums. Since the natural laws which govern the functions of life energy remain the same for all, it may well be that channelling entities have some superior methods of maintaining safety and stability at the psychic level, or it may be that the entities are not, in fact, what they are claimed to be. From surface appearances it is almost impossible to tell what the facts are.

Although as a simple researcher I do not consider myself qualified to judge the credentials of any channels or the entities who speak through them, I have been associated with those who possess the necessary qualifications. According to one such source, there are several characteristics associated with both channelling and mediumship which have to be regarded as counting against the credibility of those concerned. Not being in a position to make any judgements, I shall simply list these points as given to me.

1. Exclusivity: when it is stated that the spirit entity channels exclusively through one person and will never communicate through any other.

2. When the channel enters his/her trance states and performs the channelling without the presence of a physical control (a control is a

physically incarnate human being trained to protect the welfare of the channel/medium and any others who may be present).

3. The charging of high fees for attendance at public performances and aggressive marketing of end products such as video and audio cassettes.

4. An entity who cannot or will not be summoned through an independent channel or medium cannot be questioned as a separate being and cannot, therefore, be proven to be a distinct personality in its own right, rather than a projection of the physical instrument's inner consciousness.

Although, as I have said, I do not regard myself as an authority on the subject, the points given above impress me as sound common sense and, indeed, it is on precisely those issues that the majority of my readers question the validity of several well-known channels and the entities who speak through them. From my own experience, I have conversed with several highly advanced spirit entities through more than one medium. David, who taught me for many years through the mediumship of my former husband, has also transmitted messages to me through other mediums and is, in fact, communicating regularly with other groups entirely independent of either myself or Roland. By the same token, entities who are known to me as the guides of particular mediums have spoken to me through Roland and other mediums as well. None of these entities show any resistance whatsoever to being closely questioned as to their credibility and, in fact, they actively encourage their listeners to do so, emphasising repeatedly that we must always test, check and double-check any information given by any other being, whether that being is physically incarnated in human form or communicating from a non-physical level of existence through some human agency. Even the most talented seers, mediums and channels can have the occasional off-days when their energies are not as clear as they could be and, even though the most highly advanced of entities may be speaking through the most highly talented human instruments, the information is still being 'filtered' from a level of high energy frequency to one lower and more dense and, with the most honest intentions, errors and mistranslations have been known to occur. For these reasons alone, the Higher Ones always urge us to test everything and are always willing to be tested themselves.

Mediums, like channels, can serve as vehicles for highly evolved beings who offer words of enlightenment for the benefit and upliftment of us all. There are many similarities in what these higher beings have to say about the meaning and purpose of life and how we can best develop our own inner potential, whether they speak through mediums or through channels. That is as we should expect if they are, as they claim, expounding universal truths. There is nothing new in what these beings have to say, nor should there be, since they speak of natural energy principles that have always existed and will always continue to exist, at all levels of life. That human beings, no matter how humble in origin, can be used as vehicles for communication between the spheres is also nothing new. Countless people have served in that capacity down through the ages. Most of our major world religions are said to be founded on the teachings of some enlightened master or divinely inspired prophet. Jesus, Buddha, Mohammed, Krishna and Moses are the names that spring most readily to my mind, and there are others, in addition to innumerable 'Holy Ones', prophets, seers and spiritual leaders of varying degree. Frauds, fanatics and charlatans have also always abounded, as have alternating cycles in public opinion, ranging from the credulous to the disbelieving. So whether we call it mediumship, channelling or hocus-pocus, the phenomenon of spiritual communication is anything but a recent development. Sceptics, also, have always been with us, bless their hearts.

When asked for my opinion on the matter, I have to say that surface presentation is not an area of major importance as far as I can discern. Whether the mystics choose to wear business suits, unisex outfits or polka-dotted petticoats, whether they sit in contemplative stillness or prance like show ponies, other people will believe whatever they *choose* to believe. Sceptics will still choose to be sceptical, devotees will choose to be devoted and a whole lot of other people will wonder how anyone can make sense out of any of it. It makes no difference what others may think, it is *your* inner truth that is of most importance for you, just as my truth is of the greatest importance to me, irrespective of what anyone else may choose to believe.

The question for me with respect to channelling, mediumship and charismatic spiritual leaders is not whether we should allow ourselves to be led by one prophet or another, but whether it is wise to allow ourselves to be led by anyone at all. I believe that I will gain more by paying attention to the message rather than the messenger. We do not bow down in adoration of the telephone wires that carry messages to us, it is the content of the message and the source from which it originates that is of primary importance. If I receive a telegram, I really don't care whether the messenger who delivers it is male, female, attractive or ugly; it makes no difference to the message itself. In that sense, as far as the recipient is concerned, the messenger is only a means to an end. If I were asked, I could relate clearly where I was, the time of day and what the messenger said as he handed me the envelope containing a telegram that informed me of my grandfather's death, but I could not, for the life of me, recall the messenger's face. I cannot recall the face of the doctor who told me in 1982 that a routine test had returned a diagnosis of cancer, but I can vividly recall every word of the conversation. In matters of such crucial importance, one messenger is very much the same as another, and I see no reason why the same principle should not apply to messages from the worlds of spirit.

I am always inclined to be cautious about any philosophy that revolves around the teachings of any one person, no matter how charismatic and convincing that leader may be, especially when large amounts of money and/or property are solicited, however subtly, from the followers. That, however, is an expression of my personal preference and a matter of practicality, not a value judgement. As David pointed out to me a long time ago, a labourer is worthy of his hire, and when a person performs a fair service for someone else, he or she is entitled to fair recompense for that service, whether it be typing letters in an office, operating a switchboard, driving a truck or delivering messages from the worlds of spirit. However, he added, we are not entitled to demand excessive and unfair payment. From a personal perspective, I am a writer and no doubt I would still be a writer, regardless of my field of interest. If, instead of New Age philosophy and psychic research, my chief area of interest was centred around the sex life of the Transylvanian tree-toad, I would write books about tree-toads, their reproductive systems and their relevance to human society in general. If the release of my books coincided with a dramatic rise in the popularity of Transylvanian tree-toads worldwide, the book sales statistics would undoubtedly delight my bank manager and my publishers... not to mention my humble self. Although wealthy writers are the exception rather than the rule, few people would begrudge the fortunate ones the right to enjoy the fruits of their labour. That is a fair principle and it should apply universally, irrespective of the field of work that is carried out by the worker. It is also a fact of life that lecture tours, seminars and public gatherings have to be financed; everybody has expenses to meet and mouths to feed. However, there is a world of difference between value for money and exploitation. Along with the readers who have taken the time to write to me, I cannot see why the benefit of spiritual knowledge should be reserved for those who can afford to pay extravagant prices for it, especially when the same knowledge can be acquired with the application of a reasonable amount of time and effort, with considerably less financial outlay, from a number of readily available sources.

It seems to me that values are too often determined by price tags, which can lead to false values and lack of true understanding. Like anyone else, I see no justification for exorbitant fees, whether they are charged by a doctor, a plumber or a psychic. To be fair, however, it is well known that people have to live, and within the current structure of our society, that means having some source of income. It is no more immoral to expect fair payment for the time and energy involved in giving a spiritual service than for any other kind of work: I'm sure any clergyman would readily testify to that. Is there any reason why New Age workers, whatever their specialty (healing, astrology, etc.) should be subject to a different set of rules?

Rip-off merchants can give any profession a bad

name and, sadly, it is the many honest practitioners who suffer an unjust stigma because of the few;
yet those who are 'taken for a ride' by charlatans
must also bear some of the responsibility for their
misfortunes. If you were planning to buy a car, a
house or a block of land, would you not first shop
around and find out as much as possible about any
likely pitfalls to make sure you get a quality product at a fair and reasonable price? Is there any
reason why a person's quest for spiritual enlightenment should rate any less care and caution?

If a man spends an amount of money he can ill
afford to buy the first used car he is shown, without
first ensuring that it is mechanically and structu-
rally sound, then it falls to pieces before he has
driven it 500 metres down the street, is the sales-
man any more responsible than the buyer who
took no common-sense precautions before he
bought the vehicle? By the same line of reasoning,
if a person pays $500 to attend a public perfor-
mance by some famous guru who gives no more
useful information than could be gained from a
$10 book, is the guru to blame because the person
chose to spend that money?

The progress of your spiritual development
should always be your prime criterion. The fact
that some charismatic guru is internationally
famous adds nothing to the worth of the teachings
given . . . but it doesn't detract from them, either. If
the teachings uplift you, clarify your awareness
and help you along your chosen path, the teacher
is providing what you need, which cannot really
be valued in terms of money, but it is still wise to
remember that truth is universal, the cosmic mind
has billions of mouths to speak through, and most
of them won't stretch your credit cards to the limit.

Something else to think about with respect to
channelling, mediumship or indeed any form of

356

teaching, is lucidity: how easy (or difficult) it is for the listeners to understand what is being said. Multisyllabic words and complex phraseology are generally part of an attempt by the speaker to impress others with the idea that he/she is of superior intelligence and has greater knowledge, but in fact the best teachers are those who get their message across simply.

Very few of us carry dictionaries in our heads, and plain speech leads to clear understanding. Years ago, when I was having difficulty grasping a concept that my spirit teacher had been explaining and I was verbally berating myself for being so thick-headed, he said, 'My daughter, if the pupil is not learning, the teacher is at fault. If a teacher cannot explain his subject in language simple enough for a child to understand, he does not know that subject well enough to teach it.'

He then went on to explain the principle I had been struggling with in a way so simple that I was disgusted with myself for having failed to notice something so obvious. How often has it happened to you that a problem perplexes you for no end of time then, when the answer comes, it is so simple and obvious that you could kick yourself for not having seen it before?

Returning to the subject at hand: in my own experiences as an observer of trance communication, I have noticed that the more highly advanced entities speak simply, concisely and with almost no accent at all. Entities who dwell within levels closer to our own will sometimes speak with a colloquial accent, but the Higher Ones do not. No doubt they are perfectly capable of doing so, but since it is of great importance that they be clearly understood, why would they choose to obscure their messages with heavily accented speech? In general, if an entity retains an accent, it is usually a good indication that he/she has not advanced very far beyond the planes of earthly existence. As a parallel, think of the different speech patterns used by highly educated university professors and people with only the most rudimentary level of schooling.

One of the disadvantages that I see when it comes to public debate on the credibility of New Age phenomena is that the people selected as judges are very often self-declared sceptics who have not experienced any recognisably psychic events and whose minds are already closed. How can such people judge with any fairness, or even any real knowledge of the subject?

In a delightful book entitled *The Richest Man In Babylon* there is a tale about a man who had saved up some money, with which he planned to buy jewels from another country and make a profit on them by selling them in Babylon, where they would raise a high price. His friend the brick-maker was travelling overseas on business of his own, and it was agreed that he would buy the jewels on his friend's behalf. However, being a brickmaker by trade, the traveller knew nothing about quality jewels and a clever trickster sold him a bag of worthless stones, so all of his friend's carefully hoarded savings were lost. The moral of the story, of course, is that you do not send a brickmaker to buy jewels. You wouldn't expect the average bricklayer's labourer to judge a ballerina's standard of performance either, would you? Why, then, do people so often call upon sceptics to judge the veracity of any manifestation of psychic phenomena? You may as well ask someone who has been blind from birth to judge the quality of a painting. A sceptic's mind is made up long before he or she even sees the manifestation under question: things like that don't happen, therefore it cannot be genuine, no matter what, as far as the sceptic is concerned: therefore, the sceptic cannot really judge the psychic because his/her mind is not open to unbiased judgement.

During the previously mentioned tour of Australia by 'Mafu', I watched two television appearances by the channel, who entered a trance state and produced Mafu on request in both appearances. I cannot say whether or not I believe her performance was genuine, but there are quite a few comments I want to make about the manner in which this phenomenon was handled by the media, because it has an important bearing on the opinions of a great many members of the viewing public.

In the first appearance I saw, Mafu went through his paces, speaking in heavily accented tones and using rather complex words to explain matters that could have been explained much more simply. When the channel recovered from her trance, the president of the Australian Sceptics Association was introduced and asked to give his verdict on the channel's performance. He said exactly what I would have expected the president of a sceptics' association to say; that it was all fakery and any actress could have produced a performance equally as good, or even better. I didn't need to use any psychic skills to predict that kind of answer: what else could he be expected to say?

The second appearance was on 'Couchman', an hour-long 'open forum' debate programme in which topics of current interest are discussed on camera by guest speakers and an audience of a hundred or so people with varying points of view concerning the subject under discussion. The anchorman, Peter Couchman, does his best to present a fair and unbiased picture overall, without allowing his own opinion to influence the flow of debate. He does his job well and I enjoy his programme, so I was especially pleased to learn that Mafu was to be featured. Among the members of the audience were a number of Mafu's followers and other people of a similar disposition, including a woman who mentioned that she also functions as a channel, therefore she knows the phenomenon is genuine. Ranged in opposition to them were a number of members of the Australian Sceptics Association and others of like mind. There was also a priest and a psychiatrist.

Peter Couchman opened the programme with a brief discussion with the channel about the channelling phenomenon and her experiences. She explained, as on the previous appearance, that she leaves her body and goes into a Light, while the immensely enlightened entity Mafu uses her body as a vehicle through which to share his wisdom with us.

After stating in all fairness that he personally has no belief in anything represented by Mafu, Peter Couchman asked the channel to bring Mafu through to hold a direct debate with the audience. During the ensuing trance, questions were asked of Mafu concerning his purpose, his message for humankind and, of course, his genuineness or lack of it. I thought the situation became a trifle rowdy when one of the sceptics yelled, 'You're a fake, lady!', in the middle of the trance performance. He is, of course, perfectly entitled to his own opinion, but there are less aggressive and more rational ways in which it could have been expressed. After the trance, debate continued with the channel herself; the line of debate remaining similar throughout. The chief areas of discussion were the size of the fee for attendance at her seminar and whether or not she was faking the whole thing.

The psychiatrist seemed to think that the channel's performance could quite easily be a form of mental aberration, but as in the case of the president of the Australian Sceptics Association, his opinion held no real surprises.

I really would like to say that the believers presented a better case, but to me and everyone with whom I have discussed the programme, it seemed to degenerate into aggression and point-scoring rather than a balanced debate. I also found it interesting, and rather alarming, that amidst all the arguments as to whether or not the channel was faking, no one seemed to be aware of the possibility that the channel herself might be completely sincere and the *entity* might be an impostor. If that possibility did occur to anyone, they chose not to act upon it by issuing the kind of challenge which would have tested Mafu's credentials. Genuine and well-meaning people have been deceived by 'demons wearing angel masks' before: it is still happening, and no doubt it will continue to happen as long as people judge things on face value, wishful thinking... and prejudice. What perturbs me most about all of this is the number of sincere seekers who get hurt along the way.

Knowing there was a priest in the audience, I thought *he* might consider the possibility of possession and act accordingly, but he merely remarked that he found the channel's claim to have been initiated as a Hindu Swami after only four days of training quite interesting, since it had taken him fourteen years' study in a seminary to gain *his* qualifications. I confess to feeling some disappointment, that a priest who had studied a Bible-based religion for fourteen years would fail to act on the warning in 1 John 4 to *test* the spirits to see 'whether they are of God' by following a few simple instructions that are given in the same chapter.

It's easy for anyone to criticise and/or make derisive remarks, and I have heard quite a few people do so, not without a certain justification at times, but I have a concern that goes much deeper and involves a lot of very sincere and well-meaning people, and I think it requires some serious attention.

If a television research team as competent as that on the 'Couchman' programme could not find one person who even knows how to test for demonic possession, much less how to deal with it, what hope is there for those who are the *victims* of possession? Where do they find help? From my point of view, it is not a matter of believing in the supernatural. I live with the so-called 'supernatural' on a day-to-day basis, and for me it is a living reality. You don't believe in eggs, they are part of your everyday reality: you can see them, touch them and taste them. You *know* eggs are real... they aren't something you *believe* in. It's a rather crude comparison I know, but for me, as for countless other people, the spiritual worlds are a bit like eggs: they exist, what's to believe? Communication between those other dimensions and ours happens all the time and, in places, different dimensions can even overlap. I have seen cases of possession and I can assure you that they are chillingly real and not at all easy to behold. I know these things happen and unless this *FACT* is universally recognised and realistically treated, millions of people will continue to be hurt, and badly. That, and not thinly disguised one-upmanship, should be the kind of issue that concerns us all!

CHAPTER FOURTEEN

Astrologically Speaking The New Age — Interesting Chaos

From time to time, people ask me questions about the relationship of astrology to the unfolding of the New Age. Is there such a relationship? If so, what are the connections? How much influence do the stars really have on the events that take place in our world? These are questions that I cannot answer in any real depth, since I have not made a study of the science of astrology. I understand that all life throughout the universe exists within a matrix of living energy, through which there flows a succession of tides, currents and seasons which have an influence on all life. It stands to reason that any force powerful enough to set stars and planets in motion and keep them moving in orderly patterns must also be great enough to exert a certain amount of influence on the conditions under which we live.

Syndicated astrology columns in popular magazines have, by necessity, to make such sweeping generalisations that I can't help but regard them as being about as informative and enlightening as the messages we find in fortune cookies, but I have had my horoscope cast by more than one astrologer friend, and the results have been almost uncannily accurate, both with respect to the nature of my life circumstances from birth to the present and in their forecasts for the near future. They have also provided some valuable insights for me into my own personality characteristics, life lessons and the particular challenges that I need to overcome. Astrologers are quick to remind me that 'while the stars impel, they do not *compel*', and that while astrological tides and currents produce certain conditions and influences, we have free will, and we decide how we will work within those conditions. At this stage, my knowledge of the subject begins to waver, but because so many people have asked questions about the subject, I have been searching for some time for a way of providing answers.

Enter my friend Sandy, whose story you have read in chapter four. Astrology is one of the subjects she has studied and, more than once, she has provided me with some very useful items of information with regard to events taking place in my own life. I did not ask Sandy to write a chapter on astrology for me; I simply asked if she would like to write about what the New Age means to her, which she cheerfully agreed to do. After some time, however, she called me to say that she had been having problems, because every time she tried to organise her thoughts to write as I had asked, she had an overwhelming urge to start writing about astrology, but she didn't know if this would be appropriate.

'Your guides are smarter than both of us!' I laughed. 'I think a lot of people would be interested to read what you are feeling the urge to write. Go with the flow.'

She did, and the remainder of this chapter is the result.

As I write this, the Middle East war is unfolding live on television, right before my very eyes. I am reminded of an astrologer's reply when asked what he thought the New Age meant. 'Look around,' he said. 'If this is any indication of what it has in store, then I don't want to be around when it really begins.'

Perhaps he was right. In the last decade, many have begun to despair. Crime is so prevalent that murders and rape attacks barely attract headlines. No one who values their safety walks the streets after dark or leaves doors and windows unlocked. Children are injecting themselves with drugs, and housewives are popping Valium. Movies once considered pornographic are viewed daily in family living rooms.

In some countries, farmers are burning crops and slaughtering animals because they can't afford the upkeep, while in others, people are starving to death. Nations throughout the world are experiencing severe economic recession. Large and previously solid corporations are collapsing, and millionaires are declaring themselves bankrupt. Unemployment queues get longer every day. Big Brother computers monitor every detail about every citizen, from how much we earn to (possibly) how often we change our underwear.

Meanwhile, pollution is slowly choking us all to death, and the hole in the ozone layer continues to grow larger. Our food is bombarded with tonnes of chemicals — additives, preservatives, colourings and artificial flavourings. More and more people are developing allergies, sensitivities and food intolerances, some to the extent of having to lock themselves away in controlled environments (the phenomenon known appropriately as the 'twentieth-century syndrome'). AIDS is nearing epidemic proportions — if it hasn't achieved that dubious status already. Beaches are so polluted that some are being declared 'off-limits' to the public. Rain forests are disappearing, and entire species of animals, fish and birds are becoming extinct with each new day.

Every country in the world, it seems, is either at war, or threatening to go to war — with every other country in the world.

An ancient Eastern curse threatens the recipient with 'life during interesting times'. Perhaps all of us once received that curse in a previous lifetime, for 'interesting times' these certainly are. Was the astrologer correct when he said that these are indications of the New Age? Has the 'human experiment' failed? Is this as bad as it's going to get, or can the human race find new and even more devastating ways to wipe itself out?

It is certainly difficult to remain optimistic when the world seems to be totally out of control, but perhaps we are too close to the subject to appreciate the full implications of recent events. We need to stand back and view the scene in a more impersonal, detached way. While we are inhabiting earthly bodies, though, that's not an easy task.

An entity known as Ra is one of many disembodied souls channelling messages aimed at guiding us through these difficult or 'interesting' times. Like his counterparts, Ra is sufficiently detached to view these developments in a totally impersonal way, to the extent that he describes Earth changes as 'minor inconveniences'. This may not sound very encouraging when such 'minor' inconveniences may take the form of floods and earthquakes, nuclear wars or holocausts, but the soul is immortal and from a spiritual perspective, life on Earth is merely a testing ground.

In The Ra Material by Don Elkins, Carla Rueckert and James Allen McCarty, Ra discusses 'dimensions' and teaches that souls progress through these dimensions one step at a time in order to experience the lessons each has to offer. He goes on to say that a planet is also a living entity and therefore does not remain in one fixed dimension, but also progresses onward and upward. It would seem that planet Earth is currently experiencing a shift from third to fourth dimension, but Ra points out that it has not been an easy transition, and that it will be 'fetched with some inconvenience'. He says that 'the disharmonious vibratory complex began several years ago and will continue unabated for approximately 30 years, at the end of which, Earth will become a fourth density planet.'

What happens once Earth makes this transition, or when souls currently incarnated are poised to progress to the fourth dimension? Ra talks about 'cycles', explaining that a cycle lasts approximately 25 000 years. After three such cycles — every 75 000 or 76 000 years — those who have progressed may be 'harvested'. These souls are allowed the opportunity to seek a fourth density planet — as Earth will soon become — on which to continue learning *and growing, while those who are not ready must find a third density planet on which to repeat the cycle.*

It is interesting to note that the time periods mentioned by Ra correspond closely with astrological ages, or 'months'. Each astrological 'month' is said to come under the influence of the sign our sun occupies at the time of the Northern Hemisphere's spring equinox, which occurs around 21 March each year. The Western system of astrology uses what is known as the tropical zodiac, and within this system, the sun enters Aries at this time.

The more ancient Eastern system adjusts the zodiac in accordance with the shift in the Earth's axis (or as some believe, our universe's revolution around a central sun, Arcturus). As this occurs, our sun appears to move slowly backwards through the zodiac at the approximate rate of 1 degree every seventy-two years. After about 2160 years (72 years x 30 degrees), it moves into a new sign at the spring equinox, thereby taking about 26 000 years to complete its journey through the entire zodiac. Although Ra's estimates would appear to throw our calculations slightly out, there seems little doubt that he is referring to what we know as the astrological calendar.

Why is the approaching New Age referred to as the Age of Aquarius? According to the Eastern system of astrology, for around 2000 years our sun has been positioned in the sign of Pisces at the spring equinox, but as it continues to 'retrograde' through the zodiac, it will shortly move into the sign of Aquarius. There is no absolute agreement between astrologers regarding the exact time of this occurrence, however. Most concur that the Age of Pisces began around the time of Christ, particularly considering the use of the fish as a symbol for Christ by early Christians. This would therefore indicate that the Age of Aquarius is poised to begin.

Even if the current Age began no sooner than 1 AD, we have a mere 170 years of this Age left to us. Considering that the sun moves about 1 degree every seventy-two years, this places it a little more than 2 degrees away from Aquarius.

Anyone who was born within 2 degrees on either side of an astrological sign will know that they are referred to as being 'on the cusp', indicating that they display the characteristics of both adjoining signs... and 'cusp' people know how confusing this can be! The zodiac signs alternate between positive and negative, yin and yang, male and female qualities, and a 'cusp' person may find that they also alternate between these qualities, not being sure from one year to the next — or even one day to the next — whether they are going to display aggression or timidity, optimism or despair.

Could this be what we are ALL currently experiencing?

Another important factor to consider regarding the seemingly chaotic conditions on Earth at present is the position of the 'outer' planets — Pluto, Neptune, Uranus and, to a lesser extent, Saturn. As these outer planets move through the zodiac slowly, they create conditions which are far more profound and long-lasting than are generated by planets closer to Earth. Outer planets, therefore, tend to *influence humanity and world conditions in general, rather than individuals specifically, which is why they are often called 'transpersonal' planets.*

In 1984, Pluto (the most distant planet of which we are currently aware) entered its 'home' sign of Scorpio. The following year, Neptune rolled into Capricorn, with Uranus and Saturn following in 1989. This places three of the four outer planets in Capricorn — the sign immediately preceding Aquarius — while the other one, Pluto, has taken a twelve-year lease on its own sign.

What does all this mean? Imagine the planets as teachers — which indeed they are. At the same time, think of each zodiac sign as a subject. As a planet positions itself in a certain sign, the lessons *of that sign are taught in the* way *that planet chooses to teach them.*

If Capricorn were a subject, it would probably include economics, business education, science and political studies. Stretching this analogy a little further, we might include real estate and law enforcement on the curriculum in the same course. Prior to these planetary teachers entering the classroom marked 'Aquarius' in the mid-1990s, they are endeavouring to teach us the Capricornian subjects.

Saturn simply loves *spending time on these subjects; they are this planet's specialty. Saturn actually rules Capricorn, so the qualities of this planet and the aims of this sign are in total harmony. Imagine Saturn with glasses perched on the end of a bulbous nose and a cane in one hand, and you will understand why it has been dubbed the 'Old Taskmaster'. Saturn, like*

Capricorn, seeks order, demands discipline, and has a profound respect for tradition.

This stern old teacher also has a few tricks up his sleeve. He restricts, restrains, contains, disciplines, limits and stabilises — but is not against hurling the odd piece of chalk at a day-dreaming student or slamming his fist on to the desk if he feels that the class is not paying attention. That is precisely the way this subject has been taught in the past few years, i.e., from 1988 until early 1991.

Economic restrictions and financial restraints were certainly experienced during these years, creating testing periods of endurance. Saturn has been trying to teach us not to waste our resources or throw money away on luxuries. By the time this book is published, the economic recession should be easing, and the business sector and real estate markets once again beginning to expand. I wonder how much we have collectively gained from the Old Taskmaster's lessons?

Besides Saturn, there are other planets which need to be considered, also. For example, Uranus entered Capricorn (or began teaching the same subject as Saturn) at about the same time (1988) and will continue to do so until early 1996.

As the ruler of Aquarius, Uranus may be considered the planet of the New Age. Air and space travel, computers, astrology and crystals all come under the influence of this planet. Uranus is the eccentric teacher, the one who rarely follows the curriculum but has his own innovative ways of teaching, so that even boring subjects become interesting. That is, of

371

*course, as long as you can keep up with him.
You're never quite sure what to expect when
Uranus begins a lesson. This teacher's mind is
buzzing all over the place, and it is almost as
though he has plugged himself into an electric
light socket! In fact, he probably has, for electricity also comes within the sphere of Uranus'
influence.*

*Where Saturn seeks order, Uranus delights
in tearing it down. While Saturn believes in
tradition, Uranus thrives on revolution, and
when Saturn fights to retain law and order,
Uranus takes great pleasure in causing disrup-
tion and disorder. Is it any wonder that, while
these two planets were constantly challenging
each other in Capricorn, economic chaos
reigned supreme?*

*A planetoid known as Chiron is believed to
be acting as a mediator between these two
antagonists. (Chiron has been dubbed a 'planetoid' because it is too large to be considered an
asteroid, and too small to be called a planet.)
There is still much to be learned about the
effects of this celestial body, since it was only
discovered in 1977, orbiting between these two
outer planets.*

*If astrologers are correct in suggesting that
Chiron is mediating between Saturn (stability
and tradition) and Uranus (the new and innovative) this theory becomes highly significant as
the New Age approaches, for we will shortly
need to let go of the past and seek new and
innovative methods of survival. Another theory credits Chiron with healing abilities, and
the effects of a major transition such as the one
we are currently experiencing will certainly
make a healing body welcome.*

372

Prior to entering Capricorn, Uranus resided in Sagittarius. Traditionally considered to be the ninth house of the zodiac, Sagittarian subjects include religion, philosophy, education, publishing, travel and foreign affairs. Last time Uranus transited this sign, the Wright brothers pioneered air travel and the motor car revolutionised transportation. Throughout the 1980s, we certainly saw some revolutionary changes in Sagittarius-ruled subjects, too.

Sagittarius rules publishing, and books about computers, philosophy and the New Age were published in their thousands during those years, and Uranus stimulated minds, inspiring the search for more information about unusual subjects. Computers (Uranus) became commonplace in schools: higher education is also Sagittarius's domain. Many long-held religious beliefs (Sagittarius again) also began to undergo Uranian change during this period. People started questioning instead of merely accepting what they were told by traditional religious leaders. I don't believe this implies a loss of faith, but rather indicates that Uranus was prompting people to 'test and question' — just as Dawn's guide, David, constantly advised her to do.

'Revolution' is Uranus's middle name, and for as long as this planet dwells in the house of ambitious, business-minded Capricorn, it is hardly surprising that computers are revolutionising those areas. During this planet's previous sojourn in Capricorn, Albert Einstein raised eyebrows with his revolutionary concepts of time and matter — subjects close to Capricorn's scientific heart. This transit might even see astrology (Uranus) become accepted

by scientists (Capricorn). With any luck, Uranus should also revolutionise the area of conservation, which comes under Capricorn's influence, leading to the development of efficient waste disposal systems, while Capricorn's concern with safety should result in more careful scrutiny of Uranus-ruled electrical devices, particularly the electromagnetic radiation generated by power lines.

As you might imagine, radical Uranus is not particularly comfortable in the realistic and practical sign of Capricorn, just as our eccentric (but genius) teacher has difficulty remaining within the limitations of traditional teaching methods. Given its way, Uranus can teach us an appreciation of traditional values by bringing sudden and disruptive changes to jolt us out of our complacency. Many people would agree that it has been doing exactly that.

Four years before Uranus and Saturn joined forces in Capricorn, Neptune occupied this sign. Neptune's influence is not as obvious as Uranus's, since Neptune is located further away, and its vibrations are extremely subtle. It is a difficult planet to understand, true to its nebulous nature, for it has a tendency to weave webs of illusion around anything that comes under its sphere of influence.

Neptune governs dreams, visions, imagination, creativity, fantasy and faith. It also has rulership over liquid and gaseous substances, such as oil, alcohol, chemicals, and water — including, of course, the sea. Neptune is the quintessential 'hippie', seeing the world through rose-coloured glasses and spending his evenings in deep meditation.

As a teacher, discipline is not Neptune's strong point, and he keeps assuring his students that they will pass their exams merely by having faith in their own abilities. Study, he tells them, is totally unnecessary: paying attention in class merely stifles the imagination. He never gives homework or recommends reading material. To his credit, Neptune can increase his students' awareness of spiritual matters and turn their attention away from materialistic pursuits by showing them that there is more to life than possessions or self-centred ambition. Everyone at school adores him, but be warned: although it may not be intentional, deceit is this teacher's specialty. Neptune can be as insidious as a gas leak, and as treacherous as an underwater rip in a seemingly calm sea. This planet has the ability to cause chaos by creating illusion and confusion. While Uranus brings change through revolution, Neptune subtly weakens and scatters, quietly divides and separates, and eventually brings about complete disintegration and failure. This is a fact that his devoted students will discover for themselves when they receive their exam results!

Mystical Neptune and radical Uranus are drawing closer together: in 1993/94 they will form what is known as a conjunction, and such a conjunction only occurs once in every 172 years. The results of this phenomenon can only be guessed at, as two planets in such close proximity must compete for supremacy, each exerting its own influence in the same arena. Perhaps practical Capricorn, in whose sign this conjunction occurs, will keep these planets in line, though there is a definite possibility of large-scale social, economic and/or political upheavals. On the bright side, this conjunction could well herald the beginning of the long-awaited Age of Aquarius, for the indications strongly suggest a spiritual revolution.

In the fourteen years prior to its entry into Capricorn, Neptune resided in the sign of Sagittarius. During this time, the expansive energies of that sign allowed the planet to create the illusion of freedom and optimism. Everyone sought the 'good life', and ways to get rich quickly. Drug use (Neptune) increased alarmingly, especially in schools, which come under Sagittarius's rule.

Capricorn's tendency to restrict and restrain has helped to keep this planet under control since 1984, for unlike the Sagittarian winged horse, the Capricorn goat will not allow Neptune complete freedom to create illusions of grandeur and optimism. Capricorn prefers to focus its energies on to patience, persistence and hard work as the ways to achieve goals. If it is allowed the chance, however, Neptune has the ability to cause economic chaos through Capricorn. This may be considered as part of a testing ground; a time to prepare for the coming New Age, for it would seem that this planet offers us an opportunity to develop true and worthwhile values, as distinct from relying on false and shallow optimism.

If any one planet may be held primarily responsible for chaos, however, then Pluto is the most likely culprit. It has taken this planet almost 250 years to return to its domicile. Last time it occupied its own house (1737 to 1750) it was still unknown: it was discovered in 1930. There is a theory that planets only become visible to us when we reach the vibrationary level that allows us to be aware of them, so it is possible that Pluto's effect, last time round, was minimal.

The significance of this planet's current position is basically the intense power it generates in its own sign, for here it can function without hindrance. Pluto unleashed is a force to be reckoned with, for Pluto is an intense planet, and Scorpio is an equally intense sign.

Pluto is the professor who looks you straight in the eye, and under whose hypnotic glare you find yourself squirming. There's no getting out of homework assignments when Pluto takes the class! All the same, you can't help wondering about this strange and surly teacher — why do you feel as though you are being mentally undressed, every time he looks at you? You can't help suspecting that he gets up to some bizarre practices in private, but don't even consider asking him. This teacher is not about to reveal any of his secrets, even though he insists on knowing all of yours. Bizarre practices are quite possible with Pluto, for his secretive nature lends itself perfectly to black magic, demons and vampires. He is in his element when surrounded by criminals, gangsters and rapists, and he thrives on massacres and assassinations. Pluto claims rulership over such areas as waste, pollution, sewers, abattoirs, cesspools and pornography. War is also Pluto's domain, although the battles themselves come under the influence of Mars. Volcanoes and earthquakes relate to Pluto, as indeed does anything that is hidden below the surface.

As you may imagine, nothing seems to disgust Pluto, so-called God of the Underworld, for although this planet represents transformation and regeneration, it also feels the need to 'dig up the dirt'. Transformation, says Pluto, is never possible until the debris has been cleaned out, regardless of how disgusting it may be. Regeneration, he insists, cannot take place until deep-seated psychological, physical and spiritual scars are examined and closely dealt with, not merely covered over with Neptune's band-aid.

Scorpio, the sign ruled by Pluto and within which it is currently residing, is traditionally considered to be the eighth house of the zodiac, and governs sex, death, reincarnation, the occult, and money. In this case, 'money' refers to other people's finances, such as funds held in banks and credit unions, taxation, the stock market, insurance policies and legacies.

Scorpio allows Pluto complete freedom. For example, physiologically, Scorpio rules the anus, rectum and genitals, and Pluto vibrates in perfect tune with epidemics, plagues, and bodily excretions. AIDS may have been emerging prior to Pluto's entry into Scorpio, but it has been steadily increasing throughout the 1980s. Crime, pornography and rape also appear to be increasing. Banks and finance companies are experiencing economic chaos. Pollution is becoming more of a problem daily. What other catastrophes can this planet cause? It would sometimes appear that Pluto has no redeeming features whatsoever; that

378

doom and gloom must be expected until the planet moves on in 1995. Perhaps we should stick our heads in the sand and wait until then.

No way! Along with all of the other planets, Pluto is trying to teach us something. This planet does not allow us to gloss over anything, but demands that we look below the surface. It digs up the dirt, certainly, but it does so simply to provide us with an opportunity to clean up our act. Pluto may appear to be nothing more than a garbage bin in the eyes of the un-initiated, but just try keeping the lid on! Pluto will keep throwing the garbage back into our faces until we learn to deal with it. This puts a spotlight on that which is ugly and dirty, so that we may begin to see it more clearly and clean it up instead of sweeping it under the carpet. It probes the filth in order to show us where to let go, and it provides us with the chance to transform and regenerate.

Pluto is telling us that it is time to deal with pollution, cut down on waste, eliminate crime, expose frauds and clean up our moral stand-ards. These are just some of the areas Pluto has been spotlighting since 1984, areas which will continue to be brought to our attention throughout that planet's twelve-year stay in Scorpio, so that we will not be able to keep hiding our heads in the sand. It is encouraging to realise that more and more people are taking positive action against toxic wastes and pollu-tion, and that everyone is becoming increas-ingly aware of the importance of recycling. Pluto will continue to have a profound effect on those areas until 1995, when it moves into the more expansive sign of Sagittarius. There,

*it will attempt to bring about transformation
in religion, law and higher education by once
again probing deeply and exposing frauds.
How successful it will be in that sign is yet to be
seen, for Sagittarius promotes openness and
frankness, while Pluto moves stealthily
through the dark, dirty corridors of the underworld. Should Sagittarius actually be hiding
any secrets, Pluto will surely dig them up!*

*What does all this mean to the average Earth-
dweller poised on the brink of the brave New
Age? Simply that we are being given an opportunity to prepare. For what? Perhaps, as Ra
suggests, for advancement into the fourth
dimension, a dimension of 'compassion and
understanding, where individual differences
are ... automatically harmonised'. This seems
to be further supported by numerology, in
which the number One (a number we have
carried in our dates for a thousand years) is
about to be replaced by the number Two. One,
a masculine number, vibrates to ego, aggression, ambition and self-interest: Two, its feminine counterpart, is considered by
numerologists to be the number of co-
operation, diplomacy and harmony. It is also
interesting that Aquarius is the eleventh house
of the zodiac, and that number Eleven is the
higher vibration of number Two. Aquarius is
considered to be the sign of compassionate
humanity, and rules hopes and wishes, friends
and groups.*

*Whether we, as individuals, progress to the
fourth dimension or choose to remain in the
third depends on our actions and reactions
throughout these 'interesting' times. We can*

use the positive vibrations of these planetary aspects to clean up our act, as Pluto would say, or we can tune in to the negative vibrations and allow ourselves to be divided, separated, disrupted, restricted and discouraged. Along with increasing numbers of people around the world, I believe that we choose our own incarnations. These may be interesting times, but armed with prior knowledge of the trials in store, we must have chosen them for a reason. If Ra is correct, that reason must be to progress into the next dimension, for this entity points out that only those souls close to being 'harvestable' have been permitted to incarnate at this time.

The ancient Chinese symbol for 'crisis' also means 'opportunity'. These people obviously knew something that we are only now learning — that although a quiet and uneventful life may be pleasant for a while, it does not provide much opportunity for growth.

Has the world really gone mad? Does chaos reign supreme? Is there any hope whatsoever for humanity? I passionately believe that there is. It is my personal opinion that the New Age will be a time of peace and brotherhood. Prior to commencement at this 'university of the fourth dimension', however, we will all need to pass our entry exams, the results of which will reveal whether we are ready to let go of the old ways.

If we allow the planets to teach us to put aside petty jealousies, overcome greed and wastefulness, and practise tolerance, humility, love and compassion, then we will surely pass the test and emerge as victorious inhabitants of *the fourth dimension.* But we must remember that we are sitting for these exams at this very moment, *and that failure means repeating another term at school. (Some term — 76 000 years!)*

So... onward and upward.

(But be honest, aren't you secretly delighted to be living in 'interesting times'?)

CHAPTER FIFTEEN
Patrick's Gift

I have saved Patrick's gift until last, because I want
to give Patrick a special place in this book. Patrick
is about fourteen years old, with eyes like the sky in
summer and an aura of such clear radiance that the
air almost shimmers in his presence. His body is
crippled with cerebral palsy, but it cannot even
begin to conceal the pure, bright spirit who dwells
within.

Patrick's parents are New Age travellers and, a
couple of years ago, they taught him to meditate.
In meditation, so he told me, Patrick sits down and
draws back, away from his body, and goes to his
'favourite place', which is under a big pine tree.
There, he likes to 'just sit and think about things'.

According to his parents, and to other people
who know him, through his meditations Patrick
brings words of such inspiration that they touch
the hearts of all who hear them. A few people have
tried psychic healing on Patrick, but his parents
shake their heads, saying, 'They waste their time.
Patrick is meant to be the way he is.'

Because his body is crippled, people notice
Patrick, and because he has so much difficulty
articulating his words, people take the time to
listen to what he has to say, paying more attention
than they would normally give to the breezy

chatter of any able-bodied youngster. Therein lies a key to Patrick's gift. For those who do take the time to listen, and to think about what he says, Patrick's words bring wisdom and insight, with a quality of innocence and simplicity that most of us have all but forgotten.

I am reminded of the teaching that 'Unless you become as a child, you cannot enter the Kingdom of Heaven'. Because his disability has not permitted Patrick to undergo the process of physical development in the way most other children do, he has retained the qualities of innocence and openness that are characteristic of young children, but his mind is clear and alert and, in his meditations, his spirit is free to grow. It is as though the crippled body has protected Patrick from the 'normal' process of conditioning and kept his spirit free. Add New Age parents who actively foster the growth and expression of his spiritual qualities, and the result is a very special combination of insight, wisdom and simplicity.

Patrick has the ability to re-open in his listeners the charmed, sunlit spaces of childhood, showing by example what it is like to be 'as a child', yet not a child. For all of his child-like freshness and candour, Patrick is no immature young soul. To meet that steady, sky-blue gaze is to see the wisdom of Ages looking back at you.

When I met Patrick and his parents, they brought a gift with them. On a cassette tape, Patrick had recorded a message, gained through one of his meditation sessions. It is a gift meant for sharing. To read Patrick's words is to be reminded of the qualities so precious in youth, and to know that when we take the time to listen and cast aside the masks of 'adult superiority', there is much that we can learn from the young.

Here, just as it was given to me, is Patrick's gift, for you.

THE BEACH

The beach is God's gift,
And God's gift is love.
The waves break over the shoreline
And when you put your feet inside,
The waves sort of come around you,
Like God is hugging you.

The beach . . .
You can have fun
And no Devil can get to you,
Because the beach is a beauty to God,
And God's gift is really the real, truly, truly,
No one can describe it, it's so powerful.
Love.

Amen

by *Patrick John*

CHAPTER SIXTEEN

A Message . . .

As always, I extend an invitation for you to write and share your ideas, feelings, experiences and notions with me. In addition, my thanks to the many friends who donated time and energy with their contributions of material for this book. So many people gave such a generous response to my requests for input that I have collected much more material than can be fitted into one book, but every letter that I receive adds to the picture, like many people planting trees on a hillside, or many people lighting candles. Being only one person in certain physical respects, I cannot personally answer more than a fraction of the mail I receive, but I appreciate each letter.

I receive quite a lot of mail from people who request my assistance in some matter of personal concern to them. Again, I cannot answer each one with a personal letter, but I do my best to answer as many as possible. I also refer all requests for help to the Upstairs Management as a matter of course, but I must point out that I do not have a special-access hotline to the Almighty. The main thrust of my message has always been, '*You* can do it,' and I emphasise the necessity to reclaim the power within, which is inherent in every one of us.

I am not here for the purpose of being set up as some kind of female Messiah, New Age guru, or a leader of any kind. I neither want nor need the burden of that kind of responsibility, and I believe that it encourages people to abdicate their personal power, relying on external sources to lead them. That kind of thinking doesn't only imprison the followers, it makes cages for the leaders, too. I don't want to live in a cage, nor do I like seeing others imprisoned. I am a writer, I gather and disseminate information in the way best suited to me, and I don't particularly want to change my spots at this stage in my life.

If I had to hang a label on myself, I would describe myself as a student of life, but I would prefer not to use labels at all. I write about life, and in order to keep doing that to the best of my capabilities, I need to be in touch with life. The ideas, thoughts and feelings that you share help me to stay in touch. To me, you *are* life, in all of its richness and variety. If you feel inclined to write a letter to me, I will be delighted to hear from you.

A few necessary words of caution. I ask for consideration on my publisher's behalf. I enjoy a pleasant and friendly working relationship with the people who publish my books, and they are always most considerate towards me, but they are there to publish books, not to function as a mail-forwarding agency. People who send letters to the publisher for forwarding on to me are asking the people in the company to take on an added burden of time, effort and responsibility, which should not be theirs to carry, particularly when a more direct line of communication is available.

Should you wish to write to me, the current mailing address is:

Dawn Shelley Thomas
PO Box 787
Ulverstone
Tasmania 7315
Australia

Please remember that bulk postage is expensive: I would appreciate it if you enclose return postage with your letter if you wish me to reply. If you are writing from within Australia, please enclose an envelope and stamp for return postage. If you live overseas, you can obtain International Postal Response coupons from your post office, which can be enclosed with your letter.

I will do my best to answer but if you do not receive a personal reply, please understand my physical limitations and be assured that I do read every letter I receive, although if I start getting mailbags full of letters every day, I may need to call on some willing friends for assistance!

Thank you for sharing this book with me. I wish you Light in your heart, and upon your pathway.

ACKNOWLEDGEMENT

I am very grateful for permission to quote extracts from *The Ra Material* by Don Elkins, Carla Rueckert and James Allen McCarty, published by the Donning Company, USA, 1984.

SUGGESTED READING LIST

Cayce, Edgar. *Many Mansions* (Signet, 1978)

Clason, George S. *The Richest Man in Babylon* (Signet, 1988)

Drury, Neville. *The Occult Experience* (Fontana, 1989)

Elkins, Don; Rueckert, Carla; McCarty, James Allen. *The Ra Material* (The Donning Company, 1984)

Gawler, Ian. *You Can Conquer Cancer* (Hill of Content, 1984)

Greaves, Helen. *Testimony of Light* (CW Daniel, 1977)

Greaves, Helen. *The Wheel of Eternity* (CW Daniel, 1974)

Hay, Louise L. *You Can Heal Your Life* (Specialist Publications, 1988)

Levi. *The Aquarian Gospel of Jesus the Christ* (De Vorss, 1972)

Moody, Dr Raymond. *Life After Life* (Bantam, 1976)

Pirsig, Robert M. *Zen and the Art of Motor Cycle Maintenance* (Corgi, 1976)

Ravenscroft, Trevor. *The Spear of Destiny* (Corgi, 1974)

Szekely, Edmond. *The Gospel of the Essenes* (CW Daniel, 1979)

Dawn Hill
Lifting the Veil

'New Age awareness is not so much a matter of what you see in life, but how you look at it.'

The burgeoning New Age movement is currently taking the world by storm. In *Lifting the Veil*, Dawn Hill's third book on psychic development, Dawn turns her attention to the New Age phenomenon and its significance to us as individuals and to the world at large.

Extending the message of enlightenment delivered in the bestselling *Reaching for the Other Side* and *Edge of Reality*, Dawn lifts the veil of suspicion which has acted as a barrier between the New Age movement and the rest of the world. She dispels the myths associated with psychic activity, illuminates areas of ignorance and doubt, and explains in everyday terms the nature of the New Age and its relevance to ordinary people.

Lifting the Veil also provides deep insight into other aspects of the 'Spiritual Revolution', and includes chapters on:

• split brain research and New Age thinking
• left-brain dominance, right-brain suppression
• New Age education
• death
• cataclysms and the end of the world
• fakes, frauds and fanatics
• sex and spirituality

Dawn Hill
Reaching for the Other Side

A startling account of the psychic world – a book to change your mind – it may even change your life!

Outwardly there is nothing extraordinary about Dawn Hill. But since her late teens she has been pursuing an extraordinary subject.

Dawn's first psychic experiences left her disturbed and frightened. What was wrong with her? Why was she subject to premonitions and unbidden visions? The answers only came slowly as Dawn began to explore the spiritual world. Eventually her knowledge led her to her own spirit guide – David – who has been with her through all her past lives and will be with her when she leaves this life. David speaks to Dawn through her husband Roland, who is a trance medium. Although David's last physical incarnation was over 2,000 years ago, his spiritual teachings are timeless.

Involvement with the psychic world has led Dawn into encounters with cases of possession, psychic attack, hauntings and psychic healing. But above all, Dawn is a teacher. She presents here an absorbing, practical guide to the principles of psychic understanding. The different levels of spiritual development are explained, and exercises are included for those who wish to explore their own spiritual existence – to reach across to 'the other side'.